Introduction

Twenty-first century students work to improve their ability to proficiently and independently read a wide range of complex texts from various content areas. *Lincoln Empowered Text Collection* is a compilation of literature that provides informational texts, essays, newspaper articles, fables, legends, poetry, short stories, plays, persuasive letters, business letters, diary and journal entries, and more to students learning to read and students reading to learn alike. Even at a young age, students who engage in the careful, meaningful reading of a variety of works develop their ability to:

- Evaluate texts for story elements, literary devices, and/or text features.
- Construct effective arguments based on the content read.
- Discern authors' points of view.
- Ask questions.
- Build vocabulary.
- Gain general and content-specific knowledge.
- Build a stronger worldview through exposure to cultural and era-specific pieces.

This book's contents include all literary pieces used in Empowered courses for one grade level. For easy access, the texts are given in the order in which they appear in Empowered courses.

This collection aligns with the most recent course content at the time of printing.

Contents

The Boy Who Cried Wolf 1
adapted by Jill Fisher

Lightning of Assateague 3
written by Jennifer Tkocs

Cinderella: A Retelling 7
written by Steve Karscig

On Chestnut Street 9
written by Summer York

On the Ice – An Excerpt 10
written by Jennifer Tkocs

Jack and the Beanstalk 11
adapted by Jennifer Tkocs

The Police Report of Alfred Giant 13
written by Jennifer Tkocs

The Tortoise and the Hare 15
adapted by Summer York

From the Desk of Hare 17
written by Summer York

Sam's Lessons 18
written by Sarah Marino

The Man, the Boy, and the Donkey 20
adapted by Luke See

A Portrait of Ms. Graham 22
written by Summer York

The Love Bug 23
written by Summer York

Ollie's Outing 26
written by Jennifer Tkocs

The Extra Moment 28
written by Vincent J. Scotto

Phillip and the Shot 32
written by Luke See

Just Between Us 35
written by Vincent J. Scotto

King Arthur 38
written by Vincent J. Scotto

A Guilty Conscience 39
written by Summer York

A Close Encounter of a Different Kind 42
written by Summer York

Sleeping Beauty 45
adapted by Michael Scotto

The Runt Horse 47
written by Sarah Mario

If I Were Along on Earth 50
written by Vincent J. Scotto

Hansel and Gretel 51
adapted by Mark Weimer

Hanseled and Greteled 53
adapted by Mark Weimer

Little Red Cap: A German Folktale 55
adapted by Vincent J. Scotto

Goldilocks and the Three Bears 57
adapted by Michael Scotto

Money Management Smarts 59
written by Sarah Marino

The Scorpion 61
written by Mark Weimer

Forms of Energy 63
written by Vincent J. Scotto

The Constitution: Making Laws with Checks and Balances 67
written by Mark Weimer

Written Music Glossary 69
written by Mark Weimer

Scorpions: A Multitude of Stingers 71
written by Vincent J. Scotto

The Komodo Dragon 72
written by Luke See

Making History: Important Events in the
Civil Rights Movement 73
written by Sarah Marino

Ruby Bridges: A Brave Girl Who
Changed History 79
written by Jennifer Tkocs

Lou Gehrig 81
written by Mark Weimer

Ten Major Events of World War II 83
written by Summer York

Surrender at Appomattox 85
written by Mark Weimer

Escaped Piglet Goes on Jaunt through Town 87
written by Jennifer Tkocs

Local Girl Gets Party of a Lifetime 89
written by Sarah Marino

The Constitution: Federalists vs. Antifederalists 91
written by Vincent J. Scotto

Igneous Rocks (Third Hook) 93
written by Vincent J. Scotto

California Gold Rush 94
written by Jill Fisher

D-Day: Operation Overlord 96
written by Mark Weimer

Alternative Energy Solutions 98
written by Summer York

Desertification 101
written by Mark Weimer

Alternative Energy: A Renewable World 103
written by Vincent J. Scotto

A Brief History of Modern Dance in America:
Outline 105
written by Sarah Marino

Organic Food: Outline 107
written by Sarah Marino

First in Flight? 109
written by Summer York

Defeating Anatidaephobia 111
written by Mark Weimer

The Importance of Libraries 113
written by Luke See

The Copernicus Controversy 115
written by Jennifer Tkocs

The Battle of Hampton Roads 118
written by Mark Weimer

How the United States Was Shaped 120
written by Jill Fisher

Children Should Read for Pleasure 122
written by Summer York

Lewis and Clark: Discovering the West 125
written by Sarah Marino

Children Should Have Limited TV Time 127
written by Bryon Gill

Damaging Quake Hits Small Deleware Town 129
written by Summer York

We Shall Overcome 131
written by Summer York

Mindfulness: A Powerful Tool 135
written by Sarah Marino

Environmental Change 137
written by Vincent J. Scotto

The Dangers of Fracking: A Speech 141
written by Summer York

Expository Essay Outline 143

The Dangers of Fracking: Outline 144
written by Summer York

We Need a Playground! 146
written by Vincent J. Scotto

Editorial: Vote Peter Ash for Student Council
President 148
written by Jennifer Tkocs

Benefits of Children Learning
a Musical Instrument 149
written by Katie Catanzarite

Mummies in Ancient Egypt 150
written by Jennifer Tkocs

Energy Issues 154
written by Mark Weimer

George the Greate and Powerful 155
written by Jennifer Tkocs

The House at the End of Silver Street 158
written by Steve Karscig

The Basement 159
written by Vincent J. Scotto

Mrs. Drummond's Secret 160
written by Jennifer Tkocs

A Place I Cannot Go 164
written by Summer York

The Sparrow 165
written by Summer York

Lady Liberty 166
written by Summer York

My Favorite Season 167
written by Vincent J. Scotto

Visit Pittsburgh 168
written by Summer York

Persuasive Essay Outline 170

Essay Structure Map 171

Steven and the Turtles 172
written by Summer York

Green or Orange on St. Patrick's Day? 174
written by Summer York

The Griffin 175
written by Vincent J. Scotto

The Land Remains 176
written by Summer York

The Strange Case of Dr. Jekyll and Mr. Hyde 177
written by Vincent J. Scotto

Mega Mountaintown: Come for a Visit! 193
written by Vincent J. Scotto

Meeting at a Bus Stop 195
written by Katie Catanzarite

Wicked Storm 197
written by Byron Gill

How to Build a House of Interlocking Bricks 200
written by Vincent J. Scotto

Technical Writing Examples 201
written by Summer York

The Great Aluminum Knight 205
written by Steve Karscig

The Hat 209
written by Byron Gill

The Pacific Coast Gem:
A Memorable Tour by Train 213
written by Sarah Marino

My Not-So-Fun Trip to the Zoo 215
written by Summer York

It's Party Time 217
written by Debbie Parrish

LINCOLN EMPOWERED
TEXT COLLECTION
GRADE 5

LINCOLN
EMPOWERED

The Boy Who Cried Wolf

adapted by Jill Fisher
illustrated by Mallory Senich

Long ago there was a young shepherd boy who watched the sheep in the pasture. The pasture was located at the foot of the mountain near a dark forest. The shepherd's father used to send him to look over the sheep from sunup to sundown. Guarding the animals was not the worst job in the world. After all, the boy enjoyed being in the sunshine and fresh air. But it was hard, extremely lonely work. The boy preferred running around with his friends from the village, playing ball, or just getting into typical boy mischief.

"The sheep don't need me to look after them," the shepherd boy told his father. "All they do is munch on grass. There is nothing for me to do."

His father replied that watching the sheep was a very important job. He explained, "You must keep an eye out for the wolf that lives in the dark forest. He is big and strong, and he may sneak into the pasture and snatch one of the little lambs." Before he returned to work, the man told his son, "Shout loudly if you see a wolf. The villagers will come to help you chase the predator away and keep the animals safe."

The boy's father instructed him to never sleep on the job. The young shepherd had to sit and look out for the wolf. Time passed slowly and he grew very lonesome. He'd try to find ways to amuse himself, running up rocks, climbing trees, chasing sheep, but nothing kept him entertained for long. He began to wish the wolf would show up, if only to give him something to do.

Isolated day after day, the shepherd boy's mind often drifted away from him. On one summer day, the lonely lad began to daydream. First, he thought of his friends. He imagined them splashing in the creek and fishing. Then he started to think about how he could make his job more thrilling. All through the hot afternoon, he carefully crafted a plan that would create a little excitement and gain himself some company.

The shepherd boy sprang up and dashed as fast as he could into the village. All the while, he yelled at the top of his lungs, "Help! Wolf! The wolf is going after the sheep in the pasture!"

The villagers rushed to meet the shepherd boy. To the shepherd boy's surprise, they had brought sticks and pitchforks to scare away the wolf and save the herd. But when the villagers reached the pasture, all was peaceful. The sheep were grazing as usual. Some of the villagers decided to stay with the shepherd boy for a considerable amount of time to make sure the wolf did not return.

After a while, the shepherd boy started laughing and the villagers realized they had been tricked. They scolded the boy and told him, "Don't cry 'wolf' when there is no wolf!" Angry, they went back to the village.

Time passed and people forgot about the trick. But not the shepherd boy. He was so pleased with its success that he decided to see if the villagers would fall for it again. This time he put on a better act. He pretended the wolf had bitten his arm. He ran around holding his arm screaming, "Help, the wolf attacked me!" Again, the villagers hurried to help him.

When the villagers arrived, out of breath and sweating, they found the shepherd boy bent over in uncontrollable laughter. They grew very angry with the boy. None of them laughed with him. They scolded, "Don't waste our time."

When the boy got home, his father was furious. He was punished that evening. The shepherd boy realized he should behave himself and decided he would not trick anyone ever again.

A week later, the shepherd boy was watching the sheep in the pasture as normal. As always, he was lonely and bored. The sun was starting to set behind the trees. Then, all of a sudden, the dogs started barking and the sheep began to scamper around the pasture in fear. The shepherd boy climbed a tree to see what was going on. What he saw nearly made him fall to the ground. There was a snarling, angry wolf among the sheep!

For a few seconds, the shepherd boy could not speak. Then, louder than ever before, he cried out, "Wolf! Wolf! Wooooooollllllffff!"

The villagers heard the screams and said, "Oh, no, not the shepherd boy again." They had been fooled twice before, and they thought this was another trick. No one came to help the shepherd boy. The villagers continued to do whatever they had been doing. Sadly, the wolf scared all of the sheep away.

Later that evening, the villagers wondered why the shepherd boy had not returned with the sheep. They went looking for him and found him crying.

He said, "The wolf was here and I yelled for help. Now the sheep are all missing. Why didn't anyone come to help me?"

A wise man from the village told the shepherd boy, "We will help you find the lost sheep in the morning." He continued, "Nobody believes a liar, even when he speaks the truth."

Lightning of Assateague

written by Jennifer Tkocs
illustrated by Doyle Daigle II

I was born on the island. In fact, I thought that all ponies were. When I was just a foal, I did not know that there was anything but the island and the herd. And then, in the summer of 1909, everything changed.

I was born on a stormy morning in October. Mother named me Lightning, for the jagged white streak that wrapped around my shoulder and down my foreleg. She said it must have come into my coat with the storm as I entered the world. I was an autumn foal, which was unusual. Most foals are born in the spring, so for them, life changes before they have a chance to grow accustomed to the island.

But I lived many months on Assateague. "Mother?" I would ask. "Why aren't there any other ponies my age?"

"Shhh, now, don't worry," she told me. "It's because you're one of a kind, Lightning."

Winter was hard on Assateague Island. I was still very little, and the cold rain chilled me through my coat. But Mother taught me to find shelter under the thick loblolly pine trees. I learned to stand out of the cold ocean water when nibbling on cord grass each morning. And on days when the sun came out, I warmed up by frolicking through the marshes and practicing my whinnies.

In the spring, many foals were born. For the first time, I had playmates who were my age. It was wonderful.

But many of them talked of something that would happen in the summer. Many of them whispered about "going away," and I did not know what that meant.

Mother kept track of days for us on a rock on the shore. She added lines for days and crossed the lines for months. Soon, it was July, and my friends, the other foals, were scared.

One day, three men came to our part of the island. We saw humans often from afar. They came to look at us and point and smile. But these men came right over the fence into the thick of the herd! They did not look unkind, but they were very matter-of-fact. "Come along, ponies," they told us. "It's time to go away."

Go away, I thought. *This is what the other foals had warned me about!* I looked to Mother with fear in my eyes.

"It is time, Lightning," she said, her voice very low and soft.

"Time for what, Mother?"

"It is time for you and the other ponies to go away. You will leave the herd."

I did not want to go away. I loved my life here on Assateague Island. I loved Mother very much, and I loved the other foals I had met in the spring. I loved my favorite patch of cord grass. I loved the small waves that licked at my hooves just after sunrise.

"Where is away?" I asked Mother.

She nuzzled my shoulder on the lightning streak. "I do not know, dear. But I know there is no choice. Pay attention now. You must stay with the other foals."

I didn't want to leave the island. I didn't want to leave Mother. But the men from the mainland were very persistent. They corralled us all and kept us in a tight formation. "Time to swim, ponies!"

I saw that they had their own ponies, much bigger than us and with finer manes. The big ponies did not speak to us foals, but they nudged and nuzzled us into the water. I had never swum before, but as soon as the ground dropped away in the sea, I found that I could. Together, we moved from the island to the mainland: the men, the grand ponies, and the foals.

On the mainland, there were many other humans. One was wearing a hat and carrying a board. He was making marks on the board, much like how Mother marked the rocks to track the time. He walked up and down the shore, making marks on the board when he got to each pony.

Other men lined up to talk to the man in the hat. He would point to something on the board and they would discuss for a moment. And then there was a handshake, and a pony was given a rope, and the man guided the pony away with the rope.

The other foals were chattering as we waited. "Wonder where I'll end up!" one of them said.

"Hope there are loblollies at my new home!" said another. But I didn't understand what all of it meant.

I was near the end of the line, but at last the man with the board came to me. He looped a thick rope over my head and gave the end of it to a young man in a cap the color of the sea. "Look at that," the man said. "She's got a lightning strike across her chest! Think I'll call her Lightning!"

I wondered how the man knew my name. I wondered where we were going. He patted my shoulder as we walked. I thought, *I like this man. He seems kind.*

"Okay, Lightning," he said. "It's time to go to your new home! Going to be a bit of a ride, so let's get you settled in!"

He guided me into a large box on wheels. It was full of hay and felt very warm and safe. I was still a little scared, but I trusted the man. When I was settled in, he closed a gate behind me. The box began to move, and

I tried not to be frightened. At least now I knew what "going away" meant.

The box moved along for many hours. I wondered if it was a whole day, but I didn't have Mother's rock to keep track. Finally, it stopped. Soon the man opened the gate and led me out.

We were at a large farm. It was sunny and cheery, and although there was no sea, I could see water nearby. I started to walk toward it.

"Whoa, easy there, girl," the man said. "You'll fall right into the canal if you aren't careful!"

Canal? I wondered what that word meant. Was it the word for the water I saw? But I did not have much time to think about it. The man led me to a house just for other ponies. I had my own area, which I learned was called a "stall." The pony house was called a "barn." And the other ponies were not ponies at all, but horses. The horses told me many things I would need to know in my new life.

The horses and I were to work in the field on the farm. But my work would not begin until the fall harvest. I spent my days in the pasture.

The man was very nice, as were the horses. But I was sad. I felt lonely. I missed Assateague Island and Mother. But each day I would watch the boats come through the canal and it cheered me up.

Each boat was pulled by strong animals called mules. They looked like ponies, but the horses said they were much stronger. The mules were directed by young men who called out commands. And on some of the boats, there was another animal called a dog.

Every day I watched the boats, hoping to catch the eye of one of the mules. I wanted to be just like them someday. But none of them would even look at me. However, someone else did—one of the dogs.

"Hello there, pony!" said the dog as he leapt off the boat and bounded toward me one afternoon.

"Hello, dog," I said.

"My name is Fritz," said the dog. "I am a border collie."

"My name is Lightning," I said.

"I see you every day," said Fritz. "Have you got no work here at the farm?"

I looked down at the grass. "Not yet. But someday, I would love to be a mule!"

Fritz laughed a little dog laugh. "You can't be a mule, silly pony! You're a pony!"

"But I would like to pull the boats. I would like to have a job like that."

"Ah, well, you'd have to work very hard," said Fritz. He paced about in a small circle and then lay down in the grass. "Say, would you like to have a trainer?"

"What's that?" I asked.

"Well, I would hop off the boat every morning and help you practice to be like the mules," he said. "I'm very fast, you see, and I could catch right back up to the boat later on in the day. Those mules move so slowly!"

"Okay," I said. "Let's do it!"

"I'll be back tomorrow with a plan," said Fritz.

The next day, Fritz came back. He was carrying a large rope in his teeth. "Ready for our training?" he asked.

He looped one end of the rope over my head and looped the other end around a thick tree branch. "Okay, Lightning, pull it!" he said.

The first branch was easy. *I could pull this all day!* I thought. Then Fritz added a second branch, and a third. The branches got heavier and heavier—and harder for me to pull.

"That's enough work for today, pony," said Fritz. "Good job! Let's do it again tomorrow!"

Every day, Fritz came back to help me train. The horses looked at me like I was crazy. "Who wants to pull a boat?" they said. "Who wants to stand in that dirty water all day?"

But every day I watched the mules and saw how proud they were of their job. I wanted to be proud like that. I wanted to do something important.

"What goes on the boats?" I asked Fritz one day.

"Everything!" he said. "All of the most important things in the world! Coal to make heat. Paving stones to build roads. Meat to feed families in the villages. Everything!"

I couldn't wait to work in the canal. I knew it was just the right job for me. So every day that summer, Fritz and I worked together to build my strength.

At last, in September, the horses were preparing to help with the harvest. It was my only chance! The man came out to corral the horses and get us ready to go into the field. It was the moment Fritz and I had been waiting for.

Fritz barked and danced in a little circle to get the man's attention. "What is it, dog?" he asked. Fritz barked more and led the man to where I was standing behind the barn. I had seven big logs attached to ropes behind me. Once I knew the man was looking, I started to walk straight ahead with them behind me. I kept my shoulders and my head up, proud like I saw the mules do.

"Well, look at that," the man said. "You'll be great at pulling our carts, Lightning!"

Oh no, I thought. *That's not at all what we wanted him to think!*

"Don't worry," Fritz told me, as if he could read my mind. "I've got it!" He ran back and forth between me and the canal, barking all along.

"What's that, boy?" asked the man. "The canal? You think Lightning here would make a good canal horse?"

Fritz finally stopped pacing and sat down promptly, wagging his tail and barking. I stomped my hoof for good measure.

"Well, it sure seems like that's the plan you two have cooked up!" the man said, laughing. "I'll see what I can do!"

I was overjoyed, but there were several long days of waiting. I did not see Fritz; I stayed in the field with the horses. And then, one sunny morning, I saw Fritz bounding off of one of the boats. "You're in!" he said. "They said it this morning! You're going on the line with me!"

I kicked my hooves up in excitement. "I'm going on a canal boat!" I said. "Oh, thank you, Fritz!" We danced around the field excitedly.

"Well, it looks like you two already got the news," said the man. He came around the side of the barn. "I'll miss you, Lightning, but it seems you've found your place."

I whinnied to show my appreciation. That very day, we went to one of the locks at the canal to get me fitted for my gear and hooked up to a boat. "You did it, Lightning!" said Fritz, very proud.

"Because of your help!" I said.

We started off on the canal that day, carrying important goods to all of the towns. Each time we passed by my old farm, I whinnied and nodded to the horses there, and they whinnied back. I stood proud in the canal each day, and I let the little children of the towns come up and pat my forelock.

Fritz and I worked the canal for many years together. We made many more friends along the way and did many important deliveries. And never again was I lonely or bored. I had my purpose, and although I never forgot Assateague Island, I was very, very happy on the C&O Canal.

Cinderella: A Retelling

written by Steve Karscig
illustrated by Matthew Casper

Once upon a time, there was a girl named Cinderella who was left in the care of her stepmother. Cinderella's stepmother had two daughters of her own. The stepmother and her daughters made Cinderella their servant, while the three of them did very little work. Cinderella worked hard, but, at times, the other three women in the house frustrated her. The stepmother and her daughters considered Cinderella a lesser person. Their meanness and cruel attitudes frequently reminded Cinderella that they would rather make fun of her than have a loving and devoted family. At night, Cinderella would sleep by the cinders in the fireplace to keep warm, which is how she received her name.

Cinderella's only friends were some house mice. Cinderella was a very caring person; she tried to show everyone kindness. Cinderella fed the mice scraps of food and talked to them. The mice favored Cinderella and enjoyed being around her.

One day, while Cinderella was in the forest, she accidentally met the prince of her kingdom. Cinderella was unaware that he was the prince, and they spoke for a short while. Both Cinderella and the prince amused each other, and each liked the other's company.

After only one meeting, the prince was entranced by Cinderella's kindness and subtle beauty. Soon after, the prince decided to hold a fancy ball. In secret, he hoped that Cinderella would somehow come to the ball. He invited the entire kingdom, hoping to see her.

Hearing the news about the ball, Cinderella was eager to attend. When Cinderella told her stepmother and stepsisters about the ball, they too became excited. Cinderella assumed that she could also attend the ball, but her stepmother quickly trampled her hopes.

Devastated, Cinderella sat at home alone and talked to the mice. However, Cinderella's Fairy Godmother appeared and magically fashioned a dress, a carriage made from a pumpkin, and a coachman to drive the carriage. The Fairy Godmother gave Cinderella a pair of glass slippers to wear with her gown. The Fairy Godmother also warned Cinderella that this magic would last only until midnight.

Cinderella appeared at the ball and immediately captured the prince's attention. Together, they danced, talked, and laughed. However, just before the stroke of midnight, Cinderella quickly left. She did not want the prince to see her magic disappear. As Cinderella left the ball, one of her glass slippers fell off, and she had to leave it behind. Confused, the prince picked up the glass slipper and vowed to search the kingdom for Cinderella.

The prince asked every maiden in the kingdom to try on the glass slipper. When the prince arrived at Cinderella's residence, her stepsisters both tried on the slipper, but it did not fit no matter how hard they tried to force it. Finally, Cinderella arrived and tried on the slipper. It was a perfect fit. The prince decided to marry Cinderella, and they lived happily ever after. Due to their unkind ways, Cinderella's stepmother and stepsisters were forced to live as servants, just as they had done to Cinderella.

On Chestnut Street

written by Summer York
illustrated by D. Kent Kerr

"Did you see my awesome jump shot?" Colin asked Darius as they walked home from basketball practice.

"Yeah," replied Darius, "but it wasn't as good as my three-pointer." He stopped mid-step and shot a pretend basket. "And the crowd goes wild!" he yelled and threw his arms in the air. Colin rolled his eyes and they both snickered.

As always, though, their mood changed when they turned onto Chestnut Street. The boys fell silent and walked a little faster past the old Nelson place. Colin tried not to look at the dark stone house lurking up on the hill; it gave him the creeps.

It was a known fact among the neighborhood kids that the old house was haunted. No one had lived there for years—at least no living person. But Joey Cole swore he had seen a ghost in the attic window. Joey was a sixth grader, so he knew what he was talking about. Other kids said they heard eerie creaking and clanging sounds coming from the basement late at night. No kid had ever been brave enough to go near the place. Certainly, anyone who dared to enter the rusty gate and disappear through the overgrown trees toward the house was never coming back.

Colin had never seen any ghosts. But more than once, he was sure he had seen movement in the shadowy bushes out of the corner of his eye. He was relieved when they had left that gloomy house behind them. Colin looked at Darius and laughed nervously. As they continued down the street, Colin glanced over his shoulder toward the house. A cold shiver ran down his spine, and he couldn't shake the feeling of being watched.

On the Ice – An Excerpt

written by Jennifer Tkocs
illustrated by Sean Ricciardi

Ted O'Keefe skates down the ice with the puck. He glides over the blue line and sneaks in between two defensemen. There are thirty seconds left in the third period, and his team, the Chiefs, is down by a single goal. If the Chiefs win, they advance to the playoffs. O'Keefe knows they can score a game-tying goal to get them into overtime.

He glances around the ice at his teammates as he holds onto the puck. He spots fellow forward Larry Fitzkowski just to the side of the goal. Larry nods at him, and O'Keefe passes the puck to Larry. As soon as the shot leaves Larry's stick, O'Keefe knows that the puck is not going to get past the goalie.

O'Keefe skates in close to the goal just as the netminder deflects the puck away toward one of his own players. But O'Keefe senses where it's headed, and he spins around just in time. He intercepts the puck before it reaches the opposing player and blasts a rising shot at the net. The puck sails over the goaltender's left shoulder and into the goal. The alarm sounds; with only ten seconds left, O'Keefe has tied the game. The Chiefs force the game into overtime, and their playoff hopes remain alive.

Jack and the Beanstalk

adapted by Jennifer Tkocs
illustrated by Brittanie Markham

Once upon a time, a boy named Jack lived with his frail, elderly mother and their even frailer and more elderly cow, Bessy. Jack's mother was unable to work, which meant the family never had any money. They barely had the means to afford food each week.

"Jack, we've run out of money and resources," his mother said at last. "We have no choice but to sell old Bessy down at the market."

The next day, Jack woke early and walked Bessy down to the market at the center of town.

"Be sure to fetch a fair price for her!" his mother called after them.

Jack had only been at the market a few moments when a strange old man approached him.

"Say," the old man began, "are you selling that old cow?"

"I am," Jack confirmed. "She's old, but she's worth a good price."

"If you give me that cow," the old man said, "I'll give you these three magic beans."

"Magic beans?" Jack asked with wonder.

"Quite magical," the old man said. "It's a once-in-a-lifetime opportunity!"

Jack was quite taken by the man's proposition, and so he handed over Bessy's reins. He placed the beans in his pocket and ran all the way home.

Jack's mother was waiting by the door when he arrived.

"That didn't take long!" she exclaimed. "I'm sad to see the old girl go, but it'll be worth it to keep us fed. How much did you get for her?"

"Three magic beans!" Jack said, taking the beans from his pocket.

"Magic beans?" exclaimed his mother. "You foolish boy! How will we feed ourselves on three beans, and with winter just a few weeks away?"

"But they're magical!" Jack insisted.

"Yes, they've magically gotten you sent to your room," his mother said. "Go there and don't come out all night!"

Jack trudged off to his room, angry that his mother did not believe him.

She'll see that they're magic, he thought, tossing the beans out his window before going to bed.

In the morning, Jack rushed to the window. Sure enough, a giant beanstalk had grown from the beans! It stretched so high into the sky that he could not see the top of it.

"Ha! This will prove to Mother that I'm not foolish!" Before his mother even awoke, Jack raced down the stairs and began to climb the beanstalk.

He climbed and climbed to the very top, and there, high above the clouds, Jack discovered a magnificent castle in the sky.

This will be my golden ticket! Jack thought. *I'll find treasures here to feed Mother and myself for years!*

However, Jack had barely crept inside the door when he heard a voice bellowing down the hall.

Jack froze and peered around the wall and down the hallway. There, at the end of the hallway, sat an enormous giant. On the chair next to him sat a hen that had just laid an enormous golden egg. In the giant's lap was a majestic golden harp.

Suddenly, the giant set the harp down and stood up, sniffing the air around him.

"Fee-fi-foe-fum!" the giant hollered. "I smell the blood of an Englishman. Be he alive, or be he dead, I'll grind his bones to make my bread."

The giant turned toward where Jack was cowering behind a wall and began to walk, each step rumbling like thunder and shaking the floor.

Jack had to think fast. The giant was huge, but the boy had speed on his side. Instead of leaving through the door by which he had entered, Jack raced toward the giant and past him. The giant was taken off guard, clearly expecting Jack to run out instead of in. Jack grabbed the hen and golden harp and sprinted back to the front door of the castle.

Jack heard the giant chasing after him as quickly as he could. Luckily, Jack was much faster. He scampered down the beanstalk and raced to the barn. He placed the harp and hen on the ground and grabbed an ax.

Just as the giant was about to reach the top of the beanstalk to climb down, Jack began to hack away at it with the ax. He hacked and hacked and finally the beanstalk fell to the ground, stranding the giant in the sky.

Jack gathered up the hen and harp and ran to his stunned mother. They stood together in their front yard.

"I told you the beans were magic, Mother!" he said.

Aided by the hen's golden eggs, Jack and his mother lived happily ever after and were even able to buy back Bessy the cow.

The Police Report of Alfred Giant

written by Jennifer Tkocs
illustrated by Brittanie Markham

Ah, yes, Officer Murphy, thank you for writing down this police report. I would write it myself, but my hands are shaking far too badly to get it all down. Ah, curse that horrible intruder!

Yes, officer, my name is A. Giant. The "A" is short for Alfred. The boy who caused all this trouble, I believe, was named Jack.

This is a devastating tale of multiple offenses against me, the gentlest giant who ever lived—a tale of stolen goods, breaking and entering, trespassing, and the destruction of property. You see, when I confronted that foolish boy—and *thank you* for taking that menace into custody, by the way—he ran out my door so quickly that the door came off one of its hinges!

I apologize, sir. I am very upset, and so I am rushing too far ahead. I'll start at the beginning.

It was Tuesday morning, August the fourth—yes, yesterday. I've only now had a chance to come down to the station because…well, I had to take some time to compose myself. You see, the boy stole my very best friend: my pet hen. And I'm sure…oh, goodness, I'm sure the boy and his awful mother ate my hen. I loved that hen. I can't believe my dear friend Hennifer is gone. That's my hen's name, Hennifer.

I'm sorry. I will try not to cry for the rest of the story. This all began yesterday, right after I arrived home from my volunteer work. You see, I'm a volunteer story reader at the nearby school for blind cloud children.

People say that I have a wonderful voice for that sort of thing. I think it's so important to give back to the community, don't you?

Ah, my apologies. I'm so flustered that I keep getting off track. The story!

I had just arrived outside my home and noticed that there was this rather large beanstalk I'd never seen before. But you know how it is in the summer. Summertime is construction season, and the crews are always putting up new detours around the neighborhood. I just assumed it was something to do with them—and *not* an irresponsible young man trying his hand at advanced botany.

So, you can understand now why I didn't feel the need to report this strange new foliage. I came home and began to make breakfast for myself and my dear, dear hen, Hennifer Saint Marie. That's her *full* name. Hennifer just loves fresh grain in the morning.

This will explain one of the boy's accusations. The boy said I shouted, "I smell the blood of an Englishman."

What on earth does that even mean? It doesn't even make sense. What I clearly said was, "I smell the food of a Cornish hen!"

I was singing to Hennifer, you see, to get her excited for breakfast. Ask yourself this, officer: Why would I, a grown giant, admit to the fact that I sing to my hen about her breakfast if it weren't true?

Teenagers, on the other hand, will tell you all sorts of tall tales to avoid taking responsibility for their actions.

Regardless, that rapscallion shouldn't have been near enough to hear *any* words I said!

Well, no, officer, my door was not locked. This is a remarkably safe neighborhood. It's up in a cloud, with no roads, for goodness' sake. However, just because a door's unlocked doesn't mean you have the right to barge in uninvited!

Anyway, I was in the kitchen, and I had my harp out to play Hennifer a nice little song. I always play my harp for my pets. It eases their stress right away!

But then—*then*, officer—that awful young man raced down my hall. I had been raised by my giant mother never to run in hallways, but the boy paid no mind to common sense. It took me by surprise, and, before I knew it, he'd snatched up my harp and poor Hennifer too.

Now, I'm fit enough to jump between clouds, but I'm no runner, you see. So, I couldn't very well chase this boy.

Then, he was gone, just like that! Off with my property and my very dear Hennifer. Then, the boy chopped down that new beanstalk. I'd grown fond of it in that short time, so that was upsetting too.

So, here I am now. That's the series of events to the best of my memory.

Wait! What's that sound? It sounds just like the sweet clucking of…. You've found her! My beautiful Hennifer! She must have escaped the clutches of that evil family.

Wait. So, you mean to say that the boy gave up my hen of his own accord? Well, that is a pleasant surprise. In that case, I suppose you can downgrade the charges. Maybe just sentence the boy to a few dozen years of community service instead of throwing him in prison. Regardless, he does need to learn a lesson.

Oh, dear Hennifer, I'm so glad to see you safe. Kids today just do not understand the bond a lonely old giant can share with his dearest hen. If you ever need anything at all, officer—particularly if something is stuck on a very tall shelf—please feel free to come knocking.

The Tortoise and the Hare

adapted by Summer York
illustrated by David Rushbrook

One pleasant summer afternoon, several of the forest animals gathered in the soft grass of the meadow to enjoy the sunshine. The spring rains were over, and the work of gathering food for winter had not yet begun. It was a peaceful time. The forest creatures looked forward to passing a restful afternoon in quiet, neighborly harmony. They had just settled in when Hare happened by the gathering.

Hare could not be peaceful or restful for any amount of time. He burst into the meadow so unexpectedly as to startle old Owl from his perch upon the fencepost. A few animals grumbled at being disturbed from their afternoon naps. But Hare did not seem to notice. He spotted Tortoise in one group and hopped over to join. Bouncing to and fro, Hare loudly began one of his favorite topics.

"Tortoise, good friend, would you care to race today?" Hare asked, barely able to contain his laughter. He bounded quick circles around Tortoise, who was not amused. Hare often teased Tortoise for his slowness. Despite his slow movements, though, Tortoise's mind was quick.

"Stop laughing, Hare, or I shall be forced to race you," Tortoise replied. "And you will not laugh so rudely when I win."

At that, Hare laughed so hard that he fell on his back and clutched his stomach. "You? Win?" he asked between gasps. "You could not beat me! You are the slowest in the forest, and I am the fastest. None has ever beaten me!"

"Even you cannot win every race," observed Tortoise. Seized by a new fit of laughter, Hare rolled and flopped about on the ground like a fish. The other animals soon grew tired of Hare's bragging.

By and by, it was decided that Hare and Tortoise should race. Whoever circled the meadow and got back to the fencepost first would be the winner. The animals chattered in excitement. Although they wanted Tortoise to win, they held little hope of him beating Hare. Owl was to be the judge of the race. He perched regally again on the fencepost and waited as Tortoise and Hare took their places on the starting line.

"Racers to your marks!" Owl called out grandly. "Ready…go!" Tortoise plodded slowly over the starting line and away from the cheering crowd. After Tortoise had inched ahead, Hare scampered after him.

"Surely you can't think of winning at that sluggish pace," Hare said as he quickly approached his competitor. Tortoise paid no mind to Hare's jeering; with his brow furrowed in concentration, he fixed his eyes ahead and plodded one footstep at a time. Shrugging, Hare bounded across the meadow and was soon out of sight.

Once Hare rounded the first bend, he decided he was in no great rush. It would be some time before the laboring Tortoise came this far. He yawned sleepily and looked about him. After all, it was a rather warm day. Hare spotted an inviting patch of clover a little way off the path. He ate his fill, yawned again, and stretched. Seeing Tortoise still far behind, Hare thought he should like to steal a short nap. Surely he would wake up as Tortoise drew near, then Hare could speed past him once again. Satisfied, he curled up in a shady patch of thick grass and was soon fast asleep.

Meanwhile, Tortoise came to the first bend in the course. There, he spotted the careless Hare slumbering soundly in the grass. He crept by so as not to wake Hare. Without so much as a glance behind, Tortoise went slowly but steadily on his way.

As the orange sun began to disappear behind the trees, casting shadows across the meadow, Hare still slept undisturbed. Tortoise, on the other hand, was nearing the finish line and the waiting crowd. When they saw him, his friends gave a ringing cheer that echoed across the meadow. Hearing the cheers, Hare awoke with a start. He frantically searched the meadow for Tortoise and finally saw him near the finish line. Hare raced forward as fast as his springing legs could carry him, but it was no use. By the time Hare crossed the finish line, out of breath, Tortoise had already won. Hare hung his head in shame as Tortoise stated, "Slow and steady wins the race."

From the Desk of Hare

written by Summer York

I'm sure you've heard that fabled story of the Tortoise and the Hare. You know the one—the slow Tortoise beats the Hare in a race, even though the Hare is much faster. In the end, the Hare is shamed and the Tortoise comes out looking like the good guy. Well, that's not the whole story. Let me tell you how it really happened.

I remember it was a glorious summer day. I had spent the morning in the cabbage patch enjoying a fine meal. With a full stomach, I was feeling great. So I took myself to the meadow in search of some of my neighbors. But when I got there, everyone was lazing around. Honestly, they looked bored. It seemed wrong to waste such a lovely afternoon in that way. I thought I would join their party and liven things up a bit. I saw Tortoise and went over to him.

"Tortoise, good friend, would you care to race today?" I asked him. Now, I admit that Tortoise and I never seemed to get along. Sure, sometimes I joked about how slow Tortoise was. It was all in good fun, though. It isn't my fault if he couldn't take a joke. Not surprisingly, the old stick-in-the-mud didn't laugh.

"Stop laughing, Hare, or I shall be forced to race you," Tortoise replied. "And you will not laugh so rudely when I win." When he said that, I burst out laughing. Can you blame me? The very idea of Tortoise beating me in a race was unbelievable. But you probably know what happened next—that crazy Tortoise agreed to a race.

Well, this surprising turn of events presented a problem. On one hand, I couldn't actually race Tortoise. He would certainly lose, and I didn't want to humiliate him in front of our friends. On the other hand, though, I couldn't *not* race. It was my idea, after all. So I made a decision.

When Owl puffed himself up importantly and shouted "Go!" I let Tortoise get a head start. Then I bounded past him and across the meadow. However,

this wasn't to make him look bad; I wouldn't do that to poor Tortoise. I ran ahead to find a good spot for a nap. Let me assure you, this wasn't the accidental nap of which the fable accuses me. I only pretended to nap so that I could let Tortoise win.

I found a splendid patch of clover to have a light snack. Then I stretched out in a nice, shady spot to wait for Tortoise. Although I did snooze on and off, I was quite awake when I heard the slow-poke coming. Tortoise had no idea; he thought I had fallen asleep in the middle of the race! I would like to point out that he didn't even stop to wake me up. If I had been sleeping, Tortoise only would have won because he cheated. Now who's the bad guy?

Anyway, after a few hours of relaxing in my comfy spot, I finally heard the crowd cheering at the finish line. I sped off, making a big show of running as fast as I could to try to catch Tortoise. But I slowed down at the end to let Tortoise finish first. Then I dramatically dragged myself over the finish line and collapsed, gasping for breath. This was all for show, of course; I wasn't even winded.

Truthfully, losing the race did hurt my ego. But I suppose seeing the look of victory on Tortoise's face was worth sacrificing a win—because I'm such a nice guy. Oh, and by the way, Tortoise never said that fancy moral, "Slow and steady wins the race." He added that into the story later to make himself look even better. And now you know how the Tortoise really beat the Hare.

Sam's Lessons

written by Sarah Marino
illustrated by D. Kent Kerr

"I've been taking piano lessons for six years. I want to do something new! Please, Dad. I really want to take drum lessons, like Clay." Samantha made her argument carefully, walking around her father in circles like some kind of mad crow. Her hair, which was almost crow black, was pulled into two long braids on either side of her head. She wore black jeans and a bright green long-sleeved T-shirt that had tiny white flowers on it. While she loved clothes and shoes, she was not so much into other girly things that some of her friends were starting to like, such as make-up and cheerleading. Sam felt a strong pull toward music and rhythm, almost like there was a compass inside her that was steadily pointing to piano, and now drums.

Both Sam and her older brother, Clay, who was fifteen, had taken piano lessons since the age of five. Clay had now been taking drum lessons for four years. The "racket" (as their father called it) of his drumming in the basement would flow through the house and beat notes in Sam's chest. As she watched Clay's skills advance, she realized it was something she wanted to do as well.

"One more person drumming in this house is not acceptable to me. I'm sorry, Sam," her father was saying, rotating where he stood to follow her as she circled him. "I work all day long at a construction site, surrounded by jackhammers and machines. I don't want more noise at home."

Sam stopped abruptly and peered into her father's stern expression. His dark eyes were shadowy, but they seemed to soften a little when she peered up at him. "It's not fair," she said.

"Life isn't fair."

"But we have drums already. I've been saving money and could take lessons at the store in town. You don't have to do anything! I'll practice when you're not

here." Sam had started circling again. Her father turned and put his hands on her shoulders.

Sam shrugged him off and moved toward the back door. "Mom would let me. She would want me to pursue my dreams. You're mean!"

"Your mother cares more about her newest boyfriend than you and Clay. You don't—"

"At least she loves *someone*!" Sam shouted without thinking, then turned and fled out of the house. She ran as fast as she could down the street toward Highland Park. It was half a mile, and she ran the entire way until she came to the line of oak trees and pines where the park began. Her heart was thumping in her chest as if someone were chasing her, but she turned around and saw that her father, of course, had not followed her.

Taking a deep breath, she began to walk slowly into the park. She found a trail near the pool, which was closed for the winter, and she followed it deeper into the woods. The trees were mostly bare now. Some had a few bright yellow leaves still hanging on like misplaced mittens. Her heart felt normal again after a while, and she trudged up and down the dried-out dirt path, occasionally passing other people: families with dogs, couples, and solitary runners. Most people smiled; Sam smiled back even though she didn't feel like it.

When she could no longer see the pool, she realized she had taken a trail that she'd never been on before. At this realization, her heart fluttered a few beats. She stopped and looked around. *I can always just go back the way I came*, she thought. Feeling hungry and thirsty, she found a large rock a little way off the path and sat there eating a granola bar she happened to have in her bag. She could hear the stream off to her left and thought of taking a drink from it, when a raindrop appeared on her hand, and then another and another on her jeans. She looked up and wondered how she hadn't noticed that the sky had turned a murky dark grey.

Maybe it was the rain or not knowing her way, but teardrops began falling down Sam's cheeks. Why had she come into the woods, anyway? She couldn't remember clearly now. She just wanted to take drum lessons. Her father was unfair and rude. She would never talk to him again, she decided, and began walking back along the path.

A low rumble of thunder groaned in the distance and the raindrops became fatter and faster. She couldn't see very far ahead, and her own tears fell faster now, too. She tried running, but quickly tripped and fell, skinning her palms. As she pushed back onto her knees, she heard a rustling in the brush ahead, and then a large black and brown fur ball bounded out of the shrubs and headed toward her. Her mouth dropped and she let out a squeal. "George!" Her dog ran to her and licked her cheeks happily. She fell back onto the ground again, laughing, and saw her brother turn the path toward her. "Clay!"

"Hey, we were worried about you!" her brother said, running over to her. He grabbed her arms and lifted her up. "Didn't you hear about the storm? We need to get back. What happened with Dad?"

Sam told her brother about the fight as they walked home in the thunderstorm. George, fortunately, was not afraid of thunder—probably because he'd heard drums in the house since he was a puppy. He walked protectively by Sam's side the entire way home. She petted him every so often and stopped to hug him a few times, too. Normally, she would have taken him with her to the park, but she had left in such a stew.

"Just don't bring Mom into it. We all miss her." Clay pushed his chin-length brown hair behind his ear. He smiled at her. "I'll give you secret lessons if you promise not to tell."

"I want real lessons," she said, rolling her eyes at him. He laughed.

Their father was standing at the door waiting for them. He came down the walk and hugged Sam. "Please don't run off like that, Sam. I'm sorry," he said. "You're really serious about this drum thing?"

"Yeah, pretty serious," Sam said.

"All right. Let's go inside and talk," her father said.

As they walked through the front door, Sam smiled to herself, thinking of the first beat she might learn on the drums.

The Man, the Boy, and the Donkey

adapted by Luke See
illustrated by Sean Ricciardi

One day a young boy and his father prepared to travel into town to sell some vegetables from their farm. They took their donkey and loaded a few sacks of carrots and potatoes onto its back. The father led the donkey onto the road and started toward town with his son by his side. As they went, an old man followed behind them, walking with a cane. The two hadn't walked more than a mile when they came upon a young stranger. The man looked up at the donkey and its owners and laughed out loud at them.

"How silly you both are," said the stranger. "What is the purpose of owning such a donkey if you do not even ride him when you travel to town?" The young man shook his head and walked past the father, who frowned upon hearing this. The father stopped and thought hard until he finally made up his mind. He lifted his son onto the donkey's back so that the boy could ride upon the animal. The son balanced himself between the carrots and potatoes, and they resumed their journey.

The donkey trotted along with the father at his side holding the reins. As they passed a small farm, they ran into a group of men who were sitting in the shade. The men were taking a break from their work. As the donkey passed in front of them, a few stood and glared at the boy on the animal's back.

"What kind of son are you to make your poor father walk on foot while you yourself ride upon the back of that donkey?" one man asked. "You ought not to be so lazy and let your father ride the beast. He is your elder and a hardworking man."

The other men nodded in agreement. The boy looked down at his father and the two exchanged confused glances. Finally, the father ordered his son to get off of the donkey and handed the boy the reins. The father mounted the back of the animal and then urged it forward with his son walking alongside. The men beneath the tree congratulated the father on being stern and waved at him as he rode past. The old man followed behind slowly, still a few hundred feet to the rear of the donkey.

The father and son had not managed to go very far when they ran into more strangers on the road. This time, two old women passed by carrying baskets of fabrics and knitting tools. As the donkey approached, the father saw the ladies' disapproving looks before they even spoke a word. The younger of the two women stepped in front of the donkey and stared up at the father.

"Shame on you, sir! What kind of lazy, good-for-nothing father lets his poor son drag his feet through the dirt when he himself rides upon the back of a donkey? Why would you not let him ride upon the donkey as well?" The father quickly nodded in agreement with the women and reached down to help his son onto the donkey. He nestled the boy in between the sacks of supplies and looked down for the women's approval.

"That's much better," one said. "That's exactly how you should have been traveling in the first place!"

The father snapped the reins and the donkey continued forward, slower than before. Although their pace had slowed, the old man did not pass them but instead remained a few dozen steps behind. By the time the donkey reached town, it was nearly midday. The father and son noticed that many of the townspeople were pointing and whispering at them as they road through the square. Finally, one burly farmer marched out of the crowd and toward the donkey.

"What kind of farmer are you to treat a donkey so poorly? You have overloaded this old animal with far too much weight by riding upon it with your son. You should be embarrassed of yourselves!" With that, the man turned and trudged back toward the crowd, where others patted him on the back and glared at the father and son. The father was stunned and had no idea what to do. He got off of the donkey's back and lifted his son down as well.

He noticed that the old man who had followed them was leaning on his cane and studying the donkey. Seeing no other option, the father bent over and whispered his plan into his son's ear. He counted out loud and on three, the father and son lifted the donkey in the air with all of their might. The sacks of vegetables hung over their backs as each of them held two of the startled donkey's legs. With the animal upon their backs, they trudged through the square in the direction of the market on the other side of town.

However, the father and his son grew very weary from carrying the donkey. They had barely made it through town when they finally had to stop and rest. They set the donkey back down on its legs and slumped to the ground, each trying to catch his breath. After only a few moments, both the father and son fell asleep right on top of the vegetables.

The father awoke to find that it was nearly sunset. Both he and his son had slept the entire day away. He roused his son and the two gathered their things before they noticed that the donkey was missing. They looked all around the town, but the animal was long gone. They sadly returned to their vegetable sacks feeling completely defeated. Sitting on a low wall not far from them was the old man from the road.

He studied the father and son as they lifted their burden. "That will teach you," he said as he stood and limped past them. "If you try to please all, you will please no one."

A Portrait of Ms. Graham

written by Summer York
illustrated by Brian Cibelli

All the students had gone home for the day, but Ms. Graham still sat working at her desk. She was the sixth grade social studies teacher at Parks Middle School in downtown Baltimore. She had also recently begun a tutoring program at the school. Knowing that most students' families could not afford to pay for tutoring, she offered it for free. This meant Ms. Graham was not paid for her extra time. She did not mind, though, because test scores were already improving. Ms. Graham wanted to see her students do well. Therefore, she sometimes felt frustrated that the school had to operate with such a small amount of money each year. In fact, she had talked about her classroom's old social studies textbooks at the last school board meeting. "How can my students learn about current events from a textbook that is fifteen years old?" she had asked. However, her request for new textbooks had been denied. The school simply did not have enough money to buy new ones. Ms. Graham had been disappointed, but she was tireless when it came to her students. She would not give up so easily.

The Love Bug

written by Summer York
illustrated by Mallory Senich

Andrew Chapman had survived four whole months of sixth grade. It wasn't easy; middle school was a confusing place. To begin with, you had to wear the right clothes, sit at the right lunch table—the rules went on and on, and they could change in a flash. You had to keep up. One wrong move and you were fish food for the hungry eighth grade sharks. In the fast-paced world of middle school, Andrew quickly realized the only thing he knew for sure was that he wasn't sure about anything at all.

Furthermore—as if Andrew didn't have enough to worry about—he was becoming convinced that all of his friends had some sort of flu. They were acting strangely; instead of talking about baseball and music and the usual guy stuff, they all wanted to talk about girls. Even weirder, they wanted to talk *to* girls. A few girls had even started sitting with Andrew and his friends at lunch. Andrew wasn't sure when that had happened. Last he'd heard, girls had cooties. Apparently, now it was the guys who had some bizarre illness. Andrew wondered if he would catch it.

Andrew realized that it might be hard to avoid, though. The principal had announced last week that there would be a big dance in the gym on Valentine's Day. Since then, pink and red had invaded the halls. Everywhere Andrew looked he saw posters and giant glittering hearts advertising the dance. He found himself in grave danger of catching this bizarre flu. He wondered if his mom would let him stay home from school until Valentine's Day was over.

***

"Andrew, telephone!" Andrew's mom called from the kitchen. Andrew ran in and grabbed the handset off the counter. "It's Tony," his mom informed him.

"Hey, Tony," Andrew said into the phone.

"Hey, man," Tony replied. "Listen, I can't play football today. I have to go to the mall with Angelica instead." Andrew silently rolled his eyes. Angelica was Tony's girlfriend, which basically meant Tony had to do whatever Angelica said. And she was really bossy.

"Whatever. Maybe tomorrow," Andrew offered. "Have fun," he added sarcastically.

"Yeah, right. See ya." Tony hung up. Andrew put the handset back on the charger and shook his head.

"What's up?" asked Andrew's mom as she set a plate of brownies on the counter between them. Andrew explained the phone call.

"Tony has a girlfriend, huh?" Andrew's mom said with a smile. "It sounds like he has the love bug." She broke off a piece of brownie and popped it in her mouth.

"What do you mean?" Andrew asked.

"You know, the love bug," she said. "It happens when hanging out with a girl becomes more important than doing guy stuff."

"Oh," Andrew replied thoughtfully. So that's what all the guys at school had. "Is it contagious?" he asked with concern.

"Not exactly," his mom explained. "It's not a real illness. It just happens at a certain age."

"If what Tony has is the love bug, I don't want it," Andrew decided. His mom just laughed as she finished her brownie.

"We'll see," she said.

***

The next afternoon, Andrew and his friends were gathered in the school parking lot. They were just about to start for home when a shrill voice stopped them.

"Anthony Nucci!" It was Angelica. She stopped a little way from the group and put her hands on her hips. Tony's eyes widened. "We have to talk," she told him with a raised eyebrow and a scowl.

"Uh-oh," said Justin quietly. "My dad said it's never a good thing when a woman says that." The boys shuffled their feet and avoided looking at Tony. Having no other choice, Tony left the group and went over to Angelica. She immediately let out a torrent of words that caused her hands to flail wildly around her head. Andrew and the other boys walked away, leaving Tony at the mercy of his girlfriend.

As they left, Justin shuddered and let out a long, low whistle. They all nodded slowly in agreement. Andrew thought about what his mom had said. If that was the love bug, why would anyone want it? His mom had said it wasn't exactly contagious. Still, he hoped he wouldn't catch it.

***

The love bug was spreading rapidly with the approach of Valentine's Day. As a result, the girls were acting even odder than usual. When Jessica Dines passed Andrew in the hall, she called out, "Hi, Andrew," in a sing-song voice and then giggled loudly with her friends. Embarrassed, Andrew just ducked his head low and kept walking. It wasn't only the sixth grade girls, either; the teachers also had symptoms. Miss Avery, Andrew's English teacher, was even talking about love stories.

"Settle down, class," Miss Avery announced. "As you know, we've been discussing Greek mythology. Today we're going to learn about the Trojan War. Does anyone know how the Trojan War began?" The students shook their heads. "It all started because of love," Miss Avery informed them.

Of course it did, thought Andrew with a frown. Miss Avery explained that the Trojan War was a war that happened in Greek mythology. It began when Paris, prince of the city of Troy, fell in love with Helen, wife of King Menelaus of Sparta. Paris took Helen back to Troy with him and married her without Menelaus knowing. When Menelaus discovered this, he was so angry that he took the entire Greek army to fight Paris and the city of Troy. The war lasted ten years. In the end, Troy was destroyed, Paris was killed, and Helen went back to Sparta with Menelaus.

"They fought an entire war over love?" asked Justin in disbelief. "It sounds like a whole lot of trouble for nothing."

"Not for nothing," argued Bethany, who sat in front of Andrew. "It was for love. It's *romantic*."

"But Paris's whole city was destroyed just because he stole Helen from her husband. That's crazy!" Justin insisted. An argument soon erupted among several students about whether Paris was romantic or out of his mind. Andrew, on the other hand, was deep in thought. If the love bug could start a ten-year war and destroy a whole city, it was even more dangerous than he thought. He was convinced that he wanted nothing to do with love. He made up his mind to avoid the love bug altogether.

***

Andrew tugged at his collared shirt and wondered again why he had agreed to come. He looked around the gym as the music thumped loudly through the speakers. To Andrew, going to a dance meant standing around and trying not to look awkward. It obviously meant the same thing to everyone else—kids lined the gym walls, but the dance floor was empty.

Actually, Andrew's friends had practically forced him to come. "Everyone is going. You can't sit at home alone on Valentine's Day," they had insisted. Eventually, Andrew had agreed so that he could hang out with his buddies. However, Andrew's friends were more interested in talking to a group of girls. Among the group were Tony's girlfriend, Angelica, and Jessica Dines. Every few minutes, Andrew would catch Jessica looking at him. He noticed with some alarm that she had pretty eyes. He looked away and tugged at his collar uncomfortably.

When a slow song began to play, a few couples headed for the dance floor. Angelica begged Tony to dance with her and dragged him away before he could protest. As the group dwindled, Andrew found himself alone with Jessica. She looked up at him and smiled.

"I like this song," she said. Andrew couldn't think of anything to say. His mouth was suddenly dry, so he just nodded his head. They stood there in embarrassed silence, watching the dancing couples. Andrew struggled to think of something—anything—to say. But it was as if he had forgotten every word he ever knew. The seconds ticked by like hours. His mind raced. Just when he had finally formed a clear sentence in his mind, Jessica planted a swift kiss on his cheek and walked quickly away. He stood frozen in shock, his eyes wide. He felt his cheeks burn, and his stomach flip-flopped. He wasn't sure if he felt like laughing or throwing up. And in that moment, he knew he had caught the love bug. Surprisingly, though, he didn't mind. Maybe it wouldn't be so bad after all.

Ollie's Outing

written by Jennifer Tkocs
illustrated by Sean Kennedy

Ollie Owl was lost.

One minute, he was strolling along on his usual Tuesday afternoon nature walk. The next thing he knew, he was down a path he had never seen before.

Lovely purple flowers grew all along the path. "Oh, dear," Ollie said to himself. "These flowers are so beautiful; I know I would recognize them if I'd been here before!"

Ollie looked all around him, but nothing was familiar. How did he get so off track? He had been concentrating really hard on his strategy for the upcoming Chess Fest Tournament at school. Still, he had never just wandered away from his regular route.

"Think, Ollie, think," he told himself. "Oh, that's right. I remember how to get un-lost now! First, I must retrace my steps!"

He turned around in a small circle and realized a new problem. "Oh, dear. I can't remember which way is backward!"

Ollie looked in every direction, but all the paths looked vaguely unfamiliar. He could not remember any of them! He lifted up some plants with his beak and looked under the leaves. "Perhaps I will see my toe tracks!" he thought. "If I can just find my toe tracks, I can follow them right back to my nest."

However, there were no toe tracks to be found beneath the leaves. "Well, I certainly didn't fly out here," thought Ollie. "Where did my journey begin?"

"Hello there, young owl!" a voice called down from a tree.

"Who's there?" asked Ollie.

"It's me, Frannie Falcon!"

Ollie did not know a Frannie Falcon. He knew a Ferdinand Finch, but Ferd didn't live anywhere near here. "Who are you, Frannie Falcon?"

"Why, I'm the Captain of Avian Travel Adventures in this part of the forest!"

Frannie Falcon sounded awfully nice, but Ollie had never heard of any Avian Travel Adventure Department. "If you don't mind my asking, ma'am… what does that mean?"

Frannie flew down from her tree branch and landed in front of Ollie. "I help my fellow birds go on exciting adventure vacations."

Ollie looked down at his toes. "Oh. Well, I'm not trying to go on a vacation."

"What are you trying to do?" Frannie asked.

"My name is Ollie Owl, and I'm trying to get home," he said. "I've gotten lost."

Frannie puffed out her wings. "Lost! Why, no one gets lost in these parts of the woods! We'll figure it out together. Now, from which direction did you come?"

Ollie felt his feathers turning hot with embarrassment. "That's the part I don't know! You see, I was on my usual Tuesday afternoon walk, and I got lost in my thoughts, planning for the Chess Fest Tournament. I wasn't paying attention to where I was walking. As a result, I've ended up in a place I don't know."

"Hmm, this is a tricky one," Frannie Falcon said. "However, I'm certain we can figure it out. Let's begin at the start. Were things green where you started your hike?"

"Yes," Ollie said. "Very green."

"Very green, all right…" Frannie said to herself. She looked at Ollie again. "But were things at all blue?"

Ollie thought for a moment. "Just a few," he said. "We have some blue hydrangeas."

"But nothing was purple until you got here, correct?"

"No purple flowers, for sure," Ollie said. "In fact, where I live, we only have the blue hydrangeas and maroon chrysanthemums. Compared to here, we really don't have purple flowers at all."

Frannie Falcon's eyes lit up. "Maroon chrysanthemums!" she exclaimed. "Well that's the only answer I needed. The only place with maroon chrysanthemums in this whole forest is Glenwood Grove. Therefore, that must be where you're from!"

Ollie felt very optimistic. "Yes! That is exactly where I live! How did you know?"

"Oh, Ollie, you are in luck! I know just how to get to Glenwood Grove. Many birds like to vacation there. I can show you the way quite easily."

"Really? You could do that?" Ollie was very grateful to Frannie Falcon for her help.

"I most certainly can. You just follow me, and soon you'll be sitting right in front of your chessboard, ready to practice."

Ollie happily followed Frannie back to his part of the forest. Before he knew it, they were back at his tree.

"I'll tell you what," Frannie said. "Since you are the type of owl who is prone to distractions, I'll give you a special present." From under her wing, Frannie pulled out a small book with a photo of some trees on it.

"What's this?" Ollie asked.

"It's a map of the forest," Frannie said. "Keep this under your wing at all times on your walks. You'll never be lost again!"

The Extra Moment

written by Vincent J. Scotto
illustrated by Doyle Daigle II

Ordinary. That is how most people described me as a soccer player when I was eleven. Others may say I was even less than average. At the time, I agreed with them. I was ordinary. On top of that, I played defense. Not only do defenders never get to score goals, but they are usually blamed when the other team does. As for me, I typically kicked the ball out of bounds when I had the chance. It was much safer than trying to stop someone from taking it away from me. I did it because I was ordinary. I spent five seasons as an ordinary player—until the playoffs in my fifth year.

Back then I played for the Tigers. We spent the season scoring goal after goal against team after team. One of the best parts about having a good offense is that the defense doesn't have to do a lot of work. As an ordinary player, I liked that—too much pressure and I could just kick the ball out of bounds.

One particular team in our league, the Indians, really knew how to put on the pressure. They were the only team we lost to all season. We didn't score a single goal against them. Every time the ball came my way, the other team's player beat me. I couldn't kick it out if

I tried—and believe me, I tried. He always managed to get in the way before it went out. It was as if the goggles he wore over his glasses were magic.

After the regular season was over, the team felt accomplished even with the painful loss to the Indians. Coach Torisky couldn't have been prouder of us, but that one loss still stung a bit. It was a black smudge on our record—the only blemish on an otherwise phenomenal season.

We made the playoffs that November, but we learned that we were to face the Indians in the first round. When we got the news, it felt like someone had dropped a heavy weight on us. We were all on edge over it. The possibility of losing in the first round was tearing at my side like a small animal trying to eat its way out of my stomach.

I woke up earlier than usual the morning of the game. I can't be sure whether it was because I was excited or nervous. One thing was certain: I still felt like an ordinary player. I was worried about letting the team down, letting the coach down. Everyone had worked so hard that season. I didn't want to be the one everyone blamed for losing. My mom came in my room that morning with my freshly washed gold jersey. She smiled and asked, "Up already?"

"Uh-huh," I said with a lack of enthusiasm.

"You're going to be great today," she encouraged.

"I know," I lied with a smirk, thinking I would just be ordinary.

I took my time getting ready. I needed white underwear, black shin guards, black long socks, black shorts, a white undershirt, my gold jersey, and last but definitely not least, my lucky cleats. I wasn't allowed to wear cleats in the house because Dad said they would mess up the floors and drop dirt everywhere. Plus, the doctor said I would have knee problems if I wore them anywhere except on grass and dirt. I sure didn't want to be hobbling around like an old man before I was twenty, so I kept my cleats by the door in order to put them on just before leaving.

I sat down on the floor and started to put them on. These weren't just any cleats, they were an expensive Italian brand that we got in a clearance sale. My feet were bigger than most kids' feet, so finding the right sized cleats was already hard. The sports store happened to have one pair that fit. They had rounded studs and were lightweight, which made it easier to hold my ground when I needed to as well as easier to move quickly when necessary. The laces were so long that I had to wrap them around twice before tying them. With each wrap, I felt assured that they wouldn't let me down. Maybe they weren't actually lucky, but I thought so. I had to wait for my mom to finish getting ready, but as soon as she was, we were out the door.

As we approached the field in our blue station wagon, it felt like any other Sunday. The grass was as green as ever and still had fresh dew on it. The parents lined the sidelines with their folding chairs, anticipating when they'd need to cheer on their sons or berate the referee for calling a penalty against their team. The players were carrying duffel bags full of drinks and equipment. All was typical except for the game itself. The stakes were high today because the season was over for the team that lost and there would be no trophy for them. My worry returned as I stepped out of the car. My heart was thumping already and we hadn't even gotten to warm-ups.

Seeing my first teammates at the field always made me feel good. Even though I was an average player, no one treated me differently. We were all friends at school. Naturally, we had lots of fun together while we played. Today's game, though, was going to be work. We all knew just how serious we needed to be to win. No one goofed around; everyone was quiet. I even saw one of the boys sitting on the ground with his eyes closed and his legs crossed. It didn't seem like we were going to have any fun at all by the looks on our faces. Then Coach Torisky spoke.

"Gather around and take a knee," Coach Torisky announced. "Today we play the Indians." The team let out a collective groan.

"I won't have any of that," he emphasized. He had a seriousness in his voice that I didn't recall ever hearing before.

"We've all worked too hard this season to go into this game with a negative attitude."

"They beat us real bad, Coach," stated one of the boys. "How are we supposed to be happy?"

Coach Torisky smiled. "You get to whoop 'em today," he snapped back, raising his eyebrows high. "We're going out there to win today and I won't hear anything else about it. So what are we going to do?"

"Win!" we cheered as a team.

"Now let's get out there and make it happen. 'Tigers' on three."

We put our hands in a group around the coach and cheered, "One…two…three…Tigers!"

Well, it turns out that beating the Indians wasn't as easy as Coach had made it sound. Not only did we have trouble keeping the ball long enough to get near the goal, but we weren't exactly being positive either. Our forwards, the players in front who score goals, were busy yelling at each other for making mistakes. Our midfielders were getting too tired to run. Our defense was playing too far back and left a whole lot of the field wide open. What's worse is that even our coach was yelling. He wasn't angry that we weren't scoring goals, though; he was angry because we looked as if we weren't even the same team.

I, on the other hand, was playing as I always did. When the ball came my way, I tried to kick it out of bounds. The problem was that I was playing against the same kid with the goggles. I couldn't get the ball past him. He was right there to stop me almost every time. Each time he blocked the ball from going out, the Indians had a chance to score a goal. They scored twice before halftime because I couldn't kick the ball out of bounds without him getting it first. I didn't even feel ordinary anymore. I felt hopeless. I think we all felt that way as we came off the field for the break.

At halftime we had a few minutes to rest, eat some slices of oranges, and talk to the coach about strategy. As I sat and sucked on my couple of slices, Coach Torisky did as he always did. He talked to the forwards and midfielders. He always focused on passing and team talk. It was as if I didn't even exist. I didn't want to at the time. I just wanted the game to be over with so I could go home and forget about it. Just as the referee was about to call the players back for the second half, though, Coach called over to me.

"And you!" he exclaimed. I was baffled that he was talking to me. "When the ball comes to you, take an extra moment and think before kicking it out. Watch the side their forward goes to and turn the ball away from him. Got it?"

"But what if he—" I started to say.

"Got it?" the coach asked again, more like a command this time.

I nodded my head and went to my position on the field.

I thought about what he had said as the clock ticked in the game. I had time to think because the ball hadn't come my way for a while. Why did he tell me to do that and why hadn't he ever said it before? My mind was racing until the ball rolled in my direction. Just as I was ready to kick the ball out, I saw the boy with goggles coming. I heard Coach's voice in my head. *Take an extra moment.* I watched the boy start moving toward the sideline. He was certain that I would kick the ball out of bounds, but this time, it would turn out differently.

It felt like time slowed down for a moment. I put one lucky cleat on top of the ball and moved it toward the middle of the field, away from the sideline. The player with goggles went flying by me so fast that he slipped on the wet field trying to slow down. The whole crowd stood up to see it. Above the noise, I heard my coach yell, "Boot it!" Now, in soccer, when you hear somebody say that, it means to kick it as hard and as far as you can. Since the other player was out of my way, I took a good two steps and kicked the ball as hard as I could, extending my leg as far as I was able. I watched the ball fly as if it had wings, floating through the sky, farther and farther. For a moment, it seemed like it might not come back down. The next thing I knew, our whole team was running up the field toward the other goal. I watched from where I had kicked the ball as they ran closer. Everyone was cheering from the sideline. One of our forwards kicked the ball hard and low, just beyond the goalie's reach, and it zinged right through the net and into the trees behind the field. We had finally scored. The whole field became electrified with excitement.

Every time the ball came to me for the rest of the game, I took that extra moment to watch the other team's player. Sometimes he went left and sometimes right, but I always knew I had to do the opposite. He didn't beat me again, not even once, for the rest of the game. My team seemed to turn their playing around right when I did and we scored even more goals. For the rest of my time as a soccer player, I took that extra moment. I didn't feel ordinary anymore. For the first time, I felt *extraordinary*.

Phillip and the Shot

written by Luke See
illustrated by Mallory Senich

At six in the morning Phillip's alarm clock went off, and the first thing he thought of was his doctor's appointment after school. As he lay in bed, the alarm clock screamed at him, telling him to get up and get ready. He finally turned off the screeching alarm and got himself ready for the day. The appointment was his yearly check-up, but Phillip knew what that really meant: his yearly booster shot. The doctor would talk about some crazy disease Phillip was pretty sure never existed. He would wipe a cold little pad on Phillip's shoulder, and then it would come time for the shot: a long, scary needle. Phillip shivered just thinking about it.

His mother kissed him goodbye as he stepped outside to wait for the bus. She also reminded him that she would pick him up around eleven for his appointment. When the bus pulled up, its bold color reminded Phillip of the big yellow couch in Dr. Henderson's office. His stomach felt like a blender, mixing his fears with his breakfast as he boarded.

During the bumpy ride to school, Phillip tried to focus on his math homework; multiplication tables deserved more attention than some silly doctor. He opened his folder and focused on his homework from the night before. He double checked his math. By the time the bus pulled up to school, he'd managed to forget about the appointment—at least for the time being.

Mr. Hogan was Phillip's teacher, and he was as big as a house. He wasn't chunky—that was his mom's word for heavy people. No, Mr. Hogan was super muscular. Phillip figured that he must have been an action star before he decided to teach fifth grade.

Today Mr. Hogan wore a camouflage tie, surely left over from some epic on-screen battle. When the bell rang, everyone quieted down.

"All right, class," Mr. Hogan said, "I think you're all ready. Today is the day that we review…division!" Mr. Hogan struck a pose, flexing both arms in the air. Most of the class giggled at his performance. Phillip didn't remember a lot about division, which he had first learned about last year, but he was sure he would get the hang of it soon enough. After all, multiplication had been a piece of cake. Sure enough, he found his memories of division coming back into focus as Mr. Hogan explained the basic rules on the board. They practiced with some basic numbers first. As they worked, Phillip remembered how much he loved math; it was so definite. He liked that it had straightforward rules that he could memorize and conquer.

"I think we've all got a good understanding of the basics of division, right?" Mr. Hogan asked. The whole class nodded enthusiastically. "All right, let's go ahead and try a word problem then." Some students groaned and Phillip joined in with them. Word problems could be a real headache. It was as if word problems did their best to trip you up, sneaking around and confusing you on purpose. Phillip removed a fresh sheet of blank paper and readied himself for battle.

"Okay class, listen closely," Mr. Hogan said. "Let's say that you're a doctor and in ten days, you need to fit in twenty different appointments. Use division to tell me how many appointments you would need to schedule per day."

Phillip froze, his whole body as cold as ice. He noticed his classmates doing the math, but it was the last thing he could think about. He was already in the doctor's office, picturing Dr. Henderson laughing like a madman as he readied a giant, terrible shot. Phillip pictured himself trapped, locked down to a rusty steel chair, with no escape. In fact, he was so distracted by the daydream that he didn't notice Mr. Hogan calling his name until the third time he said it.

"Earth to Phillip!" Mr. Hogan called out. "There we are! Please, give us the answer that you came up with." Everyone looked at Phillip and he did his best not to panic. He looked at the word problem written across the board and did the division as fast as he could in his head. His brain ran at full speed toward the answer.

Finally he blurted out, "Two appointments per day?"

"Correct! Great job, Phillip. Don't look so stressed. Math should be fun, boys and girls," Mr. Hogan said. He walked over and stuck a "Math Genius" sticker on Phillip for getting the right answer. Phillip finally breathed, thankful that the problem had been a basic one. The rest of the time spent on math was blurred by thoughts of the doctor.

After math, his class moved rooms to home economics. It was a new class, also taught by Mr. Hogan. Mr. Hogan walked into the room after the whole class, the only difference now being that he was wearing a bright orange utility belt filled with sewing supplies.

"All right guys, now that we've crunched some numbers, it's time to show these patterned stitches that we mean business!" Mr. Hogan struck a trademark pose; his tiny utility belt a rubber band around his massive waist. Mr. Hogan started class off by discussing the different kinds of stitches one could use to sew together a normal seam. From there he began to review the parts of a sewing machine. So far this year, the class hadn't done any actual sewing. They had started off working in the kitchen, learning fire safety and cooking some basic meals. Sewing was next, so seeing how the machine worked was pretty interesting.

"And that's why you never try to swallow a spool, children," Mr. Hogan said, finishing up a zany story about his first time around a sewing machine. "That's just about all the parts of this here machine, save for one bit."

Mr. Hogan rummaged around his utility belt while the class quietly chattered. Phillip looked up at the clock and realized that it was already nearly eleven, almost time for his mom to pick him up.

"Here we are!" Mr. Hogan said. Phillip sat in the third row so he squinted, trying to make out what it was that his teacher was holding. "This is the most important part of the machine," Mr. Hogan noted. "In fact, you could sew all day with just this and your own two hands…the needle!" Mr. Hogan held it up again excitedly and the class nodded, taking quiet notes. Once again, though, Phillip could not focus. He knew it was silly, a teeny-tiny sewing needle, but he couldn't help but picture it as big as a sword, being waved around by Dr. Henderson.

The loudspeaker crackled to life. "Mr. Hogan," the school secretary's voice said, "Phillip Goodson is dismissed. His mother is here to get him." Some of his classmates cheered and gave him slaps on the back as he left, happy that one of them should be free from the day's classes. Phillip felt only dread.

***

He waited in the office on the big yellow couch for what seemed like an hour. Really, though, it was only a few minutes before the nurse called Phillip's name, asking him to come back to see the doctor. He waved his mom away when she asked if he wanted her to come with him—he didn't want to seem like a wimp.

As Phillip walked, he noticed something odd. The hallways and even the office were not as he had been remembering them. They seemed clean and comfortable. Dr. Henderson came into the office with a wide smile.

"How're we doing, Phil? My gosh, you're huge! Look at you sprouting up like a weed. You're going to be taller than me at your next visit," Dr. Henderson said.

Phillip was caught off guard. "Huh, yeah, I guess I might!" he said. "My dad is six-four, so I think I might end up just about his size."

"Well, I'll be," the doctor said, busying himself. "Guess you'll have to go out for basketball, am I right?" He stood right next to Phillip brushing his arm clean.

"I hadn't even thought about it, actually," Phillip replied. He pictured his own basketball hoop in the driveway at home. He was getting pretty good at shooting three-pointers. Phillip felt a light pinch and he looked down at where the doctor held his arm. Dr. Henderson was placing a bandage across his skin.

"That was just your yearly booster," the doctor said. "Always good to get that out of the way." Phillip just blinked at him. "Now, let's get to what's really important," Dr. Henderson said. "This sticker on your shirt says you're a math genius! If that's the case, we've got a lot to talk about. After all, I majored in math when I went to college."

Phillip felt so silly as the tension slipped away. Shots really were no big deal, but he had sure gotten himself worked up. "I think math is my specialty. I pretty much mastered division today," Phillip said with a smile.

Just between Us

written by Vincent J. Scotto
illustrated by Brian Cibelli

Fredrick and Edward were inseparable. Anywhere Fredrick was seen, Edward was surely nearby. It was almost like they were one person, so much so that everyone around them referred to them as "Freddie 'n' Eddie," as if it were just one name. They went to movies together, played all the same sports, and even had sleepovers almost every night. They shared everything, too: food, video games, clothes, and, most importantly, secrets. They were never able to keep secrets from each other because they knew one another so well. Edward thought he knew everything about his friend, but tonight he would learn Fredrick's biggest secret of all.

The sun was setting on their little town, the outside porch lights had begun to shine, and it was time to head back to Edward's house for dinner.

"Race you home!" shouted Edward.

"You're on, slow poke!" replied Fredrick.

The two dashed down the road toward Edward's house. They ran side by side until the house came into view. Edward leaned forward and he began to surge ahead. The house grew larger as they approached. Edward hit the driveway first, with Fredrick coming in just behind him.

"Slow poke? Guess I showed you," Edward bragged.

"I'll beat you next time, Mr. Big Shot eleven-year-old. I pulled a muscle!"

"Sure you did, Freddie."

"Rematch!"

"Beat you to the door!"

Fredrick and Edward hopped up the stairs to the porch, trying to beat each other into the doorway. They squeezed into the house at the same time, fell on the floor, and laughed at each other.

"Freddie 'n' Eddie!" a deep voice called. "It's time to wash up for dinner." It was Edward's father. His voice always filled the house when he had something to say. The two boys hurried to the upstairs bathroom to wash their hands and faces. The duo normally became quite sweaty and dirty while playing outside, so it was obvious that they should wash up a bit.

Upon finishing washing their hands, Fredrick said, "I just want to fix myself up a bit before dinner. You know how your dad is about looking good for supper."

Edward smirked and closed the door. It was no secret to Edward that Fredrick liked to look good. He knew Fredrick didn't actually care about his father's dinner table etiquette. Edward knew he'd be a while, so he walked to his room to wait for him. Edward lay down on his bed and looked at the ceiling. He rolled over to see a can of silly string, which he'd been dying to find a reason to use, sitting on his bedside table. He grabbed the can and crept out of his room toward the bathroom to spray Fredrick.

When Edward arrived at the door, he slowly turned the knob and opened it. He looked in the mirror and froze in shock. Fredrick had taken off his shirt and exposed an open cavity in his chest, filled with wires and lights! Edward watched in awe as Fredrick took out a small metal chip and inspected it. He put it back inside his chest and it snapped in firmly. Edward covered his mouth to hold in a scream, but it was too late. Fredrick had already seen Edward's reflection in the mirror.

"Eddie!" exclaimed Fredrick. Edward slammed the bathroom door and ran to his room, locking the bedroom door behind him. He scavenged frantically for a weapon to defend himself, but Fredrick was already pounding on the door.

"Eddie! Come on, dude! Let me in!"

"You're not Freddie!" he retorted. "You're a robot!"

"Now come on, Eddie. If I was a robot, I'd tell you. We're best buds! You're imagining things. You know I can't keep secrets from you!"

Edward didn't respond and continued to comb his room for a weapon. He found a pencil and held it up over his head, ready to use. Fredrick burst open the door with one big kick. The door flew off the hinges and landed on the floor. Splinters from the door frame flew everywhere.

"Ah!" yelped Edward, throwing his hands in the air and letting go of the pencil. He jumped behind the bed and hollered, "Help me, Dad! Help me!"

Fredrick held his hands out, pleading. "It's okay, Eddie. I'm not going to hurt you. Just calm down, buddy. You've got this all wrong."

Edward's father arrived at the room in a jiffy. "*What is the problem, boys?*"

"Freddie's a robot!" Edward proclaimed. "Freddie's a *certified* robot!"

Edward's father stood still, staring blankly, with his eyes wide open. He looked toward Fredrick. Fredrick shrugged his shoulders and shook his head in confusion.

"Now come on, Eddie," his father said. "What gives you that kind of crazy idea? Have you been watching those late night shows again?"

"I saw him in the bathroom, Dad," Edward said in a hurry. "He's got wires and lights inside his chest! I saw it with my own eyes. Then, he broke down my door with one kick! What kind of normal kid does that? He's a robot!"

"I'm not a robot!" Fredrick defended, finally.

"How do you explain all the circuits, then?" demanded Edward. "Huh?"

"Fredrick," Edward's father said. "I think it's time we tell him the truth."

Shocked, Edward asked, "You think it's time *we* tell *him* the truth? What's going on here?"

Fredrick sighed deeply and looked down. Edward's father sat on the bed and motioned for him to sit. Edward was hesitant, but he trusted his father. He sat on the bed and waited for Fredrick to speak.

Fredrick sat in the desk chair. "Do you remember when I got sick last year," Fredrick began, "and we couldn't hang out for like two whole weeks?" Edward nodded. He remembered every single day of it. He recalled being told that Fredrick was so sick and contagious that no one would be allowed to visit him

except his parents. "Well, what really happened is I was in an accident. I fell off my bike going down Gravel Hill—"

"You fell off your bike going down *Gravel Hill*?" Edward interrupted. "You could have died!"

"I know. I almost did. I was hurt so badly that most of my body wasn't able to be saved. My arms, my legs, even most of my organs in my chest and stomach weren't working properly. The doctors told me that I'd never live a normal life again. My parents found these doctors who were working with engineers and biologists to try out some of their new inventions. They'd never tried it on a kid before, so we volunteered. Most of my body had to be replaced with machines and computer chips so that I can function normally."

"So you *are* a robot!" Edward said confidently.

"That's incorrect, son," said his father. "Freddie isn't a robot. He's called a cyborg: part human, part machine. The parts that are machines imitate biological organs and are able to coexist and develop with the rest of Freddie's body."

Edward stared blankly for a moment.

"I know this is a bit crazy," Freddie continued, "but I really haven't changed much at all. I still can't beat you in a race, even with all of my machine parts!" They all laughed. "When we were trying to get through the door, I felt one of my processors shift, so I needed to check it out. I'm sorry you had to find out like this."

"That's okay," Edward assured. "It just really freaked me out, dude. Seriously, though: how did you keep this a secret this whole time? We're best pals and you can't keep any secrets from me!"

"You have no idea how hard it's been. Like, super hard. It's still a big secret, though. Only our parents know about it. I just want to be treated like a normal kid."

Edward's father stood up. "If the wrong people found out, we could be in a lot of trouble. Think about how you reacted—and you're his best friend!"

"I get it," Edward said, winking. "It's our little secret."

"Now that we're all good," replied Edward's father, "can we go eat some grub? I've been working on this for hours!"

They all left the room to go downstairs. Fredrick and Edward were just like normal again, but now they somehow seemed even closer than before. They shared one more secret to add to the pile, but this was the most important one they'd ever shared. The trio sat down at the table to eat, but just before anyone could take a bite, Edward's father made an announcement.

"Before I forget; if you think you're going home without fixing that door you broke, Freddie, you'd better check your circuits again!"

King Arthur

written by Vincent J. Scotto
illustrated by Sean Kennedy

There has been much debate about King Arthur. Was he a real person? Does he only exist in legends? Many admire his character and leadership skills either way. Still, many believe that he only existed in legends, particularly because several stories involve him slaying monsters. Even so, all the stories about King Arthur show that he was an unmatched warrior. The slaying of monsters may be an exaggeration of the skills of a real man. In the year 1138, one writer, Geoffrey of Monmouth, published *The History of the Kings of Britain*. This is the first known book describing King Arthur's life. Geoffrey described King Arthur as a conqueror of many regions. Geoffrey also wrote about Merlin, a wizard who advised King Arthur. Geoffrey's writings suggest supernatural happenings. They also describe King Arthur's need to expand the Arthurian Empire. Many scholars believe that most of Geoffrey's work is based on made-up happenings. Regardless, later versions of the legend of King Arthur fall in line with Geoffrey's work. More modern versions of the Arthurian legend are nearly opposite the original, however. Rather than being shown as a ruthless warrior, King Arthur is portrayed as a wise, even-tempered king with an interest in peace. The legends have changed quite a bit over time, but no one knows for sure if they are based on a real man.

A Guilty Conscience

written by Summer York
illustrated by Matthew Casper

"Did you see those adorable sparkly bracelets in the window we passed?" asked Amber. She and her friend Carissa were sitting in the crowded café, eating the last of their burgers and fries.

"We should definitely buy them!" Carissa squealed.

"But they're twenty dollars each. We won't have any money left after we pay for lunch," Amber informed her friend.

"We will if we *don't* pay for lunch," Carissa said with a devilish grin. Amber raised her eyebrows at her friend, not understanding. "We'll just wait until the waitress isn't looking, and then we'll leave," Carissa explained, as if it were the simplest thing in the world.

"We can't do that!" gasped Amber. "What if we get caught?"

"You want the bracelet, don't you?" Carissa challenged. Amber hesitated and wondered if Carissa had done this before. Amber knew Carissa didn't have very good judgment. A tiny voice inside Amber's head told her not to listen to her friend. But then she imagined strolling into the cafeteria on Monday and waving her sparkling wrist for all of her friends to admire. She could almost hear their outbursts of excitement and envy.

Amber glanced over at the waitress. Fortunately, she was at another table with her back to them, reading the lunch specials for a third time. Amber and Carissa scooted out of the booth and walked quickly to the door. Once outside, Amber let out the huge breath she had been holding. Carissa laughed.

"See, I told you," Carissa told her friend confidently. "Let's go," she said, dragging Amber by the hand. Amber looked back at the café in disbelief. She was shocked that no one came running after them yelling, "Thief!" As they walked away, Amber shushed that nagging voice inside her head that told her to go back. After all, they had gotten away with it, right? As soon as the girls spotted that glittering rainbow of colorful bracelets in the store window, Amber forgot all about the café.

∗∗∗

Amber was still wearing the bracelet when she got home later that day. Her mom noticed it immediately and frowned.

"I thought I told you not to buy anything since your birthday is next week," she said. "I gave you twenty dollars to spend on lunch."

"I didn't buy it," Amber said slowly, searching for an explanation. "Carissa gave it to me as an early birthday gift."

"Oh, that was nice of her," replied her mom. Amber forced a smile and left the kitchen before her mom could ask more questions. She had not meant to lie; the false words had tumbled out before she could stop them. Actually, she was surprised how easy it had been to lie, despite that little voice reminding her that lying was wrong. Amber shrugged.

It all worked out, she told herself as she went into her bedroom and shut the door. *No one got hurt, and I have the bracelet I wanted!* Feeling satisfied that all was well, she put the café out of her mind. Besides, she had work to do. Amber opened her closet to decide which outfits would go with her new bracelet.

∗∗∗

At school on Monday, all of Amber's friends admired her fantastic bracelet. It happened just as she had imagined—at first. However, each time someone gushed over the bracelet, she got an awful pang in her stomach. Amber tried to ignore it. But that small voice in her head kept reminding her of what she had done to get the bracelet. Every time she heard that voice, her stomach flip-flopped. By the end of the day, Amber could barely even look at the shiny trinket on her wrist.

After the last bell rang, Amber wearily climbed onto the bus and slumped down in the seat next to Carissa. She, on the other hand, chattered on and on about how her blue bracelet sparkled in the sunlight and how it brought out the color of her eyes. She didn't seem to feel guilty at all. Amber listened unhappily, wishing she could feel as carefree as Carissa did. Amber looked out the window at the passing houses and tried to tune out her friend.

∗∗∗

Amber saw her brother's car in the driveway as she got off the bus. Trevor was nineteen and worked at the diner across from the community college. He wasn't usually home in the afternoons. When Amber opened the front door, she heard Trevor complaining loudly in the kitchen. Curious, she stood unseen in the hallway to listen.

"*Another* group of college kids left without paying their bill today," Trevor told his mom. "That's the third time since Saturday!"

"How terrible," his mom said and shook her head slowly. "Don't those kids know that you have to pay their bill if they don't?"

"They either don't know or don't care." Trevor rolled his eyes. "If this keeps up, I won't be making any money at all."

"There must be something you can do," his mom said.

"Trust me, there isn't," he replied dully. "I'm not allowed to chase after the kids. And if I refuse to pay their bill, I get fired."

"It's just not right," his mom sympathized. "Maybe you should look for another job."

"It would be the same in any restaurant," Trevor told her. "A server only makes about three dollars an hour. Most of the money I earn comes from tips. I can't afford to keep getting stuck with people's bills when they sneak out without paying."

Amber, listening in the hallway, wrapped her arms around her aching stomach. She felt sick. The words echoed in her ears. *"Don't those kids know that you have to pay their bill if they don't?"* her mother had asked. No, Amber hadn't known that. If she had, she never would have let Carissa talk her into leaving the café without paying. And if the waitress wouldn't pay for their food, might she have gotten fired? Amber hadn't realized that her actions could affect other people in such a way. Trembling at the realization, she turned and went quietly to her room.

***

The next morning, Carissa had missed the bus. So Amber searched for her frantically in the hallway before the morning bell. When she finally spotted her, Amber pulled her into the bathroom.

"Did you know the waitress at the café had to pay for our food?" Amber demanded.

"So?" asked Carissa casually. She got out her lip gloss and turned toward the mirror. Amber stared at her friend in disbelief. Did she really not care at all?

"So, that's not fair!" cried Amber.

"Jeez, relax," Carissa whined, rolling her eyes impatiently. She turned back toward Amber to show she was serious. "It's over, so just forget about it."

"I can't forget about it," Amber hissed. "I feel so guilty." She paused and looked into Carissa's eyes. "I have to tell my mom."

"No way, Amber!" Carissa exploded, stamping her foot. "My dad said that if I get in trouble again, I'm grounded for a whole year. You are *not* telling *anyone*. If you do, I'll *never* speak to you again!" Carissa spun around and walked out of the bathroom before Amber could respond. Amber folded her arms and leaned against the wall, hoping the tears in her eyes wouldn't spill down her cheeks. She truly didn't want to get Carissa in trouble. But she heard that voice in her head asking if she really wanted a friend who did things that were wrong. The overwhelming weight of Amber's guilt made her sink slowly to the floor. As she hugged her knees, she knew what she had to do.

After school, Amber got off the bus and ran all the way home. When she flung open the front door, her mother looked up from the couch in surprise. Amber ran to her mother in tears. Through her sobs, Amber confessed everything. Amber's mother narrowed her eyes and frowned.

"That's very disappointing," she said seriously. "You know better than that."

"I know," said Amber between sniffles. "I heard this voice in my head telling me it was wrong, but I did it anyway."

"That voice is your conscience," her mom explained. "It will always tell you right from wrong. You have to learn to listen to it." Amber nodded as the knot in her stomach faded a bit.

Though the lecture was over, she still had to face the consequences of her actions. Amber's mother drove her to the store to return the pink bracelet. With the money, they went to the café and paid the waitress. Amber's mother also called Carissa's father, who was true to his word about grounding Carissa for a year. As it turned out, Carissa had done the same thing twice before. Amber knew she had been right to confess; however, she also knew her friendship with Carissa was probably over. Carissa would not forgive her. Carissa might even try to turn their friends against Amber. All because of one wrong decision, their friendship would most likely never be the same.

A Close Encounter of a Different Kind

written by Summer York
illustrated by Sean Ricciardi

Li and Ada were as different as night and day. Ada was the tallest girl in fifth grade, with long, light blonde hair that turned almost white in the sun. Ada played volleyball and ran on the track team. In contrast, Li was short for his age—the top of his head barely came up to Ada's shoulder. Li's features showed his Chinese heritage: black hair and tan skin. Despite their differing appearances, though, Ada and Li were best friends.

The kids at school called Li a nerd because he wore thick glasses and played a lot of computer games. But Ada thought Li was cool. He was actually the only person Ada knew who shared her love of science fiction movies. In third grade, Li had screened a few scenes from *Godzilla vs. Megalon* for show and tell. His classmates had grumbled about having to watch a silly sci-fi film from 1973. But after school, Ada had quietly asked to borrow it so she could watch the whole movie. They had been friends ever since.

As they walked down the gravel country road to Ada's house in the evening light, Ada explained a new movie she had watched about her favorite sci-fi topic: aliens.

"Then the alien supership landed in the middle of the highway, and all these alien soldiers got out and stormed the city looking for human prisoners," Ada said dramatically. "It was awesome!"

Li rolled his eyes and pushed his glasses higher on his nose. He didn't much care for aliens. In every alien movie Li had seen, the aliens didn't come to Earth to make friends; they came to destroy the planet.

Li preferred superhero movies, in which the heroes used their super powers to fight evil. At least with superheroes, you knew whose side they were on.

Li was just about to argue this point when a strange noise interrupted him. They stopped walking, and Ada turned to Li slowly with wide eyes. Then they both looked up. Above their heads came a whistling sound that was getting louder…and closer.

"Uh, what's that?" asked Li, hesitantly. The pair glanced around in confusion as the ground beneath their feet started to rumble. They crouched down so they wouldn't be knocked off their feet by the shaking earth.

"Look!" Ada shouted over the commotion. Li turned in the direction she was pointing. Above the tree line, they saw a large fireball rocketing toward the forest. As they watched, the fireball disappeared into the trees nearby and landed with an explosive bang. In an instant, silence enveloped them once again. Li and Ada remained on the ground staring into the dark forest, motionless with shock.

"D-d-do you think it was a meteor?" ventured Li in an unsteady voice. But Ada was already up and running toward the trees.

"Wait!" he yelled after her. "Maybe we should go get help—"

"Come *on*, Li," Ada cut him off. "Don't be a baby." She glided easily up the small slope that led to the forest. Li followed slowly, wrinkling his nose as he adjusted his glasses.

The two friends picked their way through the trees toward the spot where the fireball had landed. Up ahead, they saw a green glow coming through the leaves. When they parted the branches, they saw a glowing metal orb the size of Li's mom's minivan lying in the clearing. It was scuffed and smoking from the crash landing. Ada started to move closer when they heard a banging coming from the orb. Startled, they ducked behind some low bushes. What they saw next made them gasp.

With another loud bang, a door opened near the top of the orb. A green head slowly emerged. As the head turned, Li and Ada saw two large, black eyes blinking rapidly. Li whirled around to look at Ada, whose mouth formed a wide *O* before her hand clapped over it.

"What is that?" Li whispered.

"It's an alien, obviously," Ada replied in a matter-of-fact tone, unable to tear her eyes away from the scene before them.

"What if it's here to destroy the planet?" asked Li. Ada didn't respond. "Aliens are never friendly. It doesn't look friendly." The alien must have heard Li, because it turned toward them. Peering into the trees, it narrowed its black eyes and looked right at Li.

"Run!" Li jumped to his feet and ran for his life. Ada was right behind him. But with her long legs and her track experience, she was soon ahead and out of sight. Li ran blindly in the darkness, not knowing or caring where he was going. He looked over his shoulder once and saw the green alien close behind him. It was a lot taller than Li expected. Suddenly, Li's foot caught on a tree root and he hit the ground hard. He scrambled to get up and fell again. His shoelace was caught. He couldn't get away.

"Ah!" Li shrieked as the alien loomed over him. He hid his face in his trembling hands. He waited… and waited. Nothing happened. Li peeked over his fingertips, expecting the worst. Instead, the alien was closely studying Li. Then it extended a three-fingered hand and plucked Li's glasses right off of his face.

"Hey!" Li shouted in protest. The alien turned and stalked back toward the clearing. "Wait, come back! I can't see!" Li called after it. Not knowing what else to do, Li stumbled after the alien and his glasses.

Li was still complaining loudly when they reached the clearing. To Li's horror, the alien pulled out a high-tech tool and started melting the glasses.

"What are you doing? Stop!" Li screeched. The alien looked up like it was noticing Li for the first time.

"I am sorry, Earthling," it said in a strange voice, "but I need this material to repair my ship. The Defenders League thanks you for your sacrifice."

"Huh?" was all Li managed to utter.

"I am ED," said the alien, as if that were an explanation.

"Ed? Really?" Li arched an eyebrow. "That isn't a very alien-like name."

"ED stands for Earth Defender," ED explained. "I am part of a team that protects the Milky Way galaxy from hostile alien invasions. I am the Defender assigned to protect the planet Earth. I was on patrol when my ship malfunctioned and crashed." The alien turned his attention back to his work. Li crossed his arms resentfully.

"You could have told me that *before* you stole my glasses," Li huffed.

"There was no time. I must make the repairs as quickly as possible and return to my duties." Li was still miffed about having his glasses melted, but he felt important to have helped protect the planet. While ED worked, he told Li about the Milky Way Battle of 2008.

"I've never heard of that," Li informed him.

"Exactly," ED replied. "Our job as Defenders is to make sure that no hostile aliens come close to your galaxy." Li raised his eyebrows at this information.

At that moment, they heard footsteps. Li squinted and saw a blurry Ada appear through the trees. She rushed to Li in relief, but she halted at the sight of the alien. Li hastily assured her that he was okay and that ED hadn't hurt him. He explained everything Ada had missed upon disappearing.

"He's on our side," Li told her with a smile. Ada, being an alien fanatic, made instant friends with ED. She rapidly fired questions at him, wanting to know everything there was to know about the real aliens. The group continued talking until ED finished making repairs.

"I must go," ED declared. "I thank you for your help, Li."

"I guess it's okay," Li shrugged.

"If there are other friendly aliens like you, why haven't they come here?" Ada asked ED.

"Maybe they don't want to be mistaken for bad aliens," ED said thoughtfully. "I assumed that most Earthlings would not welcome beings who looked so different from themselves." After a moment, he added, "I am glad to have met two Earthlings who proved me wrong." The kids grinned.

"Just because we look different doesn't mean we can't be friends," said Ada. ED nodded his green head.

"There is one more thing I need," ED stated seriously. "No one can know about my visit. Can this be our secret?" The kids promised, and ED climbed into his ship. The green glow became brighter as the orb hummed to life. It lifted straight off the ground into the air and zipped out of sight. The kids stood watching the sky for a few more moments.

"Nobody would believe this," observed Li. Ada nodded slowly, only half believing it herself. They turned and walked back toward the road in silence. Ada wondered if they would ever see their unlikely friend again. Li was busy worrying about how he would explain his missing glasses to his parents.

— 44 —

Sleeping Beauty

adapted by Michael Scotto
illustrated by Matthew Casper

A long time ago, there lived a king and queen who wished they could have a child.

Finally, the queen had a lovely baby girl. The king was overcome with joy. He ordered a great feast. He invited his family, friends, and fellow royals. He even invited the wise fairies of the forest, who had great powers. There were thirteen fairies, but the king only had twelve golden plates to serve them. Therefore, he only invited twelve of the fairies and ignored the last one.

After the great feast, the wise fairies gave magic gifts to the baby. One gave her intelligence, another beauty, a third riches, and so on.

Just before the fairies finished giving their gifts, the thirteenth fairy stormed in. She was furious for not having been invited. She shouted out into the great hall, "In her fifteenth year, the king's daughter shall prick herself on a spindle and fall down dead!" With that, the fairy stormed off.

Everyone was shocked. The twelfth fairy, who had not yet given her gift, finally spoke. "I cannot undo what my fairy sister has done," she said sadly. "But I can help. When your baby pricks her finger, she will not die. She will only fall into a deep sleep for one hundred years. After one hundred years, she will awaken."

The king jumped into action. He ordered every spindle in the whole kingdom be burnt. He outlawed weaving and sewing altogether.

Over the years, the princess grew. She became beautiful, modest, smart, and kind. Everyone who met her loved her.

On the day of her fifteenth birthday, the princess found herself alone in the castle. She wandered about, looking into all the rooms just as she liked. At last, she found an old tower that no one used. She climbed up the narrow, winding staircase. There, she found a little door with a rusty key in the lock. She turned the key, and the door sprang open. Inside, the princess found an old woman. She was sitting with a spindle, spinning flax into yarn for sewing.

"Good day," the princess said. "What are you doing?"

"I am spinning," the old woman said.

"What is that marvelous machine?" the girl asked. She reached out to touch the spindle. In an instant, the magic spell was fulfilled. The princess pricked her finger. The old woman began to laugh. She was the thirteenth fairy! She turned herself into a blackbird and flew out of the tower.

The princess dropped down onto a bed in the tower room. There she lay in a deep sleep. Soon, everyone in the palace began to sleep. The king and queen fell asleep. The whole royal court fell asleep. The horses, the dogs, and even the flies on the wall went to sleep. Even the wind died down, and not a sound could be heard.

Outside the castle grew a hedge of sharp thorns. Every year, it grew higher, until it completely covered the castle. But all around, people told stories of the sleeping beauty inside the castle of thorns. From time to time, kings' sons came and tried to rescue her. They found it impossible. The thorns were too sharp, and they grabbed as if they had hands. Many princes were hurt trying to get to the princess.

After many, many years, a king's son ventured into the enchanted country. He had heard the story and knew of the danger. "I am not afraid," the prince said. "I will rescue this wonderful young woman."

By this time, however, the hundred years of the princess's curse had finally passed. The day had come when she was to awaken. When the prince came near the thorn-hedge, he was surprised to see it transform into nothing but large, beautiful flowers. The flowers parted on their own and let him pass.

In the castle yard, the prince saw the horses and the spotted hounds lying asleep. He went farther. In the great hall, the prince found the whole of the court lying asleep. Up by the throne lay the king and queen.

At last, the prince came to the tower. He opened the door to the little room where the princess was sleeping.

There she lay, so beautiful that he could not turn his eyes away. He stooped down and kissed her cheek. As soon as he kissed her, the princess opened her eyes and awoke.

The princess and the prince returned to the great hall. The king, the queen, and the whole court awoke. They all looked at each other in great surprise. The horses in the courtyard stood up and shook themselves. The hounds wagged their tails. The pigeons awoke and flew into the open country.

Then, the prince and the princess were married. They celebrated with the entire kingdom, leaving no one out. The two of them lived in happiness until the end of their days.

The Runt Horse

written by Sarah Marino
illustrated by Dion Williams

In a time long before this one, herds of mustangs roamed freely along the coast of the Atlantic Ocean. One particular herd roamed on an island, and in this herd, there was a runt of a horse named Ruby. She was teased continuously by the other horses: "Runty Ruby, you're no good. We should send you to the waves. You're fish food." Her mama and papa would never participate in the teasing, but sometimes they would look ashamed, lowering their heads as they made their way through the terrain with Ruby.

From the time she was young, Ruby wanted to be separate from the herd and explore the place beyond their island. As a runt, she felt like she didn't belong. She had made the mistake of making this dream known in front of Alex, the teenage horse whose bullying was the worst, and he had taunted her about it since. "You'll never make it out of here," he would say. "You would never survive. Another herd would come along and maul you, if a seagull didn't get you first!" He would laugh at his own bullying words, and then he'd continue, "Not me, though. I'm getting out soon. I'll explore and become king of another herd." As much as she considered him an enemy, Ruby was thankful she wasn't the only one who dreamed of exploring.

***

If Ruby was a runt, she was a pretty one, though. Her sleek black fur was so dark and shiny that in the sunlight, it shone a purplish color. She was smart, too, and even impressed the wise old horses who could barely trot anymore and only stood all day, talking about the time before and giving advice. One day Ruby had come walking up to a group of them by herself as they talked in hushed voices.

"Ah, Ruby, the little mare. What can we do for you?" said Xavier, the spotted old horse.

"I'm just wandering. Alex was picking on me again. He said all of the horses want me to leave," Ruby said.

"Ruby," said Xavier, "do you know why we were speaking so quietly just now?"

Ruby shook her head.

"There is some trouble beyond our coast. We cannot name it at this time. But we fear that horses like Alex will do us harm. The trouble could be serious. We might need your help," Xavier explained.

"I will try to help in any way I can," said Ruby.

"We thought so," said another wise old horse, Gertrude. "You are an important ally, Ruby. Please don't forget us. And don't mention to anyone what we've discussed."

Ruby nodded. She thought it odd that Gertrude asked her not to forget them (how could she ever?), but she smiled and didn't reply.

The old horses put their heads down and began to walk toward the ocean, a glowing silver serpent in the distance. Ruby knew this was their signal to her that the conversation had ended and she should be on her way. She turned and trotted toward the waves in the opposite direction.

***

A few days later, Ruby was galloping along the water's edge as the sun rose. The waves were music to her ears, and she kept time with them in her steps. The sun was a fiery orange pool of light just brightening the horizon over the water. Pink and purple clouds floated above. Ruby was mesmerized, so much so that she failed to see Alex running toward her.

"Ruby, my little friend. How did I guess you'd be here?" he whinnied and smiled slyly.

"Because I do this every day, maybe?" Ruby said.

"Listen, I have a plan. The herd is still asleep. We could leave, now." His beady black eyes were blinking rapidly. He stared at her, digging his two front hoofs into the sand.

"What are you talking about? Where would we go? And why would I go anywhere with you?" Ruby asked.

"So many questions. Follow me, and your questions will be answered." Alex started trotting toward a dune ten yards away. Ruby followed reluctantly.

At the top of the dune, she saw what he meant. It looked like the towns from the time before that she'd heard the wise old horses talking about—from the time before the great flood. And there! Ruby couldn't stop herself from neighing. "People!" she cried.

"That's right! I'm going to work for them. I'll get to explore and get off of this island!" Alex pranced excitedly like a colt after it's learned it can walk.

"You're wrong. They'll make you work for nothing. They'll keep you in a pen," Ruby said. "Don't you ever listen?" She snorted angrily at him.

"I've been watching them, Runty. They already have horses. See? Over there."

"But we're different. We roam on this land. We are wild. It's not the life for us, Alex."

"You don't get it. I'm going to be free and see the world! Too bad you're a runt and they wouldn't take you anyway." He began trotting toward the tents and people. Ruby followed but stayed close to the dune weeds. She tried to keep herself hidden.

Alex galloped right up to a man and woman standing near an area where some horses were grazing. There was a fence around these horses. They were big and looked tougher than any horses Ruby had ever seen.

The woman saw Alex and jumped behind the man. "How did he get out?" she asked.

"Hmm, I don't think that's one of ours," the man said. He took a long look at Alex, walking around him several times.

Alex whinnied and shook his mane. He shouted to Ruby, "See? I'll be fed and turn plump like these fellows." Sure enough, the woman brought around a bucket of carrots and apples. Alex squealed like a pig, taking large bites of everything.

Eventually, the woman noticed Ruby and alerted the man.

"Now that's strange," he said, looking at Ruby. "That's a runt horse, for sure."

Ruby suddenly had an idea. She began to droop her head and shake slightly, bending one leg as if she were hobbled. She tried to drool a bit, hoping that if she looked quite bad, the people wouldn't want her or the rest of the herd.

"I was going to go and see if these two came from a herd. We could use some others," the man said. "But they could be fit for nothing, like this runt. Nah, we'll just keep this boy. He's a machine; I can tell."

"I've got the harness ready," the woman said a few minutes later.

"Steady, steady there," the man said, petting Alex's back.

The woman threw the harness over Alex. The man grabbed it and began pulling Alex toward the pen. Alex was still chewing as he realized what was happening. He began to neigh and shake his head roughly. The man pulled harder. Ruby could take no more. She ran away, still trying to look hobbled, and then bolted after she was beyond the dune. She realized now what the wise old horses had meant.

Despite the awful teasing Alex had put her through, Ruby felt sorry for him. She ran to the old horses to tell them what she had seen. They seemed to already know. Gertrude nuzzled Ruby gently and told her she had done a good thing.

"But, Alex," Ruby began.

"Alex made his own choices," Xavier said. "We all must face the consequences of our actions. It is good to explore, but we are wild horses. That is a very different life from what we've known. You must know what you are Ruby, and you must love what you are."

From that day on, no one teased Ruby and she didn't mind being a runt. She knew she had made a difference, and when the time came, she took her place among the wise old horses.

If I Were Alone on Earth

written by Vincent J. Scotto
illustrated by Matthew Casper

Have you ever thought about what it would be like to be the last person on Earth? Some people would be scared. I would have so much fun! If I were the last person on Earth, I would play with all of the toys I wanted, stay up as late as I felt like, and go to the go-kart track every day. Oh, what fun!

As the last person on Earth, I would be able to play with whatever toys I wanted. I wouldn't have to share with anyone. If I wanted to play with one toy for a few minutes and then pick up another, I would be able to do it. Another great part is that I would never have to put my toys away. No one would be around to make me clean up. With no one to take my toys or make me put them away, I would have so much fun!

Speaking of not being told what to do, no one would be around to tell me to go to bed. I would be able to stay up as late as I felt like! No more "Time for bed!" calls across the house from my mom. I would stay out all day and all night having fun, and I would only come home to sleep when I felt like it. Since there would be no school, I would just take little naps so that I would be able to stay awake longer to play wherever I desired. I would have the most fun ever if I were the last person on Earth!

Being the last person on Earth, I would get to go to the go-kart track all the time! Since no one would be around, I would always get the best car on the whole lot. If I ever got bored of the same track, I would drive the car around on the real roads. Without any other drivers, I'd be safe to do as I pleased. The possibilities would be endless—endless fun, that is!

If I were the last person on Earth, I would have the most incredible time. I would play with all of the toys I wanted, stay up as late as I felt like, and ride go-karts every day. It would be a blast. Too bad you won't be there!

Hansel and Gretel

adapted by Mark Weimer
(adapted from "Hansel and Gretel" by the Brothers Grimm)
illustrated by Matthew Casper

In a time of great famine, a woodcutter lived in a large forest with his wife and two children. The woodcutter's wife was his second and she did not care for his son, Hansel, or his daughter, Gretel. As the famine became more severe, the family became more desperate. Soon, the wife decided that it would be best to rid themselves of the children, much to the father's dismay. Hansel and Gretel overheard the conversation from their bedroom. Gretel was very scared but Hansel reassured her that he had an idea.

The next morning, the family began the long walk into the woods. As they marched along, Hansel repeatedly dropped small white stones that he had gathered in the night. After a long while, the parents abandoned Hansel and Gretel, leaving them to starve. The two children patiently waited until the moon was bright and the stones could be seen. They began to follow the trail of stones; before morning, they arrived home. Despite the delight of the father, the wife was furious. She demanded they be taken out again by the father, only this time even farther. Just as before, Hansel awoke in the night to sneak out and gather more pebbles. However, he soon found that his door was locked. He couldn't escape.

The next day, Hansel grabbed a piece of bread and hid it in his pocket. As Hansel, Gretel, and their father marched, he dropped breadcrumbs for them to follow back home. When the moon came out that night, Hansel and Gretel could not spot a single breadcrumb. They had all been eaten by birds!

After days of wandering and getting hungrier and hungrier, Hansel and Gretel stumbled upon a cottage in the woods. To their surprise, the cottage was made of gingerbread! It had clear sugar windows and was covered with cake and icing. The children were famished; after reaching the house, they began to eat

parts of the gingerbread roof. After a few bites, they heard the front door open. An old woman peered out and saw Hansel and Gretel. Their faces were covered in crumbs from her house. She smiled and asked them who they were. It was obvious to the children that the old lady had terrible vision. It appeared as though she could hardly see—if, in fact, she could see them at all. Hansel and Gretel told the old lady who they were and that they were hungry. The old lady asked them if they would like to come inside, where they would be given lots of food and a comfortable bed on which to sleep. Exhausted and hungry, the children entered the gingerbread house.

The old lady, though, was not what she seemed. To the children's surprise, the old lady locked Hansel in a metal cage and forced Gretel into servitude. The siblings believed that the old lady was a witch of whom they had heard. There were stories of a witch who captured and ate children. Sure enough, she continued to feed Hansel, fattening him up to cook and eat him.

Every morning, she would ask Hansel to stick a finger through the cage so she could feel it. Keen to the witch's plan of eating him when he became fat, he found an old bone in the cage that he would hold out instead of his finger. The witch was continuously fooled into thinking that Hansel was too thin to be eaten. After several weeks, the witch's patience ran out. She decided to eat Hansel even if he was thin.

As the witch prepared the oven, she decided that she could eat Gretel as well. After all, Hansel had failed to gain any weight in her eyes. So the witch asked Gretel to lean into the oven to see if it was hot enough. Her cruel plan was to push the girl inside. However, Gretel was no fool. She pretended to not understand the witch's request. The witch became impatient—she could almost taste the children already. As the witch demonstrated how to lean into the oven, Gretel quickly shoved her in and slammed the door! After freeing her brother from the cage, they found a chest of precious stones and treasure. They stuffed their pockets to the brims and began home. They couldn't find their way until they came upon a large swan on a lake. The swan carried the two across the water, to a place familiar to Hansel and Gretel. The children rushed through the door and found their father, who began to cry with joy. The wife had died while the children were away. With the new wealth recovered from the witch's house, the family survived the famine and lived happily ever after.

Hanseled and Greteled

adapted by Mark Weimer
(adapted from "Hansel and Gretel" by the Brothers Grimm)

In a time of great famine, there was an old woman who lived deep in the forest. She was quite old and could no longer garden, nor could she travel to the nearest town regularly enough to purchase adequate food. She was, however, a great baker. Using half of her cherished heirloom treasure, she made one final trip into town and hired a wagon to carry massive amounts of flour, sugar, and spices back to her home. She placed the rest of her valuables in a small chest on the mantle. They were reserved for her grandchildren, who lived far away. Each day the old woman would wake and hug the small chest of treasure. Tears would run down her face. She knew she could not survive long on baked goods alone and that giving away her wealth to her kin would ensure her own demise.

To keep her spirits up, the old woman made cookies, cakes, and everything that any baker could imagine. In only a few days, she had baked so much that there wasn't enough room in her house to store the food. She had to leave several batches of cookies outside. When she awoke the next morning, the old woman saw that birds were all over the cookies. This helped her to hatch a plan. Using an old net, she flung it over the cookies and trapped several birds. She took the birds inside and prepared them for dinner. She hadn't had such a delicious dinner in weeks; she decided that she would leave more food outside the house that night.

The next day, there were rabbits eating away at the cookies! Realizing that baking might bring her a wealth of healthier food, the old woman began to bake larger and larger creations. In time, she completely transformed her home into a gingerbread house! That brought even more animals to her doorstep. There were even days when the old woman would catch more animals than she could eat. Taking some old gardening materials and fencing, she built a cage inside the house

in which she kept the extra animals until she could cook them.

One morning, after she shed tears with her remaining treasure, the old woman heard a scratching sound coming from outside. When she opened the door to look out, she saw, despite her terrible vision, two figures eating away at the roof of her house! They were children. She scolded the children, who had scared away any animals that may have been caught.

The old woman's anger, however, quickly turned to sadness. The children were very thin and she realized that they needed to eat. She graciously invited them inside for a warm meal and gave them her bed to sleep on for the night. The boy was named Hansel and his younger sister was named Gretel. Tomorrow there would surely be enough animals to capture and give the children much needed food before helping them find their way home.

The next morning, the old woman hobbled to the mantle to hug her treasure. To her horror, though, the chest was gone! She stormed to the bedroom, demanding to know where Hansel and Gretel had put her treasure. The children denied stealing anything. In a rage, the woman grabbed Hansel and threw him into her storage cage. She knew that Gretel would not go anywhere without her brother, so she put the girl to work cleaning the house. The old woman believed that by making Hansel watch his little sister do tiresome household chores, it would force him to tell her where the treasure was hidden. Despite the hard work of Gretel, though, Hansel said nothing.

She continued to feed both children more than usual as she had no place to store extra game. To her shock, Hansel did not gain weight. She checked his weight every day by squeezing his finger and became increasingly worried when he showed no evidence of being well fed. One evening, after catching a deer, the old woman made a fire in the oven and asked Gretel to check its temperature. A whole deer needed a hotter oven. Gretel appeared too confused to help, so the old woman decided to do it herself. After leaning forward into the oven, she felt a great push from behind. The little girl had pushed her into the oven and slammed the door shut! The old lady screamed at the children, calling out, "Thieves! Murderers!" Silence soon followed and the two children retrieved the treasure, which they had indeed taken and stowed. Well fed and with pockets stuffed full of treasure, Hansel and Gretel made their way home. Their father embraced them with open arms. Their stepmother had died. With their stolen wealth, the three lived happily ever after.

Little Red Cap: A German Folktale

adapted by Vincent J. Scotto

Once upon a time, there was a little girl who was loved by all who met her. Her grandmother loved her most of all. To please the young girl, her grandmother made her a fine red velvet cap. The girl loved her cap, so she wore it all the time. Before long, everyone began to call the sweet girl Little Red Cap.

One day, Little Red Cap's mother sent the girl on an errand.

"Take this cake and glass jug of cider to your grandmother," Mother said. "She is not well. She needs these to get better."

"I will hurry!" Little Red Cap replied.

"Be sure to stay on the path, or you may trip and break the glass," Mother warned. "If you do, Grandmother will have nothing to ease her illness."

Little Red Cap promised to stay on the trail. She headed into the woods toward Grandmother's house. In the woods, her walk was interrupted by a wolf. She did not know the wickedness of wolves, so Little Red Cap was not afraid of him.

"Where are you off to, little girl?" the wolf asked.

"I'm going to my grandmother's house," she replied. "It is deep in the woods."

"What's that you are carrying with you?" the wolf inquired.

"Mother and I made cake and cider. They will help Grandmother gain her strength. I must be on my way to her."

What a delicious-looking child, the wolf thought. *But how will I ensnare her and her grandmother?* Then, the wolf said aloud, "Where exactly is this grandmother's house of which you speak? I can't seem to remember any house nearby."

"Deep in the woods, down this path, under three oak trees, and behind a hedge of raspberry bushes," she explained. "You must have seen it at some point."

"It doesn't sound familiar," the wolf said, untruthfully. He then pointed off the path to a small field of colorful flowers. "I'm sure your grandmother would find freshly picked flowers to be refreshing. Their aroma is quite soothing and should help her gain strength."

"What a wonderful, thoughtful idea, kind wolf!"

Little Red Cap went off the path to pick flowers. As soon as she picked one, she saw more flower patches deeper in the woods. Each patch was prettier than the last. She drifted farther off the path, but the wolf did not follow her. He raced directly to Grandmother's house.

"Hello?" the wolf investigated. He pounded on the door. *KNOCK KNOCK!*

"Who's there?" Grandmother asked, her voice weak.

The wolf disguised his voice in a higher pitch. "It's Little Red Cap," he said. "I've brought cake and cider to help you gain strength."

"Come in, my child," Grandmother replied.

The wolf opened the door, rushed straight to Grandmother's bed, and swallowed her whole. He then found an extra gown of hers and put on her cap. The wolf closed the curtains and climbed into Grandmother's bed.

Little Red Cap gathered flowers until her arms were full. Finally, she went to Grandmother's house. To her surprise, the door to the house was opened a crack. She walked into the house and, in the darkness, called out, "Grandmother, where are you?"

"I'm here, in my bed," the wolf replied in a hoarse voice. Little Red Cap shuffled over to the bed and found the wolf with the cap pulled over his face.

"What big ears you have, Grandmother!" she said, growing uneasy.

"The better to hear you with, my dear," the wolf replied.

"What big hands you have!" she shouted, growing fearful.

"Better to grab you with, my dear."

"What a big mouth you have!" the little girl screamed.

"The better to eat you with!" the wolf snarled, and, with that, jumped out of the bed and swallowed the little girl whole. He licked his lips and yawned. His belly was so full that he decided to take a nap. He climbed back into bed and fell into a deep sleep.

All the while, a huntsman was nearby and had heard the screams of Little Red Cap. He decided to check Grandmother's house, since it was so strange to hear such screams in the woods. He went into the house and found the wolf sleeping in the bed. The huntsman had been looking for the wolf for quite some time.

"The wolf must have eaten the old woman. She may still be alive inside," the huntsman reasoned. "I'd better not shoot him."

The huntsman found a pair of scissors and cut open the belly of the wolf. He quickly spotted the bright red cap of the little girl. Little Red Cap and her grandmother escaped safely. The huntsman gathered some heavy stones, filled the wolf's body with them, and stitched him shut. When the wolf woke up, he tried to run away, but the stones inside him were so heavy that he collapsed dead.

The huntsman, Grandmother, and Little Red Cap were very happy in the end. The huntsman kept the wolf's pelt. The grandmother ate the food that Little Red Cap had brought to her, and she loved her flowers. Little Red Cap learned an important lesson: *Listen to Mother when she tells me to do something, because it might save my life.*

Goldilocks and the Three Bears

adapted by Michael Scotto
illustrated by Matthew Casper

Long, long ago, there lived a little girl called Goldilocks. Her curly hair shined as brightly as gold. She was a sweet child, but she was restless. She could never stand to be cooped up in her house.

One day, Goldilocks went for a walk in the woods. She wanted to pick flowers and chase butterflies. She ran deeper and deeper into the forest, until at last she found a small house standing all by itself. Three bears lived in the house, but right then, no one was home.

The door was open a crack, so Goldilocks pushed it open farther. The house was empty. *It wouldn't hurt anyone if I went inside*, Goldilocks thought. And so she entered and began to explore.

The three bears who lived in the house had just left for a walk. They were Papa Bear, Mama Bear, and Baby Bear. They had left bowls of hot porridge on the table to cool. Goldilocks came into the kitchen and found their porridge.

I'm so hungry, Goldilocks thought. *It won't hurt anyone if I have a little porridge.*

Goldilocks tasted the largest bowl, which belonged to Papa Bear. *Yuck!* she thought. *It's too cold!*

Goldilocks tasted the middle-sized bowl, which belonged to Mama Bear. *Ouch!* she thought. *It's too hot!*

Finally, Goldilocks tasted the smallest bowl, which belonged to Baby Bear. *Mmm,* she thought. *It's just right!* Goldilocks ate every bite of it.

Goldilocks went into the living room. She found three chairs of different sizes there. *It won't hurt anyone if I sit in these chairs*, she thought.

Goldilocks climbed into the biggest chair, which was Papa Bear's. *Yikes!* she thought. *It's too high.*

Goldilocks tried the middle-sized chair, which was Mama Bear's. *No,* she thought. *It's too wide for me to use the armrests.*

Finally, Goldilocks sat in the little chair, which was Baby Bear's. *It's just right!* she thought. However, while she was getting up, Goldilocks pushed too hard on the chair and broke it.

Goldilocks went upstairs to look around. She found a bedroom with three beds of different sizes. *Hmm, I'm growing tired,* Goldilocks thought. *It won't hurt anyone if I take a quick nap.*

Goldilocks lay in the largest bed, which was Papa Bear's. *Ugh,* she thought. *It's too soft!*

Goldilocks lay in the middle-sized bed, which was Mama Bear's. *No way,* she thought. *This is too hard.*

Finally, Goldilocks lay in the smallest bed, which was Baby Bear's. *Ahh,* she thought. *It's just right!* She fell fast asleep.

While Goldilocks slept, the three bears returned home. They came into the kitchen to eat their porridge. In an instant, Papa Bear flew into a rage. "Somebody has been tasting my porridge!" he growled.

Mama Bear looked at her bowl and grew angry. "Somebody has been tasting my porridge!" she yelled.

Baby Bear began to cry. "Somebody ate every bite of my porridge!" he sobbed.

The three bears went into the living room. Papa Bear growled, "Somebody has been sitting in my chair!"

Mama Bear shouted, "Somebody has been sitting in my chair!"

Baby Bear wept some more. "Somebody has been sitting in my chair," he cried. "They broke it all to pieces!"

The three bears went upstairs to their bedroom. Papa Bear growled, "Someone has been lying in my bed!"

Mama Bear said, "Someone has been lying in my bed!"

Finally, Baby Bear piped up. "Someone has been lying my bed—and here she is!"

At that, Goldilocks woke in a fright. She saw the three angry bears and let out a scream. The girl swiftly jumped out the window and ran away as fast as her legs could carry her. Goldilocks never returned to the three bears' little house again.

Money Management Smarts

written by Sarah Marino
illustrated by Brian Cibelli

What exactly is money management? It's not just a term for bankers! It is helpful for anyone who earns, spends, or saves money. Everyone who uses money must learn how to manage or keep track of it. Whether you need to budget your expenses or simply save for a new pair of shoes, you can benefit from learning skills in basic money management. These skills will enhance your life from now until the years past your retirement (which may seem to be a million years away!). By learning the basics when you're young, you can make managing your finances a habit you don't even need to think about. Then you can focus more of your energy on doing what you love most, whatever that may be, as you grow and change and become an adult.

The basics of money management include income, expenses, and savings. You have a certain amount of money that you earn or are given, which is your income. Most adults work part-time or full-time to earn an income. You might work as a babysitter, dog-walker, or garden helper. Or, you might receive an allowance for work you do at home to help your family. You might also receive gifts of money on certain holidays or your birthday. All of this money you take in is where money management starts. To manage money, you need some to work with.

Once you have an income, you must learn how to track your expenses and save wisely. When deciding how to spend your money, it can be helpful to think about what you need compared to what you want. It might be tempting to buy name-brand clothes and shoes and the latest video games, but are those things that you really need? You could save money by simply buying less expensive, but still stylish, clothes, or by buying some things used instead of brand-new. Figuring out how to spend your money so that your savings increase is a great skill to have in life. As one resource put it, "It's much better to have money in the bank than a closet full of designer jeans and no cash."

A good way to manage your money is by making a budget. Many financial planners, or people who are experts in money management, recommend these activities—even for adults. A budget is a document in which you write down totals for all of your sources of income and all of your expenses for a certain time period. Usually this would be a week or a month. A budget helps you to see exactly where your money goes and how much money you will have to spend and save. Without a budget, people often spend and spend and forget to save, and they end up regretting it.

Along with a budget, it is wise to create a plan for how much money you will save. It is recommended that adults save 10 to 15 percent of their earnings. You may want to save a little more, depending on what items you hope to purchase in the future. For example, if you receive twenty dollars for your weekly allowance and twenty-five dollars per week for dog-walking, you may decide to save 50 percent of your total earnings, or a little over twenty dollars. Or you might decide to save all of your dog-walking earnings and spend your allowance on new music and fun activities with friends.

You can learn to be a persistent saver by having a certain goal in mind. Perhaps there is a special item you want, like a new computer or skiing lessons. It helps to keep your goals in mind as you save. Each week, write down the amount you have saved and compare it to the total you need. Soon you will see how quickly your savings can add up. Still, no matter what savings plan you create, be sure to stick with it! Even saving a small amount each month will help. If necessary, ask a family member to keep your savings in a safe place where you will be less tempted to use them. If you plan to save over a long period, you may even want help setting up a savings account at a bank. Saving money is a key part of financial success. Once you have made it a habit, you will be a great money manager throughout your life.

In addition to saving and spending, you may wish to set some of your money aside for giving and for investing. There may be a certain cause you believe in, such as environmental issues or animal welfare. You can donate money to advance and support that cause. (You can also give your time by volunteering to help charitable organizations.) Likewise, if you're interested in investing, you can ask your family about ways you might be able to get started. You may be able to set up a savings account that earns interest. Interest is the money a bank pays on certain amounts that are registered in savings accounts.

Being a smart money manager takes time and practice, but it is worth it. While you know there are many things to do with money—spend, save, invest, give—it is important to use critical thinking skills when you manage your money. Remember to spend wisely and to save. You can find many online resources for more tips and for sample budget charts and savings plans. Also, ask your family members how they manage their money. They may have more ideas or ways you can work together to manage your income, spendings, and savings.

The Scorpion

written by Mark Weimer
illustrated by Sean Kennedy

There are few critters that can be as startling as a scorpion. A scorpion is a member of the arachnid family. That is also the family to which spiders belong. Like a spider, the scorpion has eight legs and is not considered an insect. Like all critters, creepy or not, scorpions have a purpose in the animal kingdom. They are fascinating creatures.

A scorpion has some features that one may notice in other animals. A scorpion has an exoskeleton, meaning that it does not have bones, but rather a hard outer layer that somewhat resembles armor. Like a crab, a scorpion has pincers. It uses these pincers to hold prey. When scorpions mate, they often lock pincers and dance around in circles. Many a scorpion is feared because it has a long tail with a stinger on the end. Luckily, scorpion venom is used to catch and paralyze insects. It is usually not a threat to the lives of humans. However, it never hurts to be cautious. Stings really hurt!

Scorpions can be found all over the world in both warm and cold climates. They prefer warm, dry climates and are especially fond of the desert. They are commonly found in the southwestern United States in Texas, Arizona, New Mexico, and California. Most scorpions live alone, though some are known to live together through the colder months.

Scorpions feed on various insects and arachnids. Because most scorpions are nocturnal, they mainly feed on insects and arachnids that come out at night. These include spiders, crickets, and roaches. Larger scorpions may feed on snakes, lizards, and mice. As previously mentioned, the scorpion paralyzes prey with its sting. While many people are scared of scorpions, few are a threat. Thousands of humans are stung by scorpions each year, but only four in the United States have died from stings between 1992 and 2013.

Scorpions have many predators. They must be careful of small mammals, snakes, spiders, and even other scorpions. They are larger than insects, which makes them very appealing to hungry animals. However, even their predators must be careful; a sting can be fatal to a smaller animal.

Scorpions are undoubtedly scary animals to stumble across. However, like all animals, they are here for a reason. For example, they feed on insects that often spread diseases. The scorpion is an important part of any ecosystem in which it is found.

Forms of Energy

written by Vincent J. Scotto
illustrated by D. Kent Kerr

It's Energy!

Have you ever thought about why a car coming toward you sounds different when it passes you? Perhaps you've wondered why the ice in your glass melts so quickly on a hot day. Both of these events happen because of the transfer of energy. **Energy** is moving all around you in all of the **matter** in your neighborhood, in your whole town, in the whole universe! The total amount of energy in the universe has been exactly the same since the beginning of time, and it will remain the same amount for eternity. This principle is called the law of conservation of energy. It may not seem like it, but energy is always transforming, or changing, into different types. Some of the forms of energy can be seen in action, while other forms of energy cannot. The energy itself is not truly "seen" since it exists in **particles** of matter that cannot be seen by the naked eye. However, you can observe some examples of its effects. Since observation requires more than just sight, you can use all of your senses to explore various forms of energy, how they interact with each other, and how they change matter. In this passage, you will read about a few examples of the different forms of energy.

It's Hot!

One form of energy that you can observe with your sense of touch is **thermal energy**. Thermal energy, commonly called heat energy, is the total movement of particles inside matter. It can be measured with a tool called a **thermometer**. The unit of measure used is called a **degree**. The more movement that is going on inside something, the hotter it gets; the hotter something gets, the higher the degree it will show on the thermometer. Take your hands and press them together. Then rub them back and forth as fast as you can for a few seconds. Do you feel the heat? You are taking energy from inside your body and transferring it into your hands. The rubbing is causing friction, which often turns into thermal energy. This is the same thing that happens when you sharpen a pencil. Have you ever noticed that the wood is a little bit warmer on the part that you sharpened? This is just another example of thermal energy in action. Probably the best example you can naturally observe occurs in water. When there is not much thermal energy available, water will freeze and turn to ice. When more thermal energy is transferred into the ice, it will melt and turn into liquid water. If even more thermal energy is transferred, the water will evaporate and turn into water vapor. If the thermal energy is transferred very quickly, the liquid water will boil instead and turn into steam. Can you think of more examples?

The number one object in the universe that you can observe in order to see thermal energy at work is the sun. The sun provides many forms of energy for living things to transform and use in different ways. Different places receive different amounts of thermal energy from the sun. These differences can help living things in the animal kingdom decide which environment is best for them. We measure the thermal energy inside the atmosphere, which is the air that is close to Earth's surface. Interestingly, Earth is the only place in the solar system known to have naturally liquid water, a fundamental part of life. Other planets are too cold or too hot to have liquid water. Earth is just the right distance from the sun for us to benefit from its thermal energy. You may need a jacket on certain days and short sleeves on others, but on the big scale, it is just the right amount of thermal energy.

It's Loud!

Have you ever heard music that was so loud that objects around you shook during certain parts of the song? What you experienced was sound energy in its most observable form. **Sound energy** is most often observed by your ability to hear, but sometimes you are able to feel it as well. That is because sound energy is the vibration of particles in matter. The vibration, or shaking back and forth, comes in waves. Try to imagine waves moving in the ocean and you will have a very close idea of how vibration would look. The pattern of a sound wave depends on the loudness of the sound, measured in a unit called a **decibel**, and the **frequency** of the waves, measured with a unit called a **Hertz**. This measurement determines the **pitch** of a sound; the higher the frequency, the higher the pitch. For example, a child's voice is a higher pitch than an adult's. Usually, adults are louder, too.

All matter has the ability to make sound by vibrating, as long as the waves have a **medium** through which to travel. Even the air itself is a medium. That is why sound cannot be heard in empty space. The same sound will be perceived differently when traveling through different mediums. Try saying the sentence "Science is awesome!" in an empty room. Then try saying it again while covering your mouth with your hand. It sounds very different from when you speak out in the air. The reason is because of the particles in the medium. The closer together the particles are in the medium, the more trouble the sound wave has passing through it. Your hand's particles are much closer together than the particles in the air, hence the reason it sounds so different.

Sound energy is produced from the transfer of many forms of energy. Most often, though, sound energy is converted from **kinetic energy**, which is the energy of motion. Lots of sound is produced from one piece of matter hitting another. Usually, the faster the objects collide, the louder the sound. Take your hands and very lightly clap once. Were you able to hear it well? Now hit them together as hard as you can. How did it sound that time? This idea can be applied to nearly all matter. Different particle make-ups will produce different sounds. Try experimenting a little by tapping different surfaces and objects with your hand. Listen to all of the different sounds you produce.

It's Electric!

One of the most common forms of energy that has been harnessed by people is electricity. **Electrical energy** is energy caused by the movement of electrical charges. These charges are called **electrons**, which is why the name *electrical* is used for this form of energy. Electrical energy is everywhere! Other forms of energy are transformed into electrical energy and then into more forms of energy all the time by using an **electric current**. In an electric current, electrons flow continuously in a circuit, or loop. Chemical energy from batteries (measured in **volts**) is used to move electrons and convert the energy into light in flashlights, sound in cellular phones, thermal energy in toasters, and countless others. With nuclear energy, power plants can convert massive amounts of energy into electrical energy to power entire cities. Even your body uses electrical energy to send messages to and

from the brain to control the rest of the organs. Can you believe that *you* are powered by electrical energy?

In addition to the ways humans use electrical energy, it can also be found occurring naturally in the environment. **Static electricity** does not require a connection like an electric current. It happens when electrons build up and collect on one piece of matter and then transfer to the protons of another piece of matter that is nearby. This happens in the sky with clouds. When clouds rub against each other, one can become more negatively charged (mostly electrons), and the other might become more positively charged (mostly protons). The cloud that is now mostly electrons can release a powerful **electrostatic discharge**, commonly called lightning, which quickly connects to Earth's surface. The same event happens right in front of you all the time. Try rubbing your hands on a wool piece of clothing and then touch a metallic object like a doorknob. Did you feel that? You just felt an electrostatic discharge! Your hand was the cloud and the metallic object was Earth. You just transferred lightning through your body—how shocking!

It's a Wrap!

There are many forms of energy that cause motion in and around matter. When you examine different situations and try to determine what form of energy is present, you may come to realize that many forms of energy exist at once. The transfer from one form of energy often produces many forms. The most common byproducts of energy transfers are thermal and light energies, even when they themselves are being converted. Energy fuels our lives and is continuously being converted and changed into other forms for various reasons. But one thing is for sure: nothing would ever happen without it!

Glossary

decibel: the unit of measurement for the loudness of a sound

degree: a unit of measurement for temperature

electric current: the flow of electrical charges

electrical energy: energy caused by the movement of electrical charges

electron: a subatomic particle with a negative charge

electrostatic discharge: the sudden flow of electricity between two electrically charged objects

energy: (1) the capacity of a physical system to make change; (2) power which may be translated into motion

frequency: the number of occurrences within a given time period

Hertz: a unit of measurement for the frequency of a sound wave

kinetic energy: the energy matter has because of its movement

matter: that which has mass and takes up space

medium: a substance through which sound waves may travel

particle: a tiny unit of matter

pitch: a way of describing sounds as related to the frequency of waves

sound energy: the vibration of particles in matter

static electricity: the buildup of electrical charges on matter

thermal energy: the total movement of particles inside matter

thermometer: a tool used to measure temperature

volt: a unit of measurement for potential electrical energy

The Constitution: Making Laws with Checks and Balances

written by Mark Weimer
illustrated by David Rushbrook

When the United States declared its independence from Britain, it needed to create a new government. The new nation wanted a government that would be fair and protect the freedoms of the people. It wanted to create a government based on *democracy*, a form of government that is controlled by the citizens. At that time, most governments were not elected. Most sought to limit the rights of citizens and keep the rich in power. The United States wanted a new kind of government: one that would offer opportunity to all.

For the United States, protecting the rights of individual citizens was a top priority. Thus, its founding fathers wrote a document called the *Constitution*. It defined what the federal government would be, what it could do, the rights of citizens, and how laws would be created. Importantly, the Constitution created a system of *checks and balances*. This aimed to prevent the government from becoming too powerful. As a result, the United States government is divided into three parts, or branches: the executive branch, the judicial branch, and the legislative branch. Power is balanced among the three because each branch has certain responsibilities and controls over the others, especially when creating new laws. The Constitution also stated that the creation of a new law could not conflict with the rights of the citizens.

The *legislative branch* is the largest branch of American government. This branch is also referred to as the United States *Congress*. Its main purpose is to create and revise laws. A law begins as a *bill*, or proposal for a law. For each bill, Congress debates whether or not it should become a law. If the bill is approved by Congress and signed by the president, it becomes a law. Congress is made of two separate groups called houses. The larger of the two houses is the *House of Representatives*. It is made up of 435 representatives elected from the fifty states. In the House of Representatives, states with more people living in them have more representatives. In this house, all people in the United States are represented evenly. The smaller house of Congress is the *Senate*. The Senate is also made up of representatives from each state. However, there are only two representatives per state, for a total of one hundred. In the Senate, each state is equal, no matter how many people live in it. This way, smaller states are protected and represented evenly as well. Any bill approved in the House of Representatives is sent to the Senate for a vote. If a bill passes, or is approved, by both houses of Congress, it is sent to the executive branch.

The *executive branch* is led by the president of the United States. The president acts as the representative of the United States across the world and is also the commander-in-chief of the military. The president has many people who help. He has a *cabinet*, which is a group of advisors for the president, as well as many other agencies. When a bill is given to the president from Congress, he can choose to either sign it or not sign it. If it is signed, the bill becomes a law. If it is not signed and is given back to Congress, that is called a *veto*. This means the president does not agree with what was written in the bill, and so it will not be made into a law. At this point, Congress can throw the bill away, or it can change the bill and give it back to the president. If the president still does not approve, Congress can override the president and make it into law. However, it can only do so if two-thirds of all the representatives vote in favor of the bill. This does not occur very often. It is not easy to get two-thirds of Congress to vote one way or the other.

Laws are passed often to address changes in the United States and the world. However, there are some cases in which new laws do not always work as intended.

It is the job of the *judicial branch* to determine if a law needs to be changed or removed. Usually when a citizen is charged with breaking the law, a court case will be held in his town. If the citizen believes the ruling of the court to be unfair, he can appeal to the state court and have a trial at the state level. If he believes the state court ruling to be unfair, he can appeal to the judicial branch of the United States, also called the *Supreme Court*.

The Supreme Court is the highest court in the nation, and it only takes on the most controversial cases. These cases often involve the fairness of a law itself. The Supreme Court has the power to interpret laws and decide whether or not they are fair. Any law created by the legislative branch and approved by the executive branch can be discarded by the judicial branch. If the Supreme Court decides that the law goes against the Constitution, it can remove that law. Supreme Court rulings are final and can only be overturned by the Supreme Court itself. This balance of power shows how checks and balances are built into the United States government. This helps ensure that laws will not take away any of the rights protected by the Constitution.

In the late 1700s, a government with checks and balances was a very new idea. Not everyone thought it would succeed. However, the United States Constitution became known as a tremendous achievement. In fact, many other countries adopted similar governments modeled after the United States. These countries sought to balance power and to provide, as Abraham Lincoln later described it, a "government of the people, by the people, and for the people."

Vocabulary

democracy	Senate
Constitution	executive branch
checks and balances	cabinet
legislative branch	veto
Congress	judicial branch
bill	Supreme Court
House of Representatives	

Written Music Glossary

written by Summer York
illustrated by D. Kent Kerr

bass clef: the symbol sometimes found on the second staff of a piece of music that shows the lower range of notes

eighth note: a note that lasts for one-eighth the length of a whole note; represented by a black dot attached to a line with a flag

flat: a note that is lower in pitch by half a step; represented by a symbol that looks like an italicized lowercase *b*

forte: a symbol shaped like an italicized lowercase *f* that indicates the notes should be played or sung loudly

half note: a note that lasts for half the length of a whole note; represented by an *o*-shaped symbol with a line attached to it

measure (or bar):	a segment on a music staff that designates a given number of beats, usually four
piano:	a symbol shaped like an italicized lowercase *p* that indicates the notes should be played or sung softly
pitch:	the highness or lowness of a note
quarter note:	a note that lasts for one-fourth the length of a whole note; represented by a black dot with a line attached to it
rest:	a symbol that designates an amount of silence between notes
sharp:	a note that is higher in pitch by half a step; represented by a symbol that looks like a number sign (#)
staff:	the five lines and four spaces on which musical notes are written
time signature:	the fraction at the beginning of a piece of music that regulates its rhythm; the top number shows how many beats are in each measure, most commonly four
treble clef:	the symbol on the first staff, or treble staff, of a piece of music that shows the higher range of notes
whole note:	a note that lasts for four beats; represented by an *o*-shaped symbol

Scorpions: A Multitude of Stingers

written by Vincent J. Scotto
illustrated by Sean Kennedy

Did you know that some scorpions are capable of living off of one meal for a whole year? The scorpion tends to have a bad reputation as a dangerous predator. In fact, though, of the roughly two thousand known species of scorpions, less than forty of them are fatal to humans. Venom that is deadly to some smaller animals may only cause discomfort or sickness to humans—but it all depends on the species.

The Deathstalker scorpion averages just under two and a half inches in length. It is found mostly in deserts across North Africa and the Middle East. Its name is quite misleading; while the Deathstalker is the third most venomous scorpion in the world, its sting merely sickens healthy adults. Children and the elderly are at greater risk than other groups. Still, even for them death is avoidable. Research has shown that its venom could be used to help treat brain tumors in humans. It might provide a benefit to life rather than the threat of death.

A popular pet scorpion is the Emperor scorpion. This black hunk of exoskeleton averages eight inches in length. It is one of the heaviest of the species, weighing up to thirty grams. It is one of the most feared scorpions because of its size, but this African rain forest-dwelling specimen is all show. Its sting is very similar to that of a common bee. Again, some stings can be more severe. In general, though, the sting from an Emperor scorpion is almost harmless to a human.

One scorpion that is not so harmless is the Fattail scorpion. Fattail scorpions are one of the most dangerous species of scorpions in the world. Found in arid Africa and the Middle East, this is a mid-sized scorpion. It measures just less than four inches on average. Its scientific name, *Androctonus*, originates from a Greek word that means "man killer." Its large, fat tail is a quick sign that you may not want to interact with it. Several human deaths are reported every year, but there are numerous companies that manufacture anti-venom to treat the stings.

The aforementioned species are some of the most feared in the world, yet their stings are manageable. While all are capable of causing death in humans, the examples here can be taken care of with proper precaution. They may be scary, but most scorpion stings are relatively harmless. Even the deadliest of them is easy to recognize from a distance. In the event of an emergency, most hospitals in areas where scorpions live have easy access to anti-venom. Scorpions may be uncomfortable to be around, but with proper safety measures, it is quite likely that all a person will ever experience from a sting is a little discomfort.

The Komodo Dragon

written by Luke See
illustrated by C.J. Kuehn

What if I told you that dragons actually exist? It's true! There are real dragons, and they live on a group of islands called Indonesia. You won't need to put on armor and find a sword to go defeat them, though. (And that's a lucky thing—imagine trying to get through airport security in a suit of armor! Imagine trying to fit in your seat! But don't even bother to imagine using the tiny airplane bathroom.) So, leave your suit of armor behind, take a plane to Indonesia, and you can meet a real-life dragon: the Komodo dragon, to be more exact.

Komodo dragons are large, carnivorous reptiles. However, they look a bit more like crocodiles than any storybook dragons. A Komodo dragon grows to be about ten feet long and over three hundred pounds in weight. It has a long, flat head with a big, round snout. Its skin is scaly and coarse, and it protects the Komodo dragon like a thick coat—or a suit of armor, for that matter.

Although Komodo dragons do not spit fire or fly through the air, they do have some "super" traits. For example, Komodo dragon saliva contains over fifty strands of bacteria. Because of this, a Komodo dragon's bite is almost always deadly to its prey. (Talk about a foul mouth!) On top of this deadly saliva, a Komodo dragon eats up to 80 percent of its body weight in a single feeding. That is outrageous! Next time you eat dinner, imagine eating thirty or forty times that amount—then you would be close to a Komodo dragon. Perhaps instead of "pigging out," the phrase should be "Komodo dragoning out."

Making History: Important Events in the Civil Rights Movement

written by Sarah Marino
illustrated by David Rushbrook

Introduction

Activists in the civil rights movement of the 1950s and 1960s staged many protest events that helped to end segregation in the South. These events included demonstrations, marches, protests, and sit-ins. Sit-ins were a type of protest in which demonstrators went to a segregated location and asked for equal treatment. Ordinary people took part in these events. Many were African-Americans who lived in the South. Some were white southerners who supported civil rights; others were blacks and whites from the North. In most of the events, demonstrators worked toward the goal of integration—that is, an end to segregation. Many of these events also had the goal of obtaining voting rights for blacks.

Fighting for civil rights was a daunting task. Many protesters were arrested. They were often met with physical violence by white people who did not want to see an end to segregation. To confront this abuse, civil rights activists used a strategy called nonviolent resistance. This tactic meant that activists would not act violently in their protests. Even if they were beaten up, they would not fight back. Many civil rights leaders, including Dr. Martin Luther King Jr., taught the strategy of nonviolent resistance. The strategy was not an easy one to follow, but civil rights activists tried as best they could. Their courage and dedication to the cause helped to end segregation in the South.

Montgomery Bus Boycott

One of the first significant events of the civil rights movement was the Montgomery Bus Boycott. It began on December 1, 1955, when a black woman named Rosa Parks refused to give her seat to a white passenger on a public bus. At that time in Montgomery, Alabama, most bus riders were African-American. All of the bus drivers were white, and they were frequently rude and hostile to black riders. Blacks had to enter and pay at the front of the bus, but then exit and walk to the back of the bus to enter and take a seat. Only whites could sit at the front of the bus. When the buses were very full, blacks had to give up their seats so that whites could sit. Sometimes, bus drivers would take a black person's fare and drive away before the person could re-enter at the back of the bus.

After refusing to abandon her seat, Parks was arrested (she eventually was released and charged a fine). A man named Edward Nixon heard of Parks's arrest and thought it could be used to start a campaign for civil rights in Montgomery. Nixon was the leader of the Montgomery NAACP, or the National Association for the Advancement of Colored People. This organization was founded in 1909 and is devoted to civil rights causes. Parks and her husband were both active in the Montgomery NAACP. Nixon told Parks he believed her actions could help promote a boycott of the Montgomery bus system. Parks agreed to help and promote the campaign.

Civil rights leaders felt that if they could gain enough support for the boycott, then the bus system would lose money and be forced to end segregation on the buses. However, despite the unequal and often harsh treatment African-Americans had endured, many leaders were not sure if blacks would actually boycott the bus system.

The boycott organizers worked long hours the weekend after Parks's arrest. They created and passed out flyers about the boycott. The flyers told people about Parks's arrest and told them to stop riding the buses and take part in the protest in a productive, but nonviolent, way. The boycott began on Monday, December 5, 1955. Blacks in Montgomery did support the boycott and stopped riding the buses. Black-owned taxis were asked to help provide transportation at a low cost. Many people with vehicles also joined in and took friends and neighbors where they needed to go. Other people simply walked if they were able. Also, many people in the North helped by sending money to support the boycott.

Black leaders met to form the Montgomery Improvement Association (MIA). This civil rights group would direct the boycott. They recruited the young pastor of a local church, Martin Luther King Jr., to lead the organization. This group created a list of "three demands" for the bus system. First, blacks were to be treated respectfully on buses. Second, there would be a policy of first-come, first-served for seats. Third, blacks were to be hired as drivers. People agreed to continue the boycott until these demands were met.

On December 8, King and other leaders met with officials from the bus company and the city of Montgomery. The officials said they would not agree to the demands of the boycotters. Instead, the city officials began different approaches to try to end the boycott. The first thing they did was to fine any cab driver who was not charging the minimum fare. The MIA resisted this tactic by organizing more black automobile owners to transport people to and from work. Then city officials tried to make blacks think that the boycott had ended. They put out a false story through a local newspaper. But the MIA ensured that its members were constantly informed. They knew the boycott was ongoing. Soon, police officers began to arrest blacks for walking to work, accusing them of loitering.

The boycott continued. A year later, in January of 1956, the bus company realized that its business was suffering. Store owners in downtown Montgomery were also losing money, as blacks no longer rode buses there to shop. Many in the white community refused to give in to the boycotters. On January 30, King's home was bombed. Then Nixon's home was bombed.

On February 21, city officials used an old law to arrest many of the boycotters, including King. This law said it was a crime to participate in a boycott. However, the arrests only gave more publicity to the boycott. They generated more support from other blacks and sympathetic whites in the nation.

The MIA saw that the city officials would not meet their demands. So, they decided to take their case to the courts. They filed a lawsuit stating that bus segregation was unconstitutional. The case made its way to the highest national court, the Supreme Court. Finally, in November of 1956, the Supreme Court sided with the MIA. The court ruled that bus segregation was unconstitutional. It was a monumental victory for the black community of Montgomery. But the struggle for civil rights and an end to all segregation was only just beginning.

Sit-Ins

After the Montgomery Bus Boycott, civil rights groups began to actively teach black youths (including many high school and college students) how to protest using nonviolent resistance. One of the movement's leaders was a man named James Lawson. Lawson had studied with Mahatma Gandhi in India. Gandhi had used nonviolent resistance to help India gain its independence from Britain. Inspired by Gandhi, Lawson taught students how to use nonviolence in the form of a sit-in protest. This type of protest involved going to a segregated business or public place and asking for service.

The first civil rights movement sit-in was in Greensboro, North Carolina. It happened at the lunch counter of a Woolworth's department store. On February 1, 1960, four black college students sat at the whites-only counter. They ordered coffee and doughnuts. The waitress refused to serve them because they were black. They sat there until the lunch counter closed, refusing to move, even though they were denied service. The next day they returned with forty additional students who joined the sit-in. They returned each day, and a week later, over four hundred additional students had joined in. They all took turns sitting at the lunch counter. In time, Greensboro integrated its lunch counters and other public places. This happened largely as a result of the protests.

The Greensboro sit-in gathered attention around the nation as it spurred other students to do the same elsewhere. Both blacks and whites took part in the sit-ins. By 1961, nearly seventy thousand protesters had taken part in sit-ins across the South.

Sit-in protests were nonviolent, for the most part. However, sometimes angry white customers would taunt those staging the sit-ins. At times, they would even pour food, condiments, and beverages on the protesters. At one sit-in in Nashville, Tennessee, whites fought the students sitting at the counter, hitting them and calling them names. The protesters did not react with violence; they just kept sitting. Unfortunately, they were still arrested, not the whites who had attacked them. The students did not give up their protesting, though. Eventually, the mayor of Nashville stated publicly that segregation was wrong. On May 10, 1960, Nashville began to integrate public facilities, such as those where sit-ins had been staged.

Freedom Rides

In 1947, the Supreme Court ruled that segregation was illegal on interstate buses and trains, which are buses and trains that travel from one state to another, including from northern to southern states. A ruling by the Supreme Court is supposed to be obeyed in every state. But the 1947 law was ignored by the operators of interstate buses and trains in the South. When blacks rode these methods of transportation in the South, they were still ordered to sit in "colored-only" sections. They continued to be harassed, and sometimes even arrested, if they disobeyed.

An organization called CORE, or the Congress of Racial Equality, formed in the 1940s and tried to end segregation on interstate transportation. Soon after the Supreme Court ruling, CORE had tried to integrate interstate buses by having riders refuse to sit in segregated sections. These acts of protest were unsuccessful and were discontinued. Then, during the civil rights movement, CORE leaders decided to attempt integration again. They enlisted help from another civil rights group, SNCC (Student Nonviolent Coordinating Committee, pronounced "snick"). All of the riders were trained in nonviolent resistance. They would test the Supreme Court's ruling by organizing Freedom Rides. During these rides, black and white protesters, called Freedom Riders, boarded buses and rode from state to state in the South. The riders' ages ranged from seventeen to sixty-one. Blacks sat in the front and refused to move, while the white protesters sat in the back. They also attempted to integrate places within bus stations, including waiting areas, restrooms, and lunch counters. Their goal was to defy the laws of segregation, much like the sit-in protesters had done.

On one famous ride in May of 1961, a group of Freedom Riders went from Washington, DC, to New Orleans. When the bus arrived in the town of Anniston, Alabama, people hurled stones and firebombs at the riders and beat many of them. Some of the other buses went to Birmingham, where white demonstrators awaited them and attacked them. The police commissioner did not order the police to end the violence. After the violence of this ride, President Kennedy stepped in. He ordered that federal troops ensure that riders could safely travel through the South.

In the summer of 1961, over three hundred buses made Freedom Rides. Unfortunately, the riders were still met with violence and were often arrested. Their efforts to end segregation were met with incredibly hostile and vicious attacks. But they continued in their struggle. They constantly recruited new supporters and sacrificed for the cause of integration.

The March on Birmingham

On May 3, 1963, civil rights leaders organized a protest march in Birmingham, Alabama. They wanted to demand an end to segregation in restaurants, hotels, and other businesses. The protesters were mostly teenagers (some were even younger). The police planned to arrest them. Firefighters were recruited and told to use their hoses on the protesters.

As the protesting students neared a park, firefighters began spraying them with hoses. Some of the children sat down, as they'd been taught to do, to react nonviolently. When the police and firefighters realized the protesters weren't turning back, they turned the hoses on full strength. Many of the children were swept down the street by the force. Some tried to hold on to a nearby building. One protester said, "The force of it knocked you down like you weighed only twenty pounds, pushing people around like rag dolls" (Tougas, 7). Then the police released their dogs. They had been trained to growl at and bite the demonstrators. Some adult observers began throwing things at the police to try to stop them. As the situation grew increasingly violent, the civil rights leaders agreed to end the protest and send the children home.

Some of the civil rights leaders had wanted the protest to be acted out by children because they were aiming to attract national media attention. They knew that the only way to get Americans to support the civil rights movement was by demonstrating the violence and inequality that the protesters were fighting against. They wanted the media to capture the brutality of the Birmingham police. They hoped it would shock Americans into caring about injustice in the South. Even adults in the South were often afraid to join the movement because they feared violence against their families. After the children got involved in Birmingham, though, many adults joined them.

The civil rights leaders got the media attention they were looking for. A news photographer named Charles

Moore captured a photograph of three teenagers being slammed into a building by one of the fire hoses. This image shocked people across the nation. Many Americans had not known the extent of the harsh treatment of black protesters in the South. Moore's photograph was shown in *Life* magazine, which was read by nearly half of American adults in the 1960s. It inspired support for the movement and disgust for the police brutality used on children.

Finally, after days of protests, Birmingham's business leaders realized that action was needed. The negative publicity and chaos from the protests were harming their businesses. They agreed to begin steps toward integration.

Unfortunately, peace still did not come to Birmingham. A group called the Ku Klux Klan began its own demonstrations. The Klan was an organization that used violence to promote white racism and resistance to integration. The Klansmen burned crosses and told whites to protest against civil rights. They bombed the home of Martin Luther King Jr.'s brother. They also bombed the hotel where King himself was staying. No one was injured in these bombings.

After the Klan bombings, many blacks were enraged. Some took part in a violent demonstration, abandoning the teachings of nonviolence. National leaders realized that Birmingham and other cities would continue to be plagued with violence unless a national solution was achieved. However, no real action was taken. On September 15, 1963, the Klan committed another bombing, this time at the Sixteenth Street Baptist Church in Birmingham. The bombing killed four girls, ages eleven and fourteen, who were in the restroom of the church. Three men eventually were charged with the crime.

Selma and the March to Montgomery

The Fifteenth Amendment, passed in 1870, had granted African-American men the right to vote. Still, by the early 1960s, most African-Americans living in the South were not registered to vote. They were not registered because whites in the South had found ways that they could ignore the Fifteenth Amendment and make it difficult for blacks to vote. Some areas forced blacks to take literacy tests (which white voters didn't have to take). Other areas made everyone pay a fee to vote, called a poll tax. Many blacks could not afford this fee, and thus did not register to vote. Sometimes blacks were even harassed or beaten when they tried to register to vote in the South. In January of 1965, civil rights leaders, including Dr. Martin Luther King Jr., began a campaign for voting rights in Selma, Alabama. This campaign, like most of the others in the movement, was to consist of nonviolent marches and demonstrations.

On the second day of the march for voting rights in Selma, many demonstrators were beaten or arrested by the police. In another demonstration in early February, several schoolteachers and children had joined the marchers. Many of them were arrested and put in jail for several days. The demonstrators continued to march for voting rights. On February 18, during an evening march, a police officer shot a twenty-six-year-old black man. He had been trying to shield his mother from attacks by other officers and white onlookers.

In early March, Dr. King and other leaders announced a plan to hold a fifty-mile march from Selma to Montgomery. The march would be both a protest of that young man's death and a demand for voting rights. The first day of this long march proved to be a violent one. As the demonstrators marched out of Selma, police officers blocked them on a bridge, where they beat the marchers and released tear gas. Hundreds of demonstrators were injured and hospitalized. The incident became known as "Bloody Sunday." People across the country watched news reports about the event. Dr. King wanted to continue the march a few days later, but President Johnson urged him to wait until a federal court could grant the proper protection to the marchers.

Dr. King still decided to lead a group of marchers, but they stopped at the place where the first march had ended. They knelt down in prayer and then returned to Selma instead of marching on to Montgomery. That evening, a white minister who had come from Massachusetts to support the march was attacked by a white mob. The incident further angered many around the nation. Thousands came to Selma to show support and join the march to Montgomery. The civil rights activists were determined.

On March 15, President Johnson addressed Congress. He spoke of the injustices occurring in Selma. He urged Congress to support a new Voting Rights Act, which he submitted two days later. Meanwhile, in Selma, Dr. King had been granted a court order to proceed with the march to Montgomery. The marchers would be protected by hundreds of Alabama National Guardsmen and FBI agents. They began the official journey on March 21. Thousands more Americans came to join them. Even celebrities such as the singers Harry Belafonte and Lena Horne came in to entertain the marchers. When they arrived in Montgomery, there were over twenty-five thousand demonstrators present.

In August of 1965, President Johnson signed into law the Voting Rights Act of 1965. This federal law stated that each person, regardless of race or religion, had a constitutional right to vote in any public election. He signed the law with Dr. King present. President Johnson said, "The vote is the most powerful instrument ever devised by man for breaking down injustice…." With the passage of this law, African-Americans secured the right to elect public officials who would work on their behalf at the local, state, and federal levels of government.

Conclusion

The civil rights movement included many more events than those described here. People fought day after day for over a decade to bring equality to the South. The use of nonviolent resistance was a constant theme throughout the movement. Activists met with violence, arrest, and sometimes death, but they persevered. When lunch counters, businesses, buses, and other places began to integrate, civil rights activists found hope and continued the struggle. With the passage of the Civil Rights Act of 1964 and the Voting Rights Act of 1965, there came real legal change. These laws ended segregation and secured voting rights for African-Americans. Even today, the civil rights movement and its participants inspire people as they show how ordinary citizens can join together to create positive, lasting change.

Ruby Bridges: A Brave Girl Who Changed History

written by Jennifer Tkocs
illustrated by William McCoy III

The word "segregation" describes setting people or things apart. For a very long time, governments and businesses in the United States of America segregated people by the color of their skin. This was true at restaurants, on buses, and even at schools. African Americans suffered most due to segregation. Segregation was enforced across the country, and the city of New Orleans, Louisiana, was no exception. However, in 1960, segregation in the schools of New Orleans changed forever. It happened because one brave little girl, Ruby Bridges, walked into William Frantz Elementary School. Her actions ignited the end of segregation in schools in her city.

Ruby Bridges was born in 1954 in Tylertown, Mississippi. She lived on a farm with her parents and grandparents. Her parents did not have very much money. They thought moving to a bigger city might give them a better life. The Bridges family moved to New Orleans when Ruby was four years old.

The Supreme Court had ruled in 1954 that school segregation was unconstitutional, or illegal. In 1960, though, New Orleans schools were still segregated. Black students and white students had to go to separate schools. Ruby attended an all-black kindergarten.

Things changed when Ruby was ready to enter first grade. The New Orleans school system made a test for incoming black students. This test was meant to determine if the children were eligible to attend an all-white school. The test-makers deliberately wrote the exam to be very hard. They hoped it would keep segregation alive in New Orleans schools.

At first, Ruby's parents disagreed whether or not she should take the test. Her father was afraid of what might happen if Ruby went to an all-white school. Her mother, though, thought Ruby would get a better education there. They agreed to let Ruby take the test.

Ruby Bridges was very bright. She passed the test easily, even though it was very hard. Only she and five other African American children passed the test. Ruby used to have to walk a very long distance to attend the closest all-black school. Now, though, she could walk just a short distance and attend the all-white school near her home.

But things were not easy for Ruby. The government stalled on integrating the all-white school. This meant that she had to begin the school year at her old school. Finally, on November 14, 1960, Ruby was able to attend classes at her new school for the first time.

Many were concerned that people who supported segregation would cause problems at the school.

Because of this, a judge ordered federal marshals to escort Ruby inside. This was a good idea. On Ruby's first day, many people stood outside to protest her arrival. They shouted and threw things at Ruby. The marshals protected her. Still, the chaos meant no classes could be held that day.

Ruby faced prejudice for a long time at her new school. Many white parents pulled their children out of school entirely. Ruby stayed in a single classroom by herself each day with her teacher, Mrs. Henry. Her family received threats. Her father lost his job.

Each day, though, Ruby showed up to school. Federal marshals stayed by her side. She worked hard on her lessons with Mrs. Henry. Her family still faced discrimination from many white families in their town. However, Ruby's family also began to receive notes and words of support. Some families supported integration. They helped Ruby's family by babysitting. They also found a job for her father.

Over time, the chaos calmed down. Parents brought their children back to the school. By the second year, more black students came to William Frantz. Ruby's classroom included both black and white children. She attended fully integrated schools for the rest of her time as a student.

Ruby Bridges still works to end prejudice and discrimination. She went back to the very school where her journey began to serve as a parent-community liaison. Her goal is to help end prejudice by engaging with parents. When William Frantz Elementary faced budget crises and, later, extreme water damage from Hurricane Katrina, Ruby Bridges helped raise money for the school. It has since been renovated. It reopened as a charter school, Akili Academy. Ruby Bridges still visits the students there to share her story.

Works Cited

"Biography for Kids: Ruby Bridges." *Ducksters*, www.ducksters.com/history/civil_rights/ruby_bridges.php. Accessed 15 Feb. 2017.

"Ruby Bridges Bio." *Biography.com*, www.biography.com/people/rubybridges-475426. Accessed 15 Feb. 2017.

Weible, David Robert. "New Life for the School Where Ruby Bridges Made History." *The Huffington Post*, 13 May 2014, www.huffingtonpost.com/national-trust-for-historic-preservation/new-lifefor-the-school-w_b_4956789.html. Accessed 15 Feb. 2017.

Lou Gehrig

written by Mark Weimer
illustrated by C.J. Kuehn

The story of Lou Gehrig is one of the most touching stories in sports history. He was one of the best players to ever wear a baseball uniform, but he was also a person of strong and humble character. Some call Lou Gehrig the greatest example of good sportsmanship and citizenship. Both on and off the field, Lou Gehrig was one of the greatest professional athletes to ever play sports.

Lou Gehrig was born in New York, New York, on June 19, 1903. He was nearly fourteen pounds at birth, almost double the size of a typical baby. Babies are usually between seven and nine pounds. Lou helped his mother take care of the family. He had two sisters and a brother, all of whom died while he was a child. Lou Gehrig went to Commerce High School and played baseball. Commerce High School is now Palisade

Preparatory School and has 527 students. After high school, Gehrig went to Columbia University. Columbia is one of nine colonial colleges that were created before the American Revolution.

On April 18, Babe Ruth hit the first home run on the first day that the new Yankee Stadium opened. At Columbia, Lou Gehrig struck out seventeen batters from Williams College. Williams College is in Massachusetts and its mascot is a purple cow. A New York Yankee scout had been watching Gehrig play and was impressed with his hitting power. Within two months, Gehrig signed a contract with his hometown team.

On June 1, 1925, Gehrig entered the game as a pinch hitter. He would never miss another game for fourteen years, earning the nickname "The Iron Horse." During this time, Gehrig put up some of the biggest numbers in baseball. He still holds the record for most consecutive seasons with over 120 RBI (eight seasons). For first basemen, he holds records for most RBI (1,995), most runs scored (1,888), highest on-base percentage (.447), most walks (1,508), highest slugging percentage (.632), and most extra base hits (1,190). In 1927 alone, he broke three single-season records for first basemen. He also holds the records for most RBI (184) and most runs scored (167) by a first baseman. Barry Bonds holds the record for most home runs (762). Gehrig's play was stellar and he helped the New York Yankees to win six World Series Titles. He never let the fame affect his character.

In 1938, his play began to diminish. There was a noticeable difference in his power, but there was little concern until 1939. At the beginning of 1939, his power had disappeared. In spring training, he collapsed during a game. Even his running was slower. At the end of April, Gehrig was batting .143 with one RBI. There was something very wrong. Before the game on May 2, Gehrig told the manager that he was benching himself "for the good of the team." He handed the lineup to the umpire and the crowd gave him a standing ovation. He returned to the dugout and sat with tears in his eyes. He had played in the previous 2,130 games, and though he did not know at the time, he would never play again. His record for consecutive games played stood until 1995.

Doctors told Gehrig that he had a disease called ALS, a disease of the brain, and that he would never play baseball again. He would become paralyzed, although his mind would remain sharp. The disease itself came to be known as Lou Gehrig's disease. Doctors told Gehrig that he had three years to live. He returned to the Yankees after receiving the news.

On July 4, 1939, Lou Gehrig came out of the dugout between games of a double header. He stood in front of a microphone and addressed the crowd. He began, saying, "Fans, for the past two weeks you have been reading about the bad break I got. Yet today I consider myself the luckiest man on the face of the earth." He spoke of how he had felt loved for his whole career by his teammates, his family, and even his opponents. He spoke of all the blessings of his life and concluded, "So I close in saying that I might have been given a bad break, but I've got an awful lot to live for. Thank you." He received a standing ovation for almost two minutes, and he began to cry. Babe Ruth, a teammate with whom Gehrig often did not get along, came over and hugged him. No game ever played on a baseball field compares to Lou Gehrig's farewell.

Lou Gehrig died two years later on June 2, 1941, at the age of thirty-seven. All Major League ballparks flew flags at half-staff in honor of Gehrig. His number, 4, was the first retired jersey in baseball history. He was one of the greatest men to ever play sports.

Ten Major Events of World War II

written by Summer York
illustrated by Doyle Daigle II

September 1, 1939: Invasion of Poland

In the early morning of September 1, 1.5 million German troops under the command of German dictator Adolf Hitler invaded Poland. The German air force, called the *Luftwaffe*, bombed Polish airfields. German warships and submarines attacked the Polish navy. In response to the invasion, Britain and France declared war on Germany two days later. Poland surrendered to the Germans by the end of the month.

September 15, 1940: Battle of Britain Day

In June of 1940, France surrendered to German forces. Hitler next sent his *Luftwaffe* to defeat the British Royal Air Force (RAF). The *Luftwaffe* bombed London and other major British cities. On Battle of Britain Day, the RAF fought the *Luftwaffe* and won. After this defeat, Hitler turned his attention to the Soviet Union.

December 5, 1941: Battle of Moscow

In June of 1941, Hitler's forces began an invasion of the Soviet Union called Operation Barbarossa. This operation lasted six months. Hitler tried to take Moscow, the Soviet capital. But his army was not trained to fight in severe winter conditions. On December 5, the Red Army (Soviets) attacked the Germans and held Moscow. This was the first time the German army retreated in large numbers.

December 7, 1941: Attack on Pearl Harbor, Hawaii

While Hitler spread his army through Europe, conflict arose between the United States and Japan, an ally of Germany. Japan saw the US naval fleet in Pearl Harbor, Hawaii, as a threat. In the early morning of December 7, Japanese fighter planes carried out a surprise attack on the US naval base at Pearl Harbor. After suffering heavy losses, the United States entered the war as an Allied force. The Allied Powers was an alliance of the United States, Britain, France, and the Soviet Union. The Allies fought against the Axis Powers, which included Germany, Japan, and Italy.

June 4–7, 1942: Battle of Midway

In the months after Pearl Harbor, Japanese forces gained control of several European and US territories in the Pacific Ocean. Their next target was Midway Island. However, US naval intelligence cracked the Japanese code and knew of the plans at Midway. US dive-bomber planes sank four Japanese ships, causing heavy damage to the Japanese navy. This victory gave the Allied Powers the advantage in the rest of the Pacific war.

August 8, 1942: Battle of Guadalcanal

In June of 1942, the Japanese invaded the small island of Guadalcanal in the Pacific. Two months later, US Marines secured the Japanese airfield there. But on August 8, the Japanese fought to take the airfield back. The US Marines held the airfield, fighting off several Japanese attacks. Unsuccessful, the Japanese left the island in February of 1943. This was another victory for the Allied forces.

July 5, 1943: Battle of Kursk

The Germans were still trying to gain territory in the Soviet Union. After suffering a defeat in Stalingrad, the Germans planned to attack the Red Army at Kursk. When the Germans attacked on July 5, they were stopped by the Red Army before they could gain much ground. The Soviets pushed the Germans back. This was the last attack by the Germans in the Soviet Union.

June 6, 1944: D-Day Invasion

As the war progressed, Allied forces planned an invasion of France to drive out the Germans. The large-scale assault was nicknamed Operation Overlord. On June 6, more than one hundred fifty thousand Allied troops stormed five beaches along the coast of Normandy, France. Although about four thousand Allied troops lost their lives that day, the invasion was successful. The Allies fought their way across France, forcing the Germans back toward Germany.

October 23–26, 1944: Battle of Leyte Gulf

In the Pacific war, Allied forces tried to invade the Philippines, held by the Japanese. The Allies landed on Leyte Island on October 20. On October 23, the Japanese naval fleet engaged the Allies' ships off the coast of Leyte. After four days, the Japanese had lost about twenty-five ships, a loss that destroyed their navy. The Japanese retreated from the Philippines and had to use air and land forces for the rest of the war.

May 7, 1945: Surrender of Germany

By 1945, the Allies had pushed the Japanese out of the Pacific and the Red Army had forced the Germans back to Germany. The Soviets closed in on Hitler and his military in the German capital of Berlin. On April 30, Hitler committed suicide while hiding in his underground shelter. On May 7, Germany surrendered all of its forces. World War II officially ended when Japan surrendered in August.

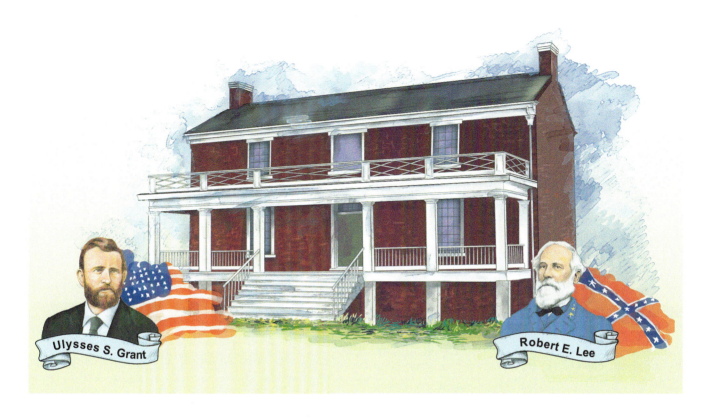

Surrender at Appomattox

written by Mark Weimer
illustrated by Sean Ricciardi

The Union army of the Potomac marched into Richmond on April 3, 1865, sending the Confederate army of Northern Virginia into full retreat. The American Civil War had lasted for four years. A final defeat of the Confederate capital caused Union General Ulysses S. Grant to send letters to Confederate General Robert E. Lee. They arranged a final surrender to help end the bloodiest conflict in the country's history. General Lee accepted Grant's invitation, and the two agreed to meet at the home of Wilmer McLean in Appomattox, Virginia.

Grant arrived at the house first and sat down at a marble-topped table in the center of the front room. He stood only five feet eight inches tall, and this was one of the few days where it was hard to smell alcohol on his breath. He drank too much, but he was effective in battle. Abraham Lincoln once said of General Grant, "Find out what Grant drinks and send a barrel of it to each of my other generals!" His war tactics mimicked his drinking. He often made haphazard decisions and ordered risky maneuvers. While some didn't work, others did. With a force that was much larger than Lee's, mistakes could be overcome. Grant was forty-three years old at the time. He had graduated from the United States Military Academy at West Point in 1843 and was twenty-first in his class. He didn't have a single grey hair. He hardly resembled a decorated general at the table. His coat was unbuttoned with mud splattered on it. He did not wear a sword or spurs on his boots. Other than his shoulder straps, which had four stars to designate his rank, he was dressed as an infantry soldier.

General Lee arrived wearing his pride and glory for all to see. Unlike Grant, the grey uniform Lee wore was brand new and spotless. It was buttoned all the way to his neck, making all six feet of him seem even taller. He towered above Grant with thick, silver hair. He wore a sword made with great skill, and its hilt was studded with jewels. His boots, with their red silk stitching, were much newer than Grant's. Lee's boot spurs glimmered in the light. He wore long leather gloves on his hands. He had a grey felt hat to match his uniform. Some would think that General Lee never had a sip of alcohol in his life. His battlefield sense was unquestionable and, despite having a much smaller fighting force, he delivered victory after victory during the course of the war. Lee did not have enough men to make a mistake, which is why in 1863, when he did make a mistake at the Battle of Gettysburg, it was a turning point in the war. Lee had also graduated from West Point and was second in the class of 1829. He was sixteen years older than Grant. However, sitting at the table, it was Grant who appeared more like the battered, defeated general.

Lee quietly entered the room in which Grant was sitting and sat down by the window, his chin held high. Grant signaled his staff to enter and witness the surrender. The two generals began to talk about the Mexican War. The Mexican War had occurred before the Civil War; in fact, in that war, both men had fought on the same side. They had met each other then and, while Grant vividly remembered Lee, Lee could not recall the appearance of Grant. Grant had been much younger during the Mexican War and their meetings at that time were short.

After talking briefly about the Mexican War, the conversation led to the terms of surrender. Lee requested that the terms be written down, and Grant began to quickly comply. After completing the terms, Grant handed the document to General Lee for review. Grant looked at Lee's sword. During surrender, it was customary for the officers of the losing army to give their swords to the victors. Both generals knew, however, that this situation was different. After the documentation was signed, the war would soon conclude; not long after, the members of the Confederate army would once again be citizens and neighbors. Grant believed that surrendering the sword would be an unnecessary humiliation. The respect for General Lee was immense, even in those who had fought against him for years. After reading through the terms, Lee further requested that his men keep their horses. Unlike those in the Union army, the Confederate cavalrymen owned their own horses. The horses were an important part of their future well-being. At about 4:00 p.m., General Lee completed a letter accepting the surrender.

The two generals, vastly different in appearance and war strategy, stood up and shook hands. Lee bowed to the Union officers in the room and left with one of his colonels. The Union officers followed one by one and stepped onto the porch. General Lee stood on the lowest step and called for his horse. Looking down, Lee clapped his hands together a few times. Union officers who were sitting outside the house all stood on their feet, aware that they were witnessing the surrender of the greatest general of the Civil War. General Lee did not seem to notice as he prepared to mount his horse. His sadness was overwhelming. Once he was seated, General Grant stepped down off the porch. In Lee's honor, Grant saluted him by raising his hat. Lee raised his hat out of respect, and rode off to inform his men of the surrender.

The surrender of the Army of Northern Virginia effectively ended the Confederacy's ability to wage war against the North during the Civil War. After Appomattox, Confederate armies all across the country began to surrender. The last surrender occurred on November 6, 1865, ending the Civil War. On August 20, 1866, President Andrew Johnson formally declared the war to be over.

Escaped Piglet Goes on Jaunt through Town

written by Jennifer Tkocs
illustrated by Mallory Senich

PORT CARVER, MASS. – A Berkshire piglet went for an unexpected romp around downtown Port Carver yesterday, leading authorities on a wild pig chase for the better part of the afternoon.

Rupert, a three-month-old Berkshire hog, was noted to be missing from his pen Tuesday afternoon around 1 p.m., according to Farmer Harold Coffey. Around the same time, Farmer Coffey noticed that much of a pile of rotten apples was missing from a trash heap behind the barn.

"If I was a speculating man, I'd say little Rupert ate up them spoiled apples and they made him go a little funny in the head," said Farmer Coffey.

Following the piglet's escape, it appeared that Rupert stumbled into Port Carver's town square. His adventure continued as he made a few rounds to the local shopkeepers.

"I saw the piglet," baker Martha Simonson of Sweets & Treats told reporters. "He wandered into the bakery, seeming a little wobbly on his trotters. He was very interested in the hot-cross buns I'd just made, so I fed him one or two."

By the time Rupert had reached the bakery, Farmer Coffey had already alerted animal control officer Stanley Bobowski, who seemed to be just a step behind Rupert's antics. "That little pig is a crafty one," Officer Bobowski said. "At every shop we stopped into, the shopkeepers told us we'd just missed him."

After leaving Sweets & Treats, the piglet was spotted trotting through the new autumn tie display at the fine menswear shop Bon Soir Monsieur. "The pig! He runs through my best ties, sticks his little pig-face into the finest green one, and canters off with it around his neck!" shop owner Claude Valmont told reporters. "But he was so charming, so proud of his achievement. I could neither be angry nor bring myself to remove the tie," the shop owner admitted. "He was still wearing it as he left my shop."

"We thought a pig in a green tie would be easy to spot," said Officer Bobowski. "But he was outsmarting us at every turn."

Rupert's trail seemed to get easier to follow after he made a brief stop at Port Carvings, the handmade furniture shop in the center of town. "The piglet ran right through my white paint," said carpenter Aiden McAdams. "You can see his little hoof prints all through my shop and out on the sidewalk."

Indeed, the meandering line of hoof prints was quite unmistakable. The little white prints led from Port Carvings in an uneven, sloppy path to the center of the square.

"We were following those pig tracks and thought we had him at last," said Officer Bobowski. "And then, they just stopped. They stopped right at the fountain."

It seemed Rupert took a short dip into the town fountain, which cleaned the paint right off his hooves. "This is a clever little pig," stated Officer Bobowski. "He knew we were getting close to catching him. So he just washed his toes to remove his prints."

Farmer Coffey began to worry during the second hour of the chase. "Officer Bobowski was giving me updates, but it just seemed like he was always one step behind that piglet," said the farmer. "We couldn't afford to lose Rupert. He's my daughters' pride and joy, that little runt. We knew he'd never get too big, so I told my girls they could keep him as a pet. Boy, were they sore at me for letting him get out!"

Officer Bobowski maintained that they were always very close to capturing Rupert. "Port Carver isn't that big of a town," he told reporters. "We knew we'd catch up to him sooner or later."

But Rupert was insistent on enjoying his day in town before letting the authorities anywhere near him. After his frolic in the fountain, he headed off to Miss Brannigan's Fine Foods shop. "He ate every last one of my truffles," owner Maria Brannigan told reporters. "I'd heard a clattering near the window of my shop. Then I looked up to see a piglet with chubby stuffed cheeks. I knew it was Rupert right away. Farmer Coffey's girls have brought him down here on his leash a few times before. I knew how much he favored those truffles."

"We were more than willing to press charges for the cost of the truffles," said Officer Bobowski, "but Miss Brannigan swore it was the biggest laugh she'd had all week. She said it was worth every penny of the cost of those truffles to see that piglet having such a grand time."

Rupert was finally apprehended at his last stop of the day, the Book Nook.

Bookshop owner Lilian Carmichael found Rupert asleep in a beanbag chair in the children's section. "One of the kids who'd been in earlier had left out a copy of *Charlotte's Web*. I came over to do some straightening up, and found the little piglet curled up in the beanbag chair with his head resting on the book."

"Ms. Carmichael called us right away when she found Rupert," reported Officer Bobowski. "But she told us we couldn't wake him just yet. She made some coffee for us and told us to wait around for him to finish his nap."

"It seemed our little Rupert had been on quite the adventure," said Ms. Carmichael. "I wanted to make sure we sent him back to Farmer Coffey fully rested."

"We brought him back to Farmer Coffey a few hours later," said Officer Bobowski. "He looked pretty happy, and he was still wearing that tie."

Farmer Coffey and his daughters were thrilled to have Rupert back. They were equally excited to hear about his travels during the day. "I'll be more careful from now on," Farmer Coffey promised reporters. "I'll make sure Rupert steers clear of rotten apples. I'll also make sure the girls keep a close eye on him when he's not on his pig leash.

"I'm just happy he's home, and I'm happy the good townspeople of Port Carver showed our piglet a fine day," the farmer added. "It's not every day a piglet gets loose. But I'm glad he came home safe and full of pig smiles."

Local Girl Gets Party of a Lifetime

written by Sarah Marino
illustrated by Brian Cibelli

July 28, 2012

PHILADELPHIA — It was the type of birthday party you read about in storybooks. Zadie Donner was turning eleven, and her parents wanted to do something very special for her. Zadie had recently recovered from a broken arm and her cat, Mittens, hadn't been seen for weeks. The Donners wanted to cheer up their only daughter. It helped that they had a very large backyard, and a modest, but sizable, three-story home.

On a sweltering late-July afternoon, this reporter (and friend of the family) found herself in that backyard. It looked like a fun expert had stormed through on a special mission. In one corner of the yard, there was a petting zoo. It was complete with two grey donkeys, two goats (one black, one white), two sheep (both white, but quite dirty), and a miniature pony. The line for the pony ride stretched halfway across the yard.

Then there was the waterslide and the swimming pool. The Donners already had the pool, but they had asked some friends in the construction business to haul in the waterslide specifically for the party.

"Zadie was so surprised when she saw it," said Mrs. Donner during the party. She then hinted, "But the real surprise will come later."

At the waterslide, daring swimmers had to climb three flights of stairs to reach its top. The slide twisted three full times before it spit them out into the pool. Zadie's teenage cousins, both certified lifeguards, watched the scene. It became fairly hectic since everyone wanted multiple rides on the slide.

Nearly all of Zadie's fifth grade class at Clover Elementary attended the affair. There were also grandparents, aunts, uncles, cousins, godparents, and friends of the family. Zadie informed me that she had only met her cousin Emma once before. (Emma and her mother had made the trip to Philadelphia all the way from Virginia.)

Whenever the partygoers got tired of the petting zoo, waterslide, and other activities, they could fill up their bellies with delicious, catered food. The options included a chocolate fountain, an ice-cream soda station, a make-your-own pizza station, a burger station, a fruit smoothie station, and a seven-tier birthday cake with pink buttercream frosting. To make Mrs. Donner happy, there was also a build-a-salad station. It had healthy vegetables like kale and artichokes. Most of the kids went right to the chocolate or the ice-cream sodas—unless a parent was nearby, of course.

The food at the party was a hit, but it was nothing compared to Mrs. Donner's big surprise. This reporter happened to be with the birthday girl when it occurred. Zadie was about to enjoy a plate of strawberries and pretzels dipped in chocolate when a certain guitar chord rang out in the yard. Then, a voice sang, "You're insecure, don't know what for. You're turning heads when you walk through the door…" Zadie dropped her plate on the ground in front of her. She looked up and her mouth opened in awe. Yes, in fact, the British teen boy band One Direction was playing on a stage behind the swimming pool! Zadie let out a scream and made a run for it, grabbing her best friend Tamara on the way. The crowd in front of the stage was already big, but they made way for the birthday girl. She got a spot to dance her heart away in front of her favorite band.

Oddly enough, the band was performing in Philadelphia that night, and they happened to know one of Zadie's aunts. She had worked for their publicist the previous year, and they adored her. She had left that job to work for Taylor Swift back in the United States. Still, the boys were happy to do her a favor and play a few songs for Zadie's party.

As the mini-concert ended, Mr. Donner and some other men set up a huge projection screen behind the stage. They planned to show a film once the sun had set.

"A movie on the big screen in my backyard!" Zadie exclaimed.

When asked how she was feeling, she said, "I'm so happy for such an amazing party. It is great to see so many family members and friends together and enjoying themselves. I'm very, very fortunate." Zadie then gave her parents enormous hugs and kisses to show her gratitude, before promptly running off to enjoy the film.

The Constitution: Federalists vs. Antifederalists

written by Vincent J. Scotto
illustrated by Sean Ricciardi

The United States Constitution is considered to be the first constitution of its kind. It was fully ratified, or approved, by all thirteen colonies in May of 1790. That was over a decade after the signing of the Declaration of Independence in July of 1776. Between those years, the young nation was hardly united at all. In fact, the Union was in danger of losing recognition as an independent nation.

Before the Constitution, America was governed by a different body of rules. They were called the Articles of Confederation and Perpetual Union. They were signed into operation by all thirteen colonies. However, the Articles left America with two major problems. First, the federal government lacked the finances to sustain itself. The Continental—the US currency at the time—was considered worthless. Also, the states were not paying all of their taxes. Some paid none at all. Second, the government lacked the ability to enforce laws. Its military could not protect the nation's sovereignty, or independence. It could not enforce its own laws of the nation. For these reasons, the Articles called for a Constitutional Convention. At this convention, delegates from every colony came together for the "sole and express purpose of revising the Articles of Confederation."

All in attendance agreed that changes were needed to protect the Union. However, not everyone agreed on how to do it. Eventually, two parties formed. One was in favor of writing a brand-new constitution. The other wanted merely to make changes to the Articles of Confederation. The party in favor of a new constitution became known as the Federalists. The party in opposition became known as the Antifederalists.

The Constitutional Convention was advertised as a meeting to revise the Articles of Confederation. However, several congressmen intended to create a new form of government altogether. James Madison, a

Federalist, had plans for major changes. He suggested that the delegates of the convention act as advisors to the states. Final passage of their proposals would be left up to the individual states. Madison and several others also proposed that nine of the thirteen states (about two-thirds) would have to pass their proposal for it to become law. This was a major point of controversy. The current Articles of Confederation required unanimous, or undivided, agreement from Congress to make amendments. Antifederalists found the desire to require only two-thirds agreement to be very suspicious. They wanted to keep the need for unanimous consent. They thought that need gave each individual state the power to govern itself. Some Antifederalists were so upset by the change that they stayed home. Patrick Henry of Virginia, the leader of the Antifederalists, was one who stayed behind. When asked why he did so, he answered, "I smelled a rat."

Another point of dispute was the election of a president. The Antifederalists argued that electing a president would be the first step toward having a monarchy with a king. To them, that was unacceptable. After all, one of the main reasons that the colonies had claimed independence from Britain was to escape the monarchy. The Antifederalists criticized the idea of a centralized government with a powerful leader. The Federalists had different ideas, though. They argued that the separation of powers would prevent a president from having total control. The Federalists believed that the president and Congress would balance one another and not allow one body to control another. The president would also be limited by his need to be re-elected every four years by the people.

Along with their concerns about the president's power, many Antifederalists worried about the loss of local and individual liberties and freedoms. They warned that a federal government with too much power would threaten the freedoms of the states, then local governments, and ultimately individuals. Some Federalists had the same concerns. Thus, they agreed that Congress would be split into two chambers. One, the Senate, would be made up of officials chosen by the state government. The other, the House of Representatives, would be elected by the people. Most agreed that this was an acceptable compromise. It gave the national government more power, but kept it from having too much.

The two groups' many conflicting ideas were a source of strife. They did agree in one area, though. They agreed that the final decision to ratify the new Constitution should be left up to the states. While several delegates still refused to sign, there was eventually enough support to pass the Constitution on to the states for a vote. However, the debate between the Federalists and Antifederalists was far from over.

On September 17, 1787, the delegates signed the new Constitution and sent it off to the state legislatures. Many leaders within the delegates wrote speeches and articles to convince the public of their cause. Early on, many of the Federalists and Antifederalists wrote their papers under pseudonyms, or false names. On both sides, most did not want to publicly share their opinions for or against the Constitution. They did not wish to influence decisions based on their reputation or status, but rather the quality of their ideas. The papers in favor of the Constitution became known as the Federalist Papers. The opposing writing became known as the Antifederalist Papers. These papers helped local governments to argue for or against passing.

Through local debates and speeches, many were able to find common ground. Almost every state agreed that, in addition to the Constitution, there should be a Bill of Rights. Several states would only sign after the Federalists promised that one would be created. By the summer of 1788, eleven states had ratified the Constitution. North Carolina and Rhode Island waited another year, but they eventually ratified as well.

The new Constitution required the election of a president, as well as senators and representatives. Several electors, or candidates, were nominated for president. In a rare agreement, though, every delegate who had a vote chose George Washington, an accomplished general and respected Federalist. Even the Antifederalists' elector, Patrick Henry, voted for Washington rather than himself. After Washington was elected, the first few members of Congress were chosen as well. The first order of business was to propose the Bill of Rights.

The United States Constitution saw quite a bit of controversy in the beginning. After some time passed, though, it was seen as a revolutionary model for democratic government. The Federalists and Antifederalists had many differences, but the compromises they made gave the United States a sturdy foundation and a strong future.

Igneous Rock (Third Hook)

written by Vincent J. Scotto

Did you know that igneous rock gets its name from the Latin word for fire? Igneous rock transforms into rock from liquid hot magma below Earth's crust. Igneous rock is the most abundant of type of rock found in Earth's crust. It comprises almost two-thirds of Earth's crust. Some forms of igneous rock cool quickly into a solid state during a volcanic eruption. Others form over millions of years. The rocks slowly push up from inside Earth toward the surface. The cooling process determines the forms of igneous rock. When the rock cools more quickly, the minerals that comprise it tend to be small. Basalt rocks are a good example. Basalt contains microscopic minerals that can look almost like glass. When igneous rock forms more slowly, its minerals tend to be larger. Granite rocks show this very well. Granite cools beneath Earth's surface. This is the main reason why it takes longer to cool. Some types of igneous rock form so slowly that their mineral clumps can be up to three feet long. This variance in cooling time is the reason there are more than seven hundred identified types of igneous rock. The "fire" rock certainly is a fascinating one!

California Gold Rush

written by Jill Fisher
illustrated by Dion Williams

It was the year 1848 when news spread about the discovery of gold in California. At that time, the average worker made approximately one dollar a day. A man working in a gold mine could earn up to thirty-five dollars a day. Some made even more! So, in the spring of 1849, what became known as the "Gold Rush" began. Thousands of people, mainly men, left their families and homes to head West in hopes of finding riches and a better life. They were known as "forty-niners" for the year in which they left. Most had never even left their hometown before.

Men traveled by land and by sea to strike it rich. They traveled from all parts of the world to gain in the wealth. The journey was extremely difficult because there was no quick and safe route. It would be one of the hardest experiences of their lives.

Many forty-niners traveled by covered wagon. They trekked across difficult land, crossed hot deserts, and climbed high mountains with their wagons, mules, and oxen. The trip took months, and the settlers were forced to face the wilderness and disease, camp outdoors, hunt for food, and cross dangerous rivers.

Others traveled by boat. But this journey was not a better experience than traveling by covered wagon.

The trip was just as dangerous. They faced similar fears, such as accidents, lack of supplies, and disease.

Most people felt that their prayers were answered when they arrived in California. However, it was not as wonderful as they had dreamed. Gold was not as easy to find as they had imagined. In fact, most forty-niners did not find much gold or make a great deal of money.

As the quest for gold grew greater, the job became more dangerous. Men began fighting over gold and the claims to mines. Some forty-niners were violently attacked or even killed during this time period. As gold became more difficult to find, foreigners such as Mexicans and Chinese—and even the Native Americans—were driven out of the camps.

The Gold Rush lasted for about ten years. Once all of the gold that could be found by hand had been discovered, there was no more money to be made. The men did not have heavy equipment to extract the remaining gold from deep in the ground. After the rush ended, many mining camps turned into ghost towns.

However, by this time, California had a prospering economy due to farming and industry. Many men stayed and built a life in the great city of San Francisco. It was a booming town with a lot of fertile land to farm.

Also, many of the miners headed to Nevada in search of silver. Sadly, a great deal of men did not make it home due to accidents during the journey or while mining. Disease also killed a lot of miners.

The California Gold Rush not only changed the lives of many people, but made California the popular state it is today. While most did not discover great wealth, people all around the world knew the story of California and its land of riches.

D-Day: Operation Overlord

written by Mark Weimer
illustrated by Doyle Daigle II

World War II began in 1939. An alliance between Russia and Germany allowed the two powers to conquer most of Europe. However, because the Germans wished to rule alone, they invaded Russia in 1941. By 1944, the Germans and Russians were in a stalemate in eastern Europe. Russian soldiers were dying by the millions. Russia waited for the United States, England, and Canada to successfully invade western Europe. A successful invasion would force Germany to fight a war in both the east and the west. This would bring a much quicker end to the war.

There was no easy way to invade western Europe. Adolf Hitler, the German military commander, had built the "Atlantic Wall." The Atlantic Wall was a series of fortifications, or defenses, along the European coast. It had obstacles that stopped boats from getting close to shore. It also had bunkers of steel-reinforced concrete, trenches, machine-guns, and artillery cannons. Because of this, the invasion needed to be well-planned.

The invasion was called Operation Overlord. In order to make it a success, extensive planning and preparation took place. The Allied forces, made of American, British, and Canadian soldiers, would launch from southern Great Britain. They would then cross the English Channel. The Germans knew that an invasion from the English Channel was probable. However, they did not know where or when the invasion was to occur.

In order to keep the Germans guessing, the Allied forces took measures to deceive the Germans. They leaked false information over the radio waves. If Germans intercepted this false information, it would confuse them. Additionally, the Allies undertook a massive effort to make the Germans believe the invasion would come at a different location. In Dover, England, Allied forces built cardboard structures to resemble a massive invasion force. The Germans had strongly considered Dover as a possibility even before the cardboard cutouts. If the radio leaks and fake army fooled the Germans, it would cause the Germans to place troops in the wrong place.

General Dwight D. Eisenhower, the Supreme Allied Commander, decided that the actual invasion would occur in a northern region of France called Normandy. The area was heavily fortified, but it offered the best beaches to make the invasion a success. Nobody knew the actual day that the invasion would take place. Because the troops had to cross the English Channel, they wanted the sea to be calm. Also, they wanted to land at low tide. A low tide would cause all of the Germans' beach obstacles to be exposed. This would prevent the bottoms of boats from being punctured. However, it would also force the soldiers to cross a great open expanse before they could find cover at the base of the cliffs. The invasion area was divided into five beaches that would be assaulted. One beach in particular, code named Omaha, was a natural geographic fortress. Many did not want to land at Omaha, but it was necessary.

The invasion was originally scheduled for early May of 1944, but the seas were too rough. The Allies had to wait a full month for the tide to be low. Finally, despite a rough sea, the decision was made to attack on June sixth. On the night of June fifth, boats loaded and prepared to depart from Great Britain. At the same time, paratroopers from the United States 101st and 82nd Airborne Divisions began to drop behind the beachfronts in France using parachutes and gliders in the night.

The airborne divisions landed in darkness behind enemy lines. Because it was nighttime, it was difficult to tell what was on the ground below. Many paratroopers landed completely in the wrong locations. They then met up with other soldiers who were from other units. Because of good training, the chain of command took over. The men regrouped and systematically destroyed railroad tracks, disabled artillery cannons, and cut wires used for communication. This caused the Germans to be unable to adequately reinforce the beaches in the morning.

On the morning of June sixth, the Allied fleet arrived at the beaches at Normandy. First, naval ships blasted the cliffs of Normandy with large guns. Then the troops were sent ashore on transports called Higgins boats. Everywhere, German resistance was strong. The greatest resistance, though, was at Omaha Beach where many of the Americans landed. Despite terrible odds and casualties, the soldiers overcame the obstacles, the cliffs, and the German bunkers built into the cliffs. Upon reaching the top, they had little trouble overrunning what seemed like a relatively small number of German soldiers. The bombardment had caused a number of German troops to retreat to safety.

As it turned out, all of the precautions the Allies had taken to hide and mislead the Germans had worked. The false radio messages and the cardboard army in Dover caused the Germans to withhold several of their best tank divisions. They were left to a completely different area of the coast. Even as thousands and thousands of Allied soldiers stormed the beaches, many German forces did not commit to Normandy. They thought the landings at Normandy might possibly not be the real attack. This may have been averted if the German commander, General Erwin Rommel, had been at the beach on June sixth. However, in a stroke of luck for the Allies, General Rommel was home for his wife's birthday on that day. This caused a delay in a German counterattack that may have pushed the Allies back into the sea. Within several days, over three hundred fifty thousand troops had landed.

The invasion was a success and it caused Adolf Hitler to divide his forces in half and fight two wars at once. The actions and preparation that led to a successful invasion ensured a quick end to World War II, the largest world war ever fought. Its success caused more triumphs for both the Russians and the western Allies. Less than a year after the invasion, Germany surrendered in 1945 on May eighth.

Alternative Energy Solutions

written by Summer York
illustrated by D. Kent Kerr

Since the time of the Industrial Revolution, people have relied on energy to meet their everyday needs. The main source of this energy has always been fossil fuels. Examples of fossil fuels include coal, oil, and natural gas. They are formed over millions of years from prehistoric plants and animals buried deep beneath the earth's surface. Fossil fuels have provided sources of energy that are inexpensive and easy to obtain. In fact, "coal, natural gas, and oil accounted for 87 percent of the world's primary energy consumption [in 2012]" (Cusick).

However, in recent years, the use of fossil fuels has become a cause of growing concern. There are two main reasons for this. First, fossil fuels are *nonrenewable resources*. This means that the supply will eventually run out. After all, fossil fuels take millions of years to form. Once they all have been used, there will be no more available to humans. Scientists debate exactly when this will happen. Most, though, agree that it will happen someday. Second, fossil fuels are harmful to the environment. Fossil fuels are often burned to make energy. When that happens, they release carbon dioxide into the atmosphere. Carbon dioxide is known as a "greenhouse gas." Greenhouse gases are gases that hold heat inside Earth's atmosphere. To a point, greenhouse gases are helpful. They hold in the heat that keeps the planet's temperature stable. However, climate scientists argue that the overuse of fossil fuels has made too much carbon dioxide. This has caused too much heat to be trapped in Earth's atmosphere. The result is warmer temperatures all over the planet. This phenomenon is known as *global warming* or *climate change*.

Many scientists fear what might happen if humans continue to use fossil fuels. They worry that global warming will increase. This would be disastrous for the planet. Despite all of this, though, fossil fuels continue to provide most of the world's energy. The US Department of Energy reports that "over the past 20 years, nearly three-fourths of human-caused emissions came from the burning of fossil fuels." According to the Environmental Protection Agency, "the burning of fossil fuels was responsible for 79 percent of US greenhouse gas emissions in 2010" (Fossil Fuels).

Due to these fears about fossil fuel usage, many are taking action. Scientific groups have begun to research and develop alternative energies. *Alternative energy* is energy generated in a way that does not deplete natural resources or harm the environment. It is also known as *renewable energy* or *clean energy*. Alternative energy comes from *renewable resources*, or resources that can replenish over time. These include the sun, water, wind, and plant life. These new energy technologies could one day replace the need for fossil fuels. That would save both nonrenewable resources and the environment.

One type of alternative energy is solar power. Solar power is obtained by collecting energy from the sun's rays. According to *National Geographic*, in a single hour, "the sun beams onto Earth more than enough energy to satisfy global energy needs for an entire year." If all of it were captured, a single hour's worth of sunlight could power the whole planet for a year! Solar power can be gathered in many different ways. One tool that collects the sun's energy is the *solar panel*. These can sometimes be seen on rooftops or in open fields. When sunlight shines on solar panels, the panels generate electricity to provide power for nearby buildings. This technology is also used in solar power plants. These power plants use the sun's energy to make electricity. A solar plant can supply power for thousands of people in an area.

Solar power has several benefits. The source of solar power—the sun—is absolutely free. The sun delivers an unlimited supply of heat and light to the entire planet. Also, solar power is pollution-free. It causes no harm to the environment. However, as of 2014, solar power accounts for "less than one tenth of one percent" of the world's energy supply (*National Geographic*). One big obstacle is the cost. Even though the sun's energy is free, the technology that collects that energy can be very expensive. However, in recent years the cost has decreased. As the technology improves, costs will continue to go down. In fact, *National Geographic* claims that "with tax incentives, solar electricity can often pay for itself in five to ten years."

Another type of alternative energy is wind power. Wind power is based on the ancient practice of using the force of the wind to generate energy. In earlier times, people captured the wind with simple tools. They used windmills to run machines and sails to travel on water. Today, wind power is gathered using a *wind turbine*. This is a tall, modern-looking windmill with two or three blades. The motion of the wind turns the giant blades. The turning creates electricity. Sometimes, hundreds of wind turbines are grouped together. This is called a *wind farm*, and it can generate a large amount of power. Smaller versions of wind turbines are also available. These can power a single home.

Wind power has many benefits. As with solar power, the source of wind power is free. As long as a wind turbine is built in an open area that gets large amounts of wind, it will provide electricity. Wind power produces no pollution, so it is environmentally friendly. Additionally, wind power is efficient. *National Geographic* claims that a single one of the largest turbines can power about six hundred homes in the United States. Because it produces clean energy, wind power is quickly gaining popularity. According to *National Geographic*, "by 2050 the answer to one third of the world's electricity needs will be found blowing in the wind."

Newer technologies like solar panels and wind turbines can provide the world with electricity. But people have other energy needs, as well, that have traditionally been supplied by fossil fuels. One such need is fuel to power vehicles. A solution that has been researched for decades is ethanol. Ethanol is an alcohol-based fuel. It is made by fermenting and distilling foods like corn and wheat. Many gas stations in the United States now sell E10, which is a blend of 10 percent ethanol and 90 percent gasoline. All vehicles manufactured today can run on E10. But new fuel blends with higher percentages of ethanol are being developed. Cars that can use these blends are being developed as well.

As a fuel, ethanol is beneficial for many reasons. Ethanol is made from renewable resources, whereas standard gasoline is not. Gasoline is made from a fossil fuel called crude oil. Also, when burned for fuel, ethanol produces less greenhouse gas emissions than standard gasoline. Therefore, ethanol is better for the environment. Despite the benefits, ethanol production has been slow in the United States. Ethanol is still more expensive to make than gasoline. However, other countries have successfully transitioned to using pure ethanol as fuel. The California Energy Commission notes that in Brazil, vehicles have been running on 100 percent ethanol for decades. As the technology improves, experts predict that more and more vehicles will be powered by ethanol.

Solar power, wind power, and ethanol are just a few examples of renewable energies. There are many others being used around the world. For example, hydroelectric power comes from moving water. Geothermal power uses the heat inside the earth to generate heat or electricity. Biomass power is created from organic matter such as plants and wastes. Biodiesel is a clean fuel made from recycled oils and animal fats. With so many alternative energies gaining popularity, a permanent solution to dangerous fossil fuel usage is not far away.

Works Cited

Cusick, Daniel and ClimateWire. "Fossil Fuel Use Continues to Rise." *Scientific American*. Nature America, Inc., 25 Oct. 2013. Web. 10 Jan. 2014.

"Ethanol as a Transportation Fuel." *California Energy Commission*. State of California, 2013. Web. 12 Jan. 2014.

"Fossil." *Energy.gov*. The US Department of Energy, n.d. Web. 10 Jan. 2014.

"Fossil Fuels." Environmental and Energy Study Institute, n.d. Web. 10 Jan. 2014.

"Renewable Energy Sources in the United States." *National Atlas of the United States*. United States Department of the Interior, 14 Jan. 2013. Web. 10 Jan. 2014.

"Solar Energy." *National Geographic*. National Geographic Society, 2014. Web. 11 Jan. 2014.

"Wind Power." *National Geographic*. National Geographic Society, 2014. Web. 12 Jan. 2014.

Desertification

written by Mark Weimer
illustrated by David Rushbrook

One-third of the world's land is covered by deserts. A growing problem in the world is that its deserts are expanding each year. This is called desertification. The Gobi Desert in China expands and covers an additional 1,400 square miles each year. It currently is threatening the city of Beijing, which is home to almost twelve million people. In the last fifty years, the Sahara Desert in Africa has spread south to cover more than 250,000 additional square miles. That new desert land is about the size of the state of Texas. Not only does desertification destroy the habitats of animals, but it also displaces many people and affects global climate. It is important to learn what causes this problem so that a solution can be found.

The greatest cause of desertification is the disappearance or removal of plants. Plants prevent erosion of fertile soil by holding good soil in place with their roots. If plants are removed from an area, the fertile soil dries up and can blow away. Plants themselves create an environment that enables seedlings to develop. They provide shade and preserve ground moisture that helps new plants to grow. When plants are removed, there is no protection and seeds cannot grow. Plants are removed in many ways. Some of these ways stem from human interference. Livestock can overgraze in dry areas, preventing new plants from growing. Overfarming can exhaust the soil, stripping it of nutrients. People also take water from underground faster than it can be replenished. This causes water shortages for people, plants, and animals alike. The combination of these factors makes it no surprise that it is very difficult for some plants to grow. However, despite the many human causes of desertification, there are ways that it can be slowed as well. Some of the desert can even be reclaimed by plant life—if people can handle the costs.

Reclaiming the desert is very costly. There is also a lack of funding to stop desertification on a large scale. This lack of help makes reclaiming more expensive than many farmers can afford. However, for those who can afford the costs and are willing to change their ways, deserts around the world can be reclaimed in many different ways.

One way to fight desertification is with a method called reforestation, which is the planting of many new trees. Some dry areas to which the desert is expanding still have an ever-shortening rainy season. During the rainy season, tree seedlings can be transplanted into areas that are threatened. This helps stop the expansion of the desert. If enough trees are planted, they begin to sustain themselves and support the growth of new plants. That makes reforestation one of the best methods available. Its results are often permanent and self-sustaining.

Another way to fight desertification is by creating windbreaks. Windbreaks are made by growing clumps and lines of trees. Without windbreaks, desert winds can blow fertile soil away and leave only infertile soil. Windbreaks prevent much topsoil from being blown away. This increases the chance of new plants being able to grow naturally.

Trenches are another way to preserve the water that is in a region. By digging trenches that contour to the landscape, water can be collected instead of running off. Water that flows into a trench is absorbed into the ground near the location where it falls. This maintains ground moisture over large areas. That, in turn, gives plants a better chance to grow.

Soil near the desert can also be fertilized using certain types of plants. Many different kinds of plants are able to take plant-loving nitrogen from the air and push it into the ground through their roots. This allows many other different types of plants to grow in the nitrogen-rich soil. Popular plants for this are called legumes, which can also be eaten. Peas, beans, peanuts, and alfalfa are examples of legumes.

Desertification will continue to be a problem until it reaches the hearts and minds of those who have the resources to fix it. Usable land is shrinking. Meanwhile, the human population is growing. Currently, the greatest obstacle to stopping this problem is money. Most of the affected areas are impoverished and overpopulated. Their limited water supplies are already exhausted due to human needs. As the climate continues to change, desertification will only worsen—unless the people of the world come together to address the problem.

Alternative Energy: A Renewable World

written by Vincent J. Scotto
illustrated by Sean Ricciardi

One of the toughest problems the world faces today is its dependence on nonrenewable resources for energy. While many people and companies use alternative energy, most of the world still relies on fossil fuels. At the moment, these fuels provide the best bang for one's buck. In other words, fossil fuels are the cheapest resources that provide lots of energy use. Since fossil fuels are a nonrenewable resource, though, they are becoming more expensive. Even worse, at the current rate of use, they will eventually disappear. As stated earlier, the world has begun to work on alternatives. These new options can supplement, or even replace, fossil fuels.

One such alternative is solar energy. Solar panels take energy from the sun's radiation. They convert it into other types of energy for power. Since the sun rises each day, its energy is an excellent way to naturally supplement the use of fossil fuels. Solar energy has some drawbacks, though. One drawback is the inverse of one of its benefits; the sun goes up each day, but it also goes down each day. Some places in the world do not even get sunlight every day. For example, there is a period every year in Alaska when the sun is not visible at all for almost a whole month. Technology in the early twenty-first century only allows for a limited amount of space to store solar energy. The best types of solar panels are also very expensive to make right now. People in many different fields are working to create solar panels that are cheaper to build and that can store more energy for conversion. In time, they might help power up the world.

Another form of alternative energy is wind energy. Wind turbines, which are gigantic fans that catch wind and spin, use the natural wind that blows in open areas. They convert the wind's kinetic energy into whatever energy is needed. Usually that energy is converted into electrical energy. In this form, it can travel long distances without too much loss. At its end point, the electrical energy is converted into something else for use. Like solar energy, wind energy happens naturally and is completely renewable. But it also has its own drawbacks. There are not many flat surfaces that have natural wind across the world. Regions without natural wind and empty space would need the energy to travel long distances, which can be costly. Wind turbines also require a great deal of space away from communities and habitats (both man-made and naturally occurring). Scientists are working on new ways to make wind energy more efficient in places where it can be used.

The most popular form of alternative energy in the early twenty-first century is biofuel. Rather than relying on iron ore, a nonrenewable resource, biofuel relies on plants and algae, which are living organisms that reproduce. Bioethanol is alcohol that is produced by plants during fermentation. This is widely used in the United States because the country has vast lands that are suited for growing crops, like corn, that can make ethanol. Many machines that use ethanol also use fossil fuels in tandem. This can improve power. Unfortunately, some regions have no space at all to grow crops. Others have only enough space to grow crops for food, not fuel. The amount of energy the world needs also becomes a problem because it takes time to grow crops. Scientists are working tirelessly to find new ways to get the best out of bioethanol fuels so that we can be less dependent on fossil fuels.

There are countless alternatives to using fossil fuels with renewable energy. All of them have their strengths and weaknesses. Eventually fossil fuels will run out. The question we have before us is a tough one because not every solution works everywhere with current technology and understanding. It will be up to new and upcoming scientists in the future to innovate and find ways to become less dependent on fossil fuels. Are you up to the challenge?

A Brief History of Modern Dance in America: Outline

written by Sarah Marino

I. Introduction
    A. Opening statement
        1. Modern dance not as popular as traditional ballet
        2. Yet, modern dance a moving art form, deserves more attention
    B. History of modern dance in America
        1. Origins in classical ballet
        2. Location and time period
    C. Brief definition
        1. Modern dance: a form of movement and expression
        2. Many famous dancers have embraced it.

II. History and origins
    A. Turn of the twentieth century: rejection of formalism/structure of classical ballet
    B. Movements were related to ballet.
    C. Many dancers had ballet training.
    D. One difference: Modern dancers did not wear restrictive ballet slippers/corsets.
        1. Corsets were tight, heavy, uncomfortable
        2. Ballet slippers were supposed to be worn too small, were uncomfortable
        3. Instead, modern dancers wear more comfortable outfits.
            a. Soft, flowing garments
            b. Often dance barefoot
    E. Locations/places where it originated
        1. California, Americans in Europe
        2. First schools and shows

III. Movement and expression
    A. Free-form movement instead of rigid ballet techniques
    B. Dance as art form and method of expression
        1. Dance should be an art, not just entertainment, as with classical ballets.
        2. Modern dancers took themselves seriously.
        3. Modern dancers made statements through their performances.
    C. Political and cultural influences
        1. Influential in modern musicals
        2. Incorporating gender, cross-cultural influences

IV. Dancers and dances
    A. Isadora Duncan
        1. Considered "founding mother of American modern dance"
        2. Upbringing in San Francisco, rebelled against ballet training at a young age
        3. Performed in Europe, started a dance school there

    B. Ruth St. Denis and Ted Shawn
        1. In 1915, started Denishawn
            a. Training center and dance company
            b. Provided training to many famous modern dancers
        2. Team helped to popularize new art form
    C. Martha Graham
        1. Studied at Denishawn, one of the best dancers there
        2. Established a new "system of movement"
            a. System called contraction and release
            b. A way of controlling and moving muscles while dancing
        3. Started own company, created several new works
    D. Paul Taylor
        1. Ties to Martha Graham
            a. Studied with her
            b. Was a soloist at her dance company
        2. Founded his own dance company, 1954
        3. Experimental, artistic performances that have received critical acclaim
    E. José Limón
        1. Established own dance company, 1946
        2. His choreographic works are thought to be "classics of modern dance"

V. Conclusion
    A. Not as popular as classical ballet but an important and influential art form
        1. Modern musicals
        2. Influential to other dance styles
    B. History to the present day
        1. Today, modern dance uses elements of various styles.
        2. Has not eliminated classical ballet, but has become another rich art form
    C. Dancers, expression, and art
        1. Many dancers have been instrumental in creating this art form.
        2. People can create new forms of artistic expression, exciting to witness
        3. Art is many things and anyone can be artistic and express themselves in a variety of ways; modern dance is one such important method of expression.

Organic Food: Outline

written by Sarah Marino

I. Introduction
    A. Opening statement
        1. Organic food better for the environment
        2. Organic food tastes better.
    B. Definition and explanation
        1. Organic: environmentally friendly method of farming
        2. Organic food has fewer preservatives/pesticides
    C. Criticism and support
        1. Critics say:
            a. Too expensive to benefit all Americans
            b. Idea of "organic" based on bogus science
        2. Supporters say:
            a. Benefits farmers
            b. Improvements making organic cheaper
            c. It's a growing industry.

II. What organic means
    A. Definition
        1. Environmentally friendly farming methods
            a. Conserve soil and water in farming processes
            b. Happens mostly on small farms
        2. Crops grown without chemical fertilizers, pesticides, and insecticides
        3. Uses natural methods of fertilizing and pest/insect control
            a. Manure
            b. Helpful birds and insects
            c. Crop rotation
        4. Organic livestock
            a. No antibiotics or growth hormones given to livestock
            b. Clean/safe living conditions for livestock
                i. Better lives for animals
                ii. Less disease
    B. Contrast to conventional farming
        1. Drawbacks of conventional farming
            a. Use of pesticides, insecticides
            b. Use of antibiotics/hormones
            c. Harm to ecosystems and livestock
        2. Use of chemicals harms soil and depletes nutrients in the soil.

    C. Better taste/quality
        1. Food grown in natural, healthy soil without residue from chemical treatments tastes better.
        2. Humans don't ingest toxic residues.

III. Criticism
    A. Like chemical pesticides, organic, natural pesticides can be harmful.
        1. Use of natural pesticides doesn't mean more nutrition.
        2. Can still be tainted with E. coli or salmonella
    B. Organic farms don't produce enough to feed all Americans.
        1. Organic harvests are smaller
        2. Even with smaller output, organic farms strain environment
    C. Higher prices aren't reasonable for what you get.

IV. Support
    A. Reduced health risks
        1. Avoids chemical pesticides, insecticides, and so on
        2. Some non-organic pesticides linked to cancer
        3. Farm workers less exposed to chemicals
        4. Consumers exposed to fewer chemicals
        5. Habitats and animals safe from chemical contamination
    B. Protection for the environment
        1. Prevents nitrogen runoff (which contaminates waterways)
        2. Builds healthy soils
        3. Protects diversity of life in nearby ecosystems
    C. Economic benefit for small farms/communities
        1. Small farms can get fairer prices for organic crops and livestock.
        2. Rural communities benefit when farms productive and profitable
    D. Reiterate taste/quality
        1. Taste test: organic produce often more fragrant and flavorful
        2. Organic means strict government farming standards have been met.

V. Conclusion
    A. Summary of definition, worth buying organic
        1. Sustainable agricultural practices
        2. Limited chemical treatments used
    B. Pros and cons
        1. Pros outweigh cons: better for environment, human health, small farmers
        2. Don't have to buy everything organic, manage cost
    C. Choice
        1. Many options for organic and conventional
        2. Research for yourself, make informed choices

First in Flight?

written by Summer York
illustrated by Sean Ricciardi

Orville and Wilbur Wright, known as the Wright brothers, are credited with achieving the first powered flight in history. They designed, built, and tested several models of early flying machines. On December 17, 1903, they tested a model called *The Flyer* at Kitty Hawk, North Carolina. That day, the Wright brothers made four successful engine-powered flights. However, the Wright brothers were not the only people experimenting with flight at the time. In fact, some say the Wright brothers' flight was not the first.

Gustave Whitehead was one such experimenter. He was born Gustav Albin Weisskopf in Germany in 1874. As a young man, he worked in mechanic shops and on ships. But his real dream was to build a flying machine. Whitehead came to the United States in 1895. He began building gliders for the Aeronautical Society in Boston. He continued to improve his designs, hoping to one day achieve flight. Eyewitness accounts and newspaper articles document three successful flights by Whitehead. All of these occurred before the Wright brothers' flights in 1903.

While Whitehead was living in Pittsburgh, Pennsylvania, he added a steam engine to his glider design. According to author Megan Adam, Whitehead's assistant Louis Darvarich gave a statement saying, "In approximately April or May, 1899, I was present and flew with Mr. Whitehead on the occasion when he succeeded in flying his machine, propelled by steam motor, on a flight of approximately a half mile distance." In Connecticut, Whitehead reportedly flew on two more occasions. In August of 1901 in Bridgeport, witnesses claim Whitehead made four successful flights in one day in a model called *No. 21*. The event was reported in the local *Bridgeport Herald*. Then on January 17, 1902, onlookers saw Whitehead fly *No. 22* over Long Island Sound.

If these statements are true, then Whitehead flew more than four years before the Wright brothers did. Besides eyewitness statements, though, no other evidence of these flights has been found in photographs or scientific records. Because of the lack of evidence, many critics claim that these stories are made up. They argue that Whitehead never actually flew. But according to the article "The Case for Gustave Whitehead," Paul Jackson, editor of *Jane's All the World's Aircraft*, believed he found a photograph in 2013 proving that Whitehead was indeed the first to fly. Nevertheless, most critics are still not convinced. None of Whitehead's flights have been officially recognized.

William O'Dwyer, a retired Air Force officer, believes the flights of Whitehead and others are not recognized for another reason. He discovered a contract stating that "the Smithsonian [Institution] agreed to ignore all other claims of flights before the Wright brothers" in exchange for the Wrights' plane *The Flyer* (White 49). However, the people involved have not admitted to this. There could be many reasons why flights before Kitty Hawk have been ignored. But some consider the eyewitness accounts of Gustave Whitehead's flights as proof enough that the Wrights may not have been the first to fly.

Works Cited

Adam, Megan. "The Flights." *Gustave Whitehead's Flying Machines*. June 2006. Web. 10 March 2014.

"The Case for Gustave Whitehead." *Wright Brothers Aeroplane Company*. Web. 10 March 2014.

White, Thomas. *Legends and Lore of Western Pennsylvania*. Charleston: The History Press, 2009. Print.

Defeating Anatidaephobia

written by Mark Weimer
illustrated by Mallory Senich

There are many things in the world that people fear. Many people fear public speaking. Others fear spiders, small spaces, or high places. These are all very common fears. Some fears, though, are much less common. One of the most awful fears known to humans is anatidaephobia (*ah-NA-tuh-dee-foh-bee-a*). Like all phobias, anatidaephobia is no laughing matter. What makes it such a terrible fear is that it can affect people anywhere, anytime. It is not a fear brought on by seeing a spider or by being in a high place. It is a constant fear. For some, it never goes away. It is important to know the warning signs, symptoms, and possible causes of this dreaded fear. This way, you can recognize and treat it as quickly as possible. This guide will help you identify and treat anatidaephobia. Hopefully, it will help you avoid this illness and understand more about those who suffer from it.

Anatidaephobia is the fear that no matter where you are or what you are doing, you are being watched by a duck. While some consider this affliction absurd and perhaps even funny, it is very serious! A duck, known for its feathers, bill, and webbed feet, is a very mobile creature. Not only can a duck swim and walk, but it can also fly. It can watch you from the air, water, or land. Ducks can even dive underwater for short periods of time. Ducks can be anywhere, anytime, watching!

Do you think you may have this fear? You may have a fear of ducks if, when the word "duck" is spoken, your mouth becomes dry and you find it harder to breathe. You may feel tense or trapped. If this happens to you, you may already suffer from anatidaephobia. In some cases, you may have to see a doctor. However, a good education can help you to treat your anatidaephobia as well. The key—and this is very important—is to avoid ducks at all costs.

There are certain surefire ways to prevent a duck from watching you. To keep the watchful eyes of a duck away from you, it is important to know more about them, and especially to know what ducks themselves dislike. Recently, my colleague, a hunter, tried to conduct an interview with a duck. The duck would not answer his questions, but the feathered floating menace did reveal some of its own fears. My hunting friend learned that ducks' first and foremost fear is the clothing pattern plaid. This must be the truth. My friend was dressed in an all-plaid hunting outfit at the time, and the dastardly duck flew away in terror the moment it saw him.

If ducks do not like plaid patterns, then it must also be true that they dislike checkers, sewer grates, and whole Belgian waffles. Anything with a pattern of squares or crossed lines will most likely repel a duck. Therefore, it is safe to assume that ducks hate addition symbols as well as multiplication signs, crossed fingers, and the lowercase *t*. One thing ducks love, on the other hand, is bread. For safety's sake, one should **never** carry bread if one does not want to be watched by a duck—unless, of course, you have already cut your bread into the shape of a letter *t*.

Avoiding ducks is no easy task. They are small and can survive in many climates. They can fly, swim, dive, and walk. They can even run by flapping their wings while walking on the ground. Worst of all, ducks can attack with their eyes at any time. However, armed with knowledge, it is possible to create a situation that a duck would not want to watch or even be *near*. Combining one, two, or more of a duck's dislikes will surely keep you out of its sight. If you find yourself in dire fear that a duck is watching, your wisest course of action would be to take these safety steps. First, dress up in a plaid suit (preferably with the pockets stuffed full of Belgian waffles). Second, go to the county courthouse and have your name changed to something terrifying, such as "Otto," "Attila," or "Etttttthan." As soon as you finish, immediately cross all of your fingers and toes. Lastly, begin adding numbers at the top of your lungs. If you take these steps, there is a very good chance that any nearby duck will flee at the sight of you.

If you fear geese, however, that is an entirely different story.

The Importance of Libraries

written by Luke See
illustrated by Sean Ricciardi

It seems that everything today is digital. Even books you might want to read can be downloaded to a tablet or a smartphone. Knowledge is right at your fingertips every day. If you want to do research, you do not always have to go to the local library. Instead, you could use your computer. With all of these advances in technology, it can be easy to forget just how useful libraries are to individuals and communities. Libraries may get brushed aside as being less important than they were in the past. Too often, libraries are forced to close their doors and shut down. However, the public library is a vital part of a town for many reasons.

First, the library is not just a place to rent books, but a place to gather. Nearly every library hosts various reading groups that take place within its walls. People of all ages set times to meet and discuss new novels or poetry. These types of clubs help a community to thrive. In addition, the library can be a resource to other groups. A library can use its space to host a community service fair or a chess club, for example. Every library is full of friendly staff; most staffs are open to any experience that strengthens a town and spreads knowledge. Ask the local librarian about any community events or clubs. Surely you will learn about all sorts of opportunities that you did not even realize existed.

Second, the library is a great example of sustainability. Think about how much waste an average person creates. After reading the morning paper, eating breakfast, and checking the mail, the average adult has probably already discarded a handful of stuff. In today's world, too much seems dispensable. The library is a place of preservation. Each library collects and protects books so that they may exist and be shared and enjoyed for decades. Chances are that your local library has books that are older than your oldest friends and relatives. The library not only preserves resources, like paper and ink, but also knowledge itself. If it were not for some written works, certain types of information would not exist today. Some libraries hold books that are so rare or old that they are worth thousands of dollars.

Third, the library provides so much more than just books. Personal computers have become very popular in the last two decades. During the time when computers were still very expensive and not widespread, many people used the local library as a place to experience this new technology. Today you can still visit a library to use a computer or the Internet. As technology advances, so do libraries—oftentimes right on the cutting edge. A library may also have special equipment, such as a microfiche machine. A microfiche machine allows you to look at newspapers from hundreds of years ago. A lot of library technology is vital to researchers.

Fourth, the library gives every person free access to knowledge. One of the beautiful things about libraries is that every man, woman, and child can belong. Applying for a library card is a great opportunity that is also free. Once you are a member, you can use the facilities, check out books, or just come in to relax and read. Such activities are often taken for granted; however, not everyone can afford a computer or to have the Internet at home. People also may not have enough money to purchase all of the books that they really want to read. The local library welcomes members of the community and encourages them to educate themselves in any way. Just as some people cannot afford books, some cannot afford education. The library is like a university that any person can attend. The library is a resource that can be used to learn as much as one can. In that way, the library is a teacher, always waiting to give knowledge to those who desire it. At its core, a public library is a building full of valuable education that is totally free!

Fifth, the library is a great place to teach life skills. For many young people, getting a library card is one of their first steps toward personal responsibility. Getting a driver's permit or license does not happen until high school. However, one can become a member of the local library at any age. Once you go in and sign up, you will get your very own card that allows you to check out books and use the facilities. Your library card is very important and it is your responsibility to take care of it and use it well. This is a great lesson as you grow into early adulthood. Simply holding the card is just part of the job, though. You will be expected to take good care of the books that you use or borrow. You will also need to make sure that you return any borrowed books on time and keep track of your late fees if you do not. Such responsibilities might seem small, but they are good practice for other challenges down the road.

Finally, the library is necessary to a community because a library champions a great cause: reading. The ability to read is a wonderful asset that people are fortunate to have. Even a century ago in the United States of America, the ability to read was not something that was guaranteed. Public schools were not always available. Some people lived their entire lives without learning the alphabet. As times change and technology flies forward, people can never forget the importance of the written word. This goes hand in hand with the library. No computer screen or electronic reader will ever give the same feeling as that of opening a new book. The library is a portal to thousands of adventures in worlds of fantasy, research, and excitement. The local library encourages reading and makes it available to everyone, and that is something worth celebrating and protecting.

The Copernicus Controversy

written by Jennifer Tkocs
illustrated by Mallory Senich

When we study astronomy today, we recognize a *heliocentric* model of the solar system. In this model, the sun sits in the center of the solar system. Earth and the other planets *orbit*, or revolve, around it. While this may seem obvious to us, it was not always so. Centuries ago, astronomers believed that Earth was the center of the planetary system. In the early 1500s, a man named Nicolaus Copernicus discovered the truth. He published the very first papers to show evidence of a heliocentric model. In his lifetime, though, many did not believe Copernicus's claims. In fact, the idea that our solar system is heliocentric was not widely accepted until decades after Copernicus's death.

Nicolaus Copernicus was born on February 19, 1473, in Torun, Poland. His father died when he was ten years old. From that point on, he was raised by his uncle. This uncle was a *cleric*, or religious leader, in the Catholic Church. Education was very important in his uncle's eyes, so in 1493, Nicolaus began to attend the University of Cracow. He went there to study painting and mathematics. Although he did not formally study astronomy there, his interest in the subject began to grow.

When he returned from the university, Copernicus was elected as a *canon* at a cathedral in Frombork, Poland. This was an administrative position in the Catholic Church. It gave the young man a steady income, as well as the chance to continue his studies for as long as he pleased.

Copernicus went to the University of Bologna in 1496. He intended to study canon law, or the rules of the church. However, two important things happened that influenced his pursuit of astronomy. First, he met astronomy professor Domenico Maria Novara. Novara was the first person Copernicus met who had ideas that challenged the current understanding of astronomy. Second, Copernicus began to study the Greek language. Most astronomy texts of the time were written in Greek, not Latin, so this opened up much new research to him.

In 1501, Copernicus attended medical school at the University of Padua. This also allowed him to add to his astronomy knowledge. Italian medical schools at the time incorporated both astronomy and astrology into their lessons. Scholars believed that the planets and stars directly influenced living things on Earth. Alongside lessons about illness and epidemics, Copernicus's professors taught lessons about the phases of the moon, the paths of comets, and changes in the weather.

After medical school, Copernicus continued to study astronomy on his own. He was also very busy, though, with his church duties. Additionally, he had to care for his uncle, who had grown sick. Finally, in 1510, Copernicus left his uncle and moved back to Frombork. There, he worked more directly on his astronomy studies.

Copernicus completed his first essay, called *Commentariolus*, between 1510 and 1514. In the essay, Copernicus introduced a radical new theory: that the universe was heliocentric.

Until this point, most astronomers followed "classic astronomy." It was originally based on statements by the ancient philosopher Aristotle. Aristotle stated that the universe was made up of seven planets. Earth was the center of this universe. The other six planets were the moon, the sun, Mercury, Venus, Mars, and Jupiter. Aristotle believed that these six "planets" revolved around Earth. This was called a *geocentric* model of the universe.

Another philosopher, Claudius Ptolemy, refined Aristotle's theory in the second century. He made some slight changes, but he still pictured Earth to be at the center of the universe. For over a thousand years, Ptolemy's geocentric theory was thought to be the best description of how the planets existed and moved in the night sky.

Between Ptolemy's time and that of Copernicus, a few philosophers and astronomers did try to challenge the geocentric model. However, none received much attention. One astronomer, Aristarchus, even suggested that Earth and other planets might revolve around the sun. His work may have given Copernicus some inspiration. However, it was Copernicus who first established the scientific evidence to support this theory.

Copernicus saw that Ptolemy's model sought to build upon and more fully explain Aristotle's theory. However, he noticed inconsistencies between the two. Ptolemy's model showed the general positions of the planets at any given time, but it wasn't very precise. Copernicus realized that if he changed the center of the universe to be the sun instead of Earth, it would correct this problem. He also determined that the moon did revolve around Earth, but that the other "planets" did not. Copernicus's theory stated that the sun was stationary, or unmoving, in the center of the planetary system. The other planets revolved around it.

Copernicus gave copies of his manuscript to friends and fellow astronomers. It was never formally printed, though. He viewed it as a mere introduction to the idea of a heliocentric planetary system. His full statement would be a much larger work. He called it *De revolutionibus orbium coelestium*, which is Latin for *On the Revolutions of the Heavenly Spheres*.

On the Revolutions was published in 1543. In this work, Copernicus reintroduced his theory of the heliocentric universe. He also expanded on the theory. He showed the order of the planets based on their distances from the sun. Copernicus also showed that each planet moved on its own path. In addition, he showed how each planet traveled around the sun in a different length of time. This was the first time such a clear system had been identified in the planetary realm. It seemed to solve many of the problems with Ptolemy's model.

However, many rejected Copernicus's research. Scholarly critics claimed that he failed to fully explain why Earth would orbit the sun. Some objected on religious grounds. In Copernicus's time, the Roman Catholic Church had a very strong influence over what people believed to be true. Some members of the Church believed that a heliocentric planetary system went against the teachings of the Bible.

Even the man who printed Copernicus's work believed it went against the Bible. The man who printed *On the Revolutions* was a Lutheran minister named Andrew Osiander. Before publishing the book, Osiander secretly included a note stating that the information in Copernicus's book was merely a hypothesis and was not to be interpreted as true. Osiander did not sign his name to the note. Because of this, many believed it to have come from Copernicus himself. Copernicus was quite ill at the time of the book's publishing, which left him unable to defend his work.

Copernicus had dedicated his book to the current Pope, the leader of the Roman Catholic Church. Yet that won him no favors from the Church. In fact, after Copernicus's death, the Church actually banned *On the Revolutions*. It remained on the forbidden book list for nearly three centuries.

In the early 1600s, an astronomer named Galileo began to promote Copernicus's theory. Galileo also worked to make an improved kind of telescope. With this creation, one could finally see Copernicus's theories at work in the sky. At that point, the heliocentric planetary model finally gained popularity. Despite this, astronomers and religious scholars still tried to disprove Copernicus—even as late as the nineteenth century.

Nicolaus Copernicus's heliocentric model of the planetary system is the model that is still used today. In his lifetime, though, Copernicus never saw the fruits of his labor. He died in May of 1543, just after the publication of *On the Revolutions*. He was buried in an unmarked grave in Frombork. There his remains stayed until the year 2010. In that year, the Catholic Church finally reburied Copernicus. The Church blessed his remains and gave him a full ceremony—one much more fitting for a man who literally changed how we saw the universe.

The Battle of Hampton Roads

written by Mark Weimer and Jennifer Tkocs
illustrated by Doyle Daigle II

Despite its bloodshed and destruction, the American Civil War (1861–1865) led to many developments in technology. Some of these developments increased America's military power. One newer technology was put to the test in the Battle of Hampton Roads. In this battle, two ironclad ships attacked one another. Ironclads were wooden ships that were plated in metal armor. The armor prevented cannonballs from causing the level of damage they would to regular ships. Each side in the Civil War—the Confederacy in the South and the Union in the North—had its own ironclad, though each ironclad was designed differently. The Confederates named their ironclad the CSS *Virginia*. The Union ironclad was the USS *Monitor*. The two ironclads met in battle on March 9, 1862. This date marked the first time two ironclads had fought directly in combat.

The two ironclads were built using different approaches and for different purposes. The Confederacy built the CSS *Virginia* in order to break a Union blockade. A blockade is a military strategy in which one side cuts off supply lines to the enemy. The Union had surrounded the southern states with its fleet. The Union intended to choke the Confederacy until it ran out of resources for fighting. In response, the Confederacy built the CSS *Virginia*. Confederates salvaged an old Union steamship, the USS *Merrimack*. The Union had sunk the *Merrimack* at the beginning of the war so that the Confederacy could not use it. However, they failed to destroy the ship.

The Confederacy rebuilt the *Merrimack* as the CSS *Virginia*. A ram was mounted to the front of the *Virginia*, and 10 guns pointed out of ports in the ship's sides, front, and back. The Confederacy covered the ship in iron to make it strong enough to break through the Union's blockade. Meanwhile, the Union built the USS *Monitor* in response to news that the Confederacy was building an ironclad. The design of the Union ship was much different. Instead of having many guns, the *Monitor* had only two. They were mounted in a revolving turret that could point in any direction. The guns were larger than the guns on the *Virginia*. The only parts of the ship that were visible above the water were the gun turret and a small smokestack.

The CSS *Virginia* caused a great deal of damage on the first day of the Battle of Hampton Roads. The battle began on March 8, 1862, where the James River meets the Chesapeake Bay in Virginia. The *Virginia* entered the harbor from Norfolk with several other ships to attack the Union blockade. The Union had five warships in the water and several other supporting ships. The *Virginia* wasted little time, heading right for the Union warships. The Union fired at the *Virginia*, but the cannonballs bounced off its side. The *Virginia* then rammed the warship USS *Cumberland*, sinking it. The *Virginia* set its sights on the USS *Congress* next. In a panic, the captain of the *Congress* ran the ship aground and surrendered. The USS *Minnesota* ran aground as it was leaving a Union fort to enter the battle. However, the tide was going down by that time. Because the *Virginia* sat very low in the water, its captain decided to wait until the next day to attack the USS *Minnesota*.

When the *Virginia* retreated inland for repairs, the Union took action to turn the tide of the battle. The USS *Monitor* steamed into Hampton Roads and prepared to protect the USS *Minnesota*. When the *Virginia* returned on March 9, it attacked, despite not really knowing what the *Monitor* was due to its strange appearance. The battle between the vessels lasted for hours. The two ironclads bombarded each other at close range, but neither gained the upper hand in the battle. Finally, by chance, a shot from the CSS *Virginia* exploded when it hit the pilothouse of the USS *Monitor*. The explosion blinded the ship's commander. This forced the *Monitor* to withdraw for a time. The commander of the *Virginia* believed the *Monitor* was leaving in defeat. While he wanted to attack the *Minnesota*, the day had grown late, and the *Virginia* needed extensive repairs. As a result, the *Virginia* also withdrew. When the *Monitor* returned to the battle, the *Virginia* was gone. Both sides thought they had won.

The battle between the *Monitor* and the *Virginia* did not change the tide of the Civil War. It did, however, change the future of naval technology. It sent other countries into a panic because their wooden ships were vulnerable to the new ironclad vessels. By the war's end, the United States boasted one of the strongest, most technologically advanced militaries on the planet. Other countries began equipping their navies with ironclads as well.

Works Cited

"Hampton Roads." *Civil War Trust*, www.civilwar.org/learn/articles/hampton-roads. Accessed 14 Nov. 2017.

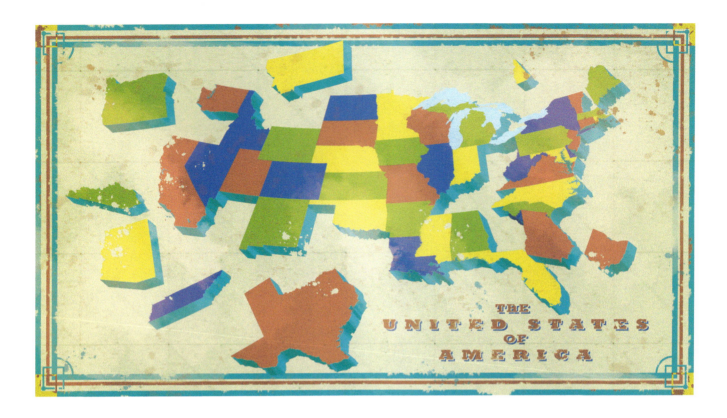

How the United States Was Shaped

written by Jill Fisher
illustrated by Josh Perry

In 1776, the year of its founding, the United States of America consisted of only thirteen colonies. Today, however, America is composed of fifty states. Forty-eight of these states are located between two countries and three large bodies of waters. These states are known as the continental, or mainland, United States. The nation of Canada borders the mainland to the north, while Mexico meets its southern border. The bordering bodies of water are the Pacific Ocean on the west, the Atlantic Ocean on the east, and the Gulf of Mexico along parts of the south. The remaining two states are separate from the mainland. The forty-ninth state, Alaska, is divided from the mainland by Canada. Alaska is located about five hundred miles northwest of the state of Washington. The fiftieth state, Hawaii, is even farther away. Made up of a group of islands in the Pacific Ocean, Hawaii is over two thousand miles southwest of California.

Each of the fifty states has a unique shape and size. Many factors affected the crazy borders of the jigsaw puzzle that make up the United States. Some borders were created by natural elements, such as rivers, lakes, volcanoes, and mountain ranges. However, military battles, historical events, railroads, the government, and more played a hand as well.

Mother Nature helped to create some of the more oddly-shaped states with her enormous mountain ranges, dangerous volcanoes, great lakes, and powerful rivers. Twelve states have borders that are marked by active or potentially active volcanoes. They are Alaska, Arizona, California, Colorado, Hawaii, Idaho, New

Mexico, Nevada, Oregon, Utah, Washington, and Wyoming. Many other states are divided by rivers. For example, the southern part of Ohio is lined by the Ohio River. This river marks the border between Ohio and the states of West Virginia and Kentucky.

Over time, some rivers have shifted due to erosion. That makes some parts of states appear to be on the wrong side of the rivers that originally marked their borders. For example, part of Indiana's border was originally marked by the Wabash River. Today, though, there are small parts of Indiana that are on the wrong side of this river. They look like they are part of Illinois due to the Wabash River gradually shifting over a long period of time. Obviously, this can be quite confusing.

Another reason for confusing borders between the states is human error. Long ago, when the states were created, men surveyed the land using transit and compass, chronometer, and astronomical readings. They also relied on information from previous surveys. They did the best they could with the given tools and situation. The border between the states of Georgia and Tennessee is still debated today. People say the original border is incorrect and needs to be changed. It is believed that the surveyor started at the wrong location. In fact, there are some homes that use Georgia addresses, even though they are technically in the state of Tennessee.

State boundaries have also been formed by historical events, such as the Louisiana Purchase, the creation of the Mason-Dixon Line, and the Oregon Treaty. The Mason-Dixon Line, for instance, takes its name from two surveyors named Charles Mason and Jeremiah Dixon. They helped to settle a dispute in colonial times over where Pennsylvania ended and where the colonies to the south of it began. The line these men mapped forms the southern border of Pennsylvania and the western border of Delaware. It sets these states off from Maryland and West Virginia (which was still part of Virginia when the line was drawn).

Look carefully at a map of America. You will notice how the states on the eastern side of the country have crooked borders and widely varying sizes. The states farther west look more like organized squares with straight lines. That is because people occupied the eastern side early in the country's history, with each state making its own rules. However, as the United States expanded westward, the American government made laws about how to form the states. In fact, most borders beyond the original thirteen colonies were created by Congress, which gave the states a more uniform shape and size. Often, they used the lines of longitude and latitude to determine the size and shape of each state.

Some states are very large while others are tiny. As the states were being formed, many people believed that all states should be the same size. In fact, back in 1786, Thomas Jefferson predicted the large territory of California would crumble into smaller states. Despite border battles, the gold rush, and even earthquakes, that did not happen. Another large state, Texas, was created with the intention of dividing it into five smaller states. Obviously, that did not happen either.

It is clear that many forces have affected the size and shape of each of the states. Over time, Mother Nature will continue to change the earth, and there may be more historical events that change the shapes of the states. Will the map of the United States ever look different than it does now? Only time will tell.

Children Should Read for Pleasure

written by Summer York
illustrated by David Rushbrook

"Adolescents entering the adult world in the 21st century will read and write more than at any other time in human history," stated Moore and fellow researchers (qtd. in Clark and Rumbold). Yet, in recent years, scholars have noted a major decrease in reading for pleasure among children. Reading for pleasure is reading that one chooses to do in one's free time beyond what is required. Today's children are choosing to spend their spare time with modern technologies. These include television, video games, and the Internet. "Where children might have picked up a book, now screens fill their time. The result is that those moments where reading took root and flourished are diminishing," said Alison David. However, studies have proven that childhood reading for pleasure has many important, lasting benefits. This article will discuss three of these: it aids academic performance, fosters personal development, and creates a lifelong interest in reading.

First, children should read for pleasure because it aids academic performance. A study by the Institute of Education (IOE) showed the gains that children who read for pleasure can make. They regularly had more success in vocabulary, spelling, and math than those who did not read often. Better vocabulary and spelling skills may be expected. Reading for pleasure helps children to practice skills in reading, writing, vocabulary, spelling, text structure, and more. "When children read for pleasure…they acquire, involuntarily and without conscious effort, nearly all of the so-called 'language skills'" (Clark and Rumbold). But how does reading for pleasure improve math scores? The IOE study shows that it develops a child's ability to concentrate and understand new information. These skills can improve performance in all school subjects. Dr. Sullivan, who conducted the IOE study, claims that this study proves the importance of childhood reading for pleasure even in today's digital world. Children do not gain the same educational benefits from television or the Internet as they do from reading.

Second, children should read for pleasure because it helps them grow as people. Literacy, or the ability to read and write, is an essential part of life. That part begins with early childhood reading. The Department for Culture, Media, and Sport notes that "people cannot be active and informed citizens unless they can read. Reading is a prerequisite for almost all cultural and social activities" (qtd. in Clark and Rumbold). Literacy gives children the tools they need to be successful throughout their lives. Even further, reading for pleasure develops a child's sense of self. Denise von Stockar claims that "reading contributes in a concrete way to the very sense of our lives." The article "10 Reasons Why You Should Read to Your Kids" explains that reading for pleasure nurtures many positive abilities. These include language development, social skills, confidence, imagination, empathy, and communication. All of these contribute to one's personal growth. In addition, reading for pleasure allows a child to establish personal beliefs and values. Barbieri determined that "seventh-grade girls read for personal reasons: to clarify their beliefs, to find out who they are, and to discover that they are not alone" (qtd. in Cullinan). Children who gain an early confidence and sense of self are more likely to succeed in school and later in life. Reading for pleasure can help make this happen.

Third, children should read for pleasure in order to become lifelong readers. Reading is a skill that improves with practice. According to Cunningham and Stanovich, "reading amount and reading achievement are thought to be reciprocally related to each other—as reading amount increases, reading achievement increases, which in turn increases reading amount" (qtd. in Clark and Rumbold). In other words, frequent early experiences with reading lead to a more positive attitude toward reading throughout one's lifetime. Research shows that a love of reading often begins in childhood. Without an early foundation, adults are less likely to read for pleasure. O'Leary claims, "If the classroom is the only place a child reads, writes and has ongoing exposure to books and stories, then that child is at risk of growing up a reluctant reader or, worse, a nonreader. To develop good reading habits that will last a lifetime, a child must be surrounded by books, stories and reading, not only in the classroom, but in the home, the community and beyond." When children read for pleasure, it creates a lifelong interest in reading.

As the current research shows, reading for pleasure during childhood is very important. It provides more than improved reading skills. It helps academic performance, fosters personal development, and promotes lifelong reading habits. Reading for pleasure as a child is a smart way to achieve academic and personal success later in life.

Works Cited

"10 Reasons Why You Should Read to Your Kids." *Early Moments: Sharing the Gift of Reading*. Sandvik Publishing, n.d. Web. 4 Jan. 2014.

Clark, Christina and Kate Rumbold. "Reading for Pleasure: A Research Overview." National Literacy Trust, Nov. 2006. Web. 2 Jan. 2014.

Cullinan, Bernice E. "Independent Reading and School Achievement." *American Association of School Librarians*. American Library Association, 2000. Web. 3 Jan. 2014.

David, Alison. "Should we be worried about the decline of children's reading?" *The Guardian*. Guardian News and Media Limited, 1 Nov. 2013. Web. 2 Jan. 2014.

O'Leary, John Daniel. "Creating a Love of Reading." Copian: Connecting Canadians in Learning, n.d. Web. 4 Jan. 2014.

"Reading for pleasure puts children ahead in the classroom, study finds." *Institute of Education*. University of London, 2013. Web. 2 Jan. 2014.

von Stockar, Denise. "The Importance of Literacy and Books in Children's Development." International Board on Books for Young People, June 2006. Web. 3 Jan. 2014.

Lewis and Clark: Discovering the West

written by Sarah Marino
illustrated by David Rushbrook

In the winter of 1803, the US Congress agreed to fund an expansion project of President Thomas Jefferson. The project would fund a group of explorers to go on an expedition to survey the unmapped West. Jefferson's main goal for the project was to make contact with western Native Americans and create trade with them. Finally, Jefferson also wished to gain knowledge of the plants and animals that lived in the West, as it was uncharted territory. Congress provided $2,500 for the expedition (which would be worth nearly $40,000 in 2014). President Jefferson named the traveling group the Corps of Discovery. The Corps was to be led by Meriwether Lewis, Jefferson's personal secretary, and William Clark, Lewis's friend. Lewis was a captain in the US Army.

Before setting out on the journey, Lewis went to Philadelphia to learn various skills from the nation's best scientists. He was trained in mapmaking, land surveying, botany, mathematics, anatomy, and medicine, among other subjects. While in Philadelphia, he also procured many tools and items needed for the trip. These included rifles, a chronometer (a kind of timekeeper), a sextant for navigation, blankets, medicines, food, and candles. Lewis also got ink and journal paper for taking notes. Lastly, Lewis purchased items to be used in gift exchanges with Native Americans. Exchanging gifts was important to many native cultures. Some of the gift items included mirrors, beads, scissors, and tobacco. The Corps of Discovery carried some 3,500 pounds of goods.

Lewis set out on the first part of his journey in the summer of 1803. He crossed the Appalachians and stayed for a time in Pittsburgh. There, he built a keelboat to take his cargo down the Ohio River to Indiana where he picked up his partner, William Clark. The two were joined by some additional soldiers, Clark's African-American slave York, and Lewis's Newfoundland dog Seaman.

The team spent the winter of 1803–1804 at Camp Dubois, near St. Louis. While there, the two leaders recruited more men for the Corps of Discovery. They also gathered additional provisions for the rest of their group. In May of 1804, the group began their westward journey up the Missouri River.

While traveling, Lewis and Clark wrote in their journals and made maps of the terrain. They were also responsible for naming new waterways, such as streams and rivers, as well as plants and unknown animals that had not been encountered before. In July they came to the mouth of the Platte River, in present-day Nebraska. There they had their first meeting with western Native Americans. The natives were from the Oto and Missouri tribes. While there, one of the members of the expedition suffered from appendicitis and died. He was the only member of the Corps to die during the trip.

As the group traveled up into present-day North Dakota, the landscape of the plains came into view. There were fewer trees and more tall grasses. There was a multitude of buffalo and many groups of prairie dogs. To prepare for the winter of 1805, the Corps built Fort Mandan near a few native villages. During this time, the group became friendly with the tribes and some English and French fur traders who had been there for years. One French trader, Toussaint Charbonneau, became an interpreter for the group. Lewis and Clark asked him to continue on in the expedition. Accompanying Charbonneau was his young Shoshone wife, Sacagawea, who was pregnant. Her baby was born that February and the two also journeyed west with the travelers. This traveling party consisted of thirty-three members. After that, no one else came or left. Those thirty-three constituted the "permanent" party that would make the entire journey to Oregon and back.

In the spring of 1805, the group headed west into present-day Montana. They encountered enormous herds of buffalo, grizzly bears, and the Great Falls of the Missouri River. Heading southwest, near the Montana-Idaho border, they came upon the lands of the Shoshone tribe. Sacagawea recognized some landmarks and was reunited with her brother when they reached the tribe's village. Lewis explored the area and reached the summit of the ridge of the Continental Divide.

The group next had to travel through the Bitterroot Mountains in the Rockies. They dealt with freezing weather and dangerous terrain. Still, they managed to get through the mountains. After doing so, they came across the territory of the Nez Perce tribe, with whom they traded to get additional supplies.

From there, the group built canoes and traveled down the Columbia River into present-day Oregon. When they glimpsed Mount Hood and the Pacific Ocean, they realized that their journey was complete. They had traversed the entire West and had reached the opposite coast of the United States. The group spent the summer in northwest Oregon and built Fort Clatsop. It was named after the Clatsop native tribe that resided in the area. That tribe provided the expedition team with information to help them survive the winter. Before departing, Lewis and Clark left Fort Clatsop and its remaining furniture and provisions to the Clatsops' chief, Coboway.

The Corps began its trek home in late March of 1806. They reached Fort Mandan in North Dakota in August, where they parted ways with Charbonneau and Sacagawea. On September 23, 1806, the group reached St. Louis and considered their journey complete.

The Lewis and Clark expedition changed America. They generated new knowledge of the West and all it contained. The maps they created and the new waterways and landforms they found helped to turn the uncharted territory into a known terrain. In addition, they discovered new species of vegetation and animals, findings that enhanced the knowledge of the scientific community. Their expedition also established peaceable relationships with many friendly Native American tribes of the West. The roughly two-and-a-half-year journey of over four thousand miles was accomplished with little violence and death, and with great industriousness and success.

Children Should Have Limited TV Time

written by Bryon Gill

According to scientific studies, children should limit their time each day in front of a television or other screen. Too much time in front of a screen may lead to obesity, stunted social development, and bullying behaviors.

Children develop best when they interact with people. Time in front of a screen is time when children cannot learn from each other, parents, or teachers. One study about the effects of screen time took place at an outdoor education camp and lasted for five days. While at the camp, children were not allowed to spend any time in front of a screen. As a result, the children improved at picking up on emotional cues when interacting with others (Uhls et al.).

Another study found that children who spend too much time in front of the TV or other screen gain more weight than those who do not ("Television Watching"). Some theorize that simply sitting down so much is the cause. Others point a finger at junk food marketing. Several trial programs have shown that reducing screen time can help children to lose weight, whether the problem is the screen itself or just sitting without moving for too long.

Finally, according to the PEACH project, children who spend too much time in front of a screen may develop psychological problems ("Screen Time Linked"). This study found that spending more than two hours per day in front of a screen caused higher levels of psychological difficulty. This was true even in children who were otherwise physically active. This means that the problems that these children had can be attributed to the screen time itself, not just sitting for long periods of time.

In the report "Managing Media: We Need a Plan," the American Association of Pediatrics recommends that children between the ages of three and 18 spend no more than two hours in front of a screen each day. The evidence that excessive screen time creates problems for children is very strong. The more that parents and children follow these guidelines, the healthier children will be.

Works Cited

"Managing Media: We Need a Plan." *AAP.org*, 13 Oct. 2013, www.aap.org/en-us/about-the-aap/aap-press-room/pages/managing-media-we-need-a-plan.aspx. Accessed 19 Feb. 2017.

"Screen Time Linked to Psychological Problems in Children." *EurekAlert!*, 11 Oct. 2010, www.eurekalert.org/pub_releases/2010-10/uob-stl100510.php. Accessed 19 Feb. 2017.

"Television Watching and 'Sit Time.'" *Obesity Prevention Source*, 20 Oct. 2012, www.hsph.harvard.edu/obesity-prevention-source/obesity-causes/television-and-sedentary-behavior-and-obesity/. Accessed 19 Feb. 2017.

Uhls, Yalda T., Minas Michikyan, Jordan Morris, Debra Garcia, Gary W. Small, Eleni Zgourou, and Patricia M. Greenfield. "Five Days at Outdoor Education Camp without Screens Improves Preteen Skills with Nonverbal Emotion Cues." *ScienceDirect.com*, www.sciencedirect.com/science/article/pii/S0747563214003227. Accessed 19 Feb. 2017.

Damaging Quake Hits Small Delaware Town

written by Summer York
illustrated by D. Kent Kerr

Thursday, September 26, 2013

Four people were hospitalized yesterday after a 5.3-magnitude earthquake struck the small coastal town of Meriton, Delaware.

The earthquake began at 2:34 p.m. and lasted for almost nine minutes. The quake was most severe in Meriton, though it was felt by surrounding communities. Geologists report the quake struck about one mile off the coast of Meriton in the Atlantic Ocean. The small town was at the epicenter.

Residents heard chaotic sounds of crashing and falling debris on and around Main Street. An office worker was hospitalized for injuries sustained while evacuating Meriton Savings and Loan Bank. Annie Green, 35, suffered a concussion from falling debris when she exited the bank.

"I was in line at the bank when the shaking started," said Green. "I have never felt anything like that before. No one knew what was happening."

Green described the shaking as a soft vibration at first. The pens rattled on the desks and the line divider ropes swayed. "I thought maybe a plane was flying low overhead." But within seconds, the tremors grew more intense. Books and stacks of papers fell to the floor. Customers and bank employees held on to the teller counter to steady themselves.

Green explained that she and other customers ran outside in a panic. In the street, small pieces of tile and shingles started to fall from rooftops.

"I heard someone on the street yell, 'Earthquake!' and we ran back into the bank to escape the falling debris," Green said. She was hit in the head with debris but managed to enter the bank and take shelter under the marble countertop.

George Dell, 54, was also in the bank when the quake started. He stumbled to the grocery store he owns next to the bank to help his customers.

"I had to make sure everyone in my store was safe," Dell said. At the height of the quake, Dell saw items falling from the store's high shelves. He heard soup cans splattering as they hit the floor and glass shattering in the street. Dell and his customers huddled in the paper products aisle, away from the windows and heavy merchandise. No one in the store was injured.

Three maintenance workers were also hospitalized for injuries sustained while helping visitors evacuate Meriton Pier. Rodney Jones, 29, head of the maintenance staff at the pier, suffered minor cuts and bruises from falling debris.

"It was risky on the pier, with the carnival rides and food stands shaking," Jones said. "I was trying to get everyone off the pier and onto the beach." The pier's carnival rides were closed for the season, so no one was on the rides at the time of the earthquake. But the pier's thirty-foot-tall Ferris wheel shook dangerously. A few lightbulbs shattered and a popcorn cart overturned during the tremor. The names and injuries of the other two hospitalized maintenance workers have not been released.

Dan Evans, mayor of Meriton, was dining at the Main Street Café as the quake began. Coffee cups and plates clattered to the floor. Mayor Evans said patrons sought shelter in the kitchen of the café. No one was hurt when a street lamp fell through the café window, spraying glass into the dining area.

"There has never been an earthquake in Meriton," explained Mayor Evans. "Citizens weren't sure how to react." Fortunately, the Meriton School District practices regular earthquake drills, so the faculty and students were prepared. Hoover Elementary and George Washington High School received little damage during the quake.

Mayor Evans said in a press conference this morning that the town sustained minor damage. He cited the greatest danger as downed power lines throughout the area, which left about three dozen residents without power. Crews expect to restore power to all citizens by this evening.

The US Geological Survey reports that while an earthquake in Delaware is unlikely, it is not impossible. An earthquake can happen anywhere at any time, so everyone should be prepared.

Mayor Evans plans to conduct earthquake preparedness training courses at the Meriton Community Center in the coming weeks.

We Shall Overcome

written by Summer York
illustrated by David Rushbrook

A fifteen-year-old black girl was arrested for not giving up her seat on a bus to a white man. A black United States Air Force veteran was blocked from enrolling in the University of Mississippi by a violent mob. Four young black girls were killed when a hate group bombed a Baptist church. It can be difficult for young people to imagine such a world. Yet not so long ago, this was the reality for African-Americans.

As late as the 1960s, parts of the United States were segregated. Segregation is the separation of people of different races or ethnic origins. It is a form of discrimination, which is unfair treatment. African-Americans were not allowed to eat at the same places as white people. They had to use separate bathrooms, drinking fountains, swimming pools, and other public facilities. They were prevented from voting in elections. They were not even allowed to attend the same schools as whites. Many people, including some lawmakers, believed that segregation was right. But there were some who stood up against such injustice. They envisioned a world in which all people were treated equally. Their efforts inspired a social movement that changed the course of history. It was called the civil rights movement. Dr. Martin Luther King Jr. was among the leaders of this movement.

"The ultimate measure of a man is not where he stands in moments of comfort and convenience, but where he stands at times of challenge and controversy."

Martin Luther King Jr. was born on January 15, 1929. His given name was Michael King Jr., after his father. The King family lived in Atlanta, Georgia. King's father and grandfather were ministers at the Ebenezer Baptist Church. King, his older sister, and his younger brother were raised in a family with strong religious faith. His father changed his name to Martin Luther King Sr., in honor of the fifteenth century religious leader Martin Luther. His son Michael's name was then changed to Martin Luther King Jr.

Like most African-Americans at this time, the King family experienced segregation. While growing up, King attended segregated schools. This means that he went to schools that were only for black children. King was such a good student that he skipped ninth grade and eleventh grade. At only fifteen years old, he went to Morehouse College in Atlanta. Morehouse was an all-male, all-black college at the time.

At first, King was not interested in becoming a minister like his father and grandfather. But in his third year of college, he changed his mind. He was influenced by Dr. Benjamin Mays, then president of Morehouse College. Mays was a minister and a social activist who openly criticized segregation. In 1948, King graduated from Morehouse College with a degree in sociology. He enrolled in Crozer Theological Seminary in Pennsylvania. A seminary is a school at which a person studies to become a minister. Crozer had mostly white students at the time, but King was determined to do well. He graduated first in his class in 1951.

King went on to attend Boston University, where he earned a doctorate degree in theology in 1953. He met Coretta Scott in Boston, and they got married in 1953. The couple moved to Montgomery, Alabama, where King became the minister of the Dexter Avenue Baptist Church. Over the next ten years, they had four children.

"Faith is taking the first step even when you can't see the whole staircase."

In the 1950s, the civil rights movement was in its early stages. Leaders in the African-American community were starting to speak out against segregation. Then, on December 1, 1955, a black woman named Rosa Parks took action. She brought national attention to Montgomery when she refused to give up her seat on a bus to a white man. She was arrested and fined. Her boldness brought local civil rights leaders together to plan a city-wide boycott of the bus system. Among them was Martin Luther King Jr., who was chosen to lead the protest. He proved to be an energetic speaker who motivated many people to support the boycott. After more than a year, the city of Montgomery did away with segregation on public transportation.

King quickly became a well-known advocate of civil rights throughout the South. He taught his followers that using nonviolence was the best means of protest. He once wrote, "Nonviolent direct action seeks to create such a crisis and foster such a tension that a community which has constantly refused to negotiate is forced to confront the issue." King's goal was to bring attention to the issues of segregation and racism so that people could no longer ignore them. He drew inspiration from Mahatma Gandhi, a civil rights leader in India. Gandhi is famous for using nonviolent civil disobedience to stir political and social change. In 1957, King and other civil rights leaders founded the Southern Christian Leadership Conference. This organization helped spread King's message of nonviolent reform throughout the United States.

"Darkness cannot drive out darkness; only light can do that. Hate cannot drive out hate; only love can do that."

In 1960, King and his family moved to Atlanta, Georgia. There, King joined his father as a minister at the Ebenezer Baptist Church. His commitment to the civil rights movement remained strong. His message of peaceful protest continued to spread. African-Americans, and even some whites, held nonviolent demonstrations in several US cities. Some of the methods used were boycotts, marches, and sit-ins. A boycott is when a group of people refuses to buy a product or use a service, which has negative effects on a business. A march is when a group of people walks from one location to another while chanting or singing a message. A sit-in is when protestors sit in seats at a business and refuse to move. King supported these methods and often participated.

However, these peaceful demonstrations did not always end peacefully. Protestors were often arrested. King himself was arrested and jailed several times for his involvement in protests. In 1963, King was arrested in Birmingham, Alabama. While in jail, he wrote "Letter from a Birmingham Jail." It was a letter directed toward white clergymen who urged King to end his fight for civil rights. In this letter, King defended the struggle for social justice for all people. He wrote, "Injustice anywhere is a threat to justice everywhere." This letter was later published in newspapers, magazines, and books. King endured criticism and harsh treatment for his efforts. His home was attacked several times. He also received several death threats toward himself and his family. But the difficulties only strengthened his resolve.

"We must accept finite disappointment, but never lose infinite hope."

By 1963, the civil rights movement had gained the support of people throughout the country. King and other leaders planned a march in Washington, DC, to promote equality for all people. On August 28, more than two hundred thousand supporters attended the March on Washington. In front of the Lincoln Memorial, King gave his inspiring "I Have a Dream" speech. He said, "I have a dream that my four little children will one day live in a nation where they will not be judged by the color of their skin but by the content of their character." The March on Washington aroused so much attention that the US government was forced into action. The following year, Congress passed the Civil Rights Act of 1964. This act made segregation illegal in the United States.

Unfortunately, not everyone supported the Civil Rights Act. Tensions reached their height in Alabama in 1965. Police officers became increasingly violent against civil rights demonstrators. On March 7, protestors gathered in Selma, Alabama, for a march to promote African-Americans' right to vote. The marchers were stopped by police and state troopers. When they refused to leave, the officers attacked them. Many people were severely injured. The event, which became known as "Bloody Sunday," angered the nation.

In response, King organized a second march two days later. The marchers were angry at the police brutality, but they chose to protest peacefully. King and more than two thousand people marched to the site of the attack. When they arrived, they were again met by law officers. Instead of starting a violent confrontation, though, King asked the marchers to kneel and pray. After the prayer, they turned around and marched back. The nonviolent demonstration of faith said more than any act of violence could. On August 6 of that year, President Lyndon B. Johnson signed the Voting Rights Act of 1965. This act outlawed unfair rules that prevented African-Americans from voting.

"Returning violence for violence multiplies violence, adding deeper darkness to a night already devoid of stars."

King expanded his efforts to other US cities during the next few years. He spoke about issues besides segregation, including poverty, labor laws, and the Vietnam War. On April 3, 1968, he attended a protest in Memphis, Tennessee. King gave a speech to supporters. He told them, "I've seen the promised land. I may not get there with you. But I want you to know tonight that we, as a people, will get to the promised land." The next day, King was standing on the balcony of his room at the Lorraine Motel in Memphis. He was shot and killed by a man named James Earl Ray. King was only thirty-nine years old.

"An individual has not started living until he can rise above the narrow confines of his individualistic concerns to the broader concerns of all humanity."

The world will never know what Martin Luther King Jr. could have accomplished if he had lived. But in his short lifetime, he made a lasting impression. He is best remembered for his leadership efforts during the civil rights movement. In 1964, King was awarded the Nobel Peace Prize. He was the youngest man to ever receive the award. King received honorary doctorate degrees from many respected universities. He wrote books about his work, including *Why We Can't Wait* and *Where Do We Go from Here: Chaos or Community?* King's writings and speeches have also been collected and published in numerous books. A national holiday to honor King is celebrated on the third Monday of January each year. Many schools, parks, and other public places in the United States are named after King.

The Martin Luther King Jr. Memorial opened in 2011 near the National Mall in Washington, DC.

"No one really knows why they are alive until they know what they'd die for."

The work that Martin Luther King Jr. began is not over. People all over the world still suffer from the effects of prejudice and hatred, but King's dream lives on through the works of people who continue to fight for equality. In their voices that refuse to be silenced echo King's message of hopeful inspiration: "We shall overcome."

Mindfulness: A Powerful Tool

written by Sarah Marino
illustrated by Matthew Casper

Do you ever lose focus when you are studying? Do you ever get caught up in worrisome thoughts? Do you ever eat too much junk food and then wonder why you did? What if there was a practice you could begin that would help you to concentrate for longer periods of time, worry less, and have more control over your impulses? Well, there is!

Mindfulness is a way of increasing your concentration and your awareness of the present moment. It is a skill that is most frequently taught through meditation practices and yoga. Mindfulness can be described as "paying attention on purpose, in the present moment, and nonjudgmentally." When you practice mindfulness, you can avoid getting lost in your random thoughts and impulses. Instead, you focus on something in the present moment. This brings your attention to some specific purpose. For example, most meditation practices teach beginners to focus on their breath. The instruction might be to count to five as you inhale, noticing how your chest and belly rise. Then count to five as you breathe out, exhaling from your lungs. You simply focus on your breathing with the intent to sharpen your attention and not let your mind wander. The goal is to help you focus more on whatever you're doing, instead of losing concentration.

The key to mindfulness is learning when you're not paying attention. When you realize you have lost concentration of your breathing and your mind is lost in thought, that is mindfulness! You catch yourself and go back to focusing on whatever it is you are supposed to be paying attention to. One author and promoter of mindfulness, Susan Kaiser Greenland, advises making mindfulness a habit by checking in with yourself every so often while you go about your daily activities. Ask yourself the following questions to make sure your attention is where it should be: "Has my mind wandered or become dull? Am I paying attention to my homework, or am I thinking about the past or future? Am I alert or have I faded into a sleepy state of mind?"

Several research studies have shown that mindfulness practice can be very beneficial. It can help to reduce stress, improve emotional balance, and boost focus and memory. It may even help you to sleep better and do well on tests. In addition, mindfulness practice can reduce anxiety and make you feel happier and more at ease. Finally, learning to be mindful can help you to be calmer, more patient, more alert, and less likely to act on your impulses.

Mindfulness can help you to be a better observer of your own thoughts, feelings, and experiences. This might seem like common sense. Aren't we already aware of ourselves and our experiences? It might surprise you, but until you start a mindfulness practice, you probably will be unaware of how much you are missing! When you slow down and learn to observe yourself, you can keep calm and learn to watch certain impulses and feelings. For instance, maybe you are a worrywart or you have trouble concentrating on your homework and would rather play video games or eat cookies. Maybe you start worrying about an upcoming test and how you won't have enough time to study, and then your worry grows until you are having this whole daydream where you have failed the test and flunked fifth grade! While it is just a worry, such thoughts can be distracting and make you feel distraught. Learning to be mindful can help you to observe these thoughts and urges before you act on them. Without mindfulness, we often act on our urges without giving them much thought. Through mindfulness practices, such as meditation, you can learn to just observe an urge or a worry without getting caught up in it.

Mindfulness is a skill. Like any skill, it takes practice to learn and improve. A good way to practice is by making it a habit. The creator of the *Zen Habits* blog, Leo Babauta, recommends practicing mindfulness every day for two minutes, until you can gradually increase the time.

Here's a common exercise to use: Start by sitting in a comfortable position in a quiet spot. (Don't get too comfortable, or you will fall asleep!) You can close your eyes or leave them open. Bring your attention to your breathing. Feel the breath come into your nose as you inhale. Feel your chest and tummy rise. Then observe your chest fall as you exhale. Your mind will wander as thoughts and memories arise. When that happens, just observe those thoughts, and then bring your attention back to your breath. A good tip to remember is to think of your thoughts and feelings as clouds in the sky. Many mindfulness training guides use this instruction as a way to help you notice your thoughts and feelings as things that are within you and that can be observed. Do this every day for two minutes and you will soon be a mindfulness expert!

Remember that this practice is very difficult at first. Sometimes you might not be able to focus even on one full breath without thoughts distracting you. That is okay. The goal is not to stop thinking; that will never happen! The goal is to realize when you have lost focus and bring your attention back to concentrating on your breath. This practice will develop your concentration skills and make you a better, calmer observer of yourself and your surroundings. This is a skill you can use in everyday life, as being a calm observer enables you to participate in life without simply reacting to it based on various emotions.

There are many other mindfulness exercises you can try. Your local library may even offer meditation training or yoga classes. If you're interested, be sure to check out your options. The reasons for being mindful are plenty. Nurture your inner observer and get started today!

Environmental Change

written by Vincent J. Scotto
illustrated by D. Kent Kerr

Environments can change due to a wide range of causes. These changes can be major or minor, rapid or gradual. Nature can cause changes to an environment, while other changes are caused by humans. Living things can cause changes, and so can nonliving things. These changes can be positive or negative. Some events can actually cause both positive and negative changes at the same time. This essay will explore a number of the factors that can change environments from across the spectrum.

Many nonliving things can have an effect on the environment. Some of these things do not even involve any kind of living thing. For example, an environment can change because of events that occur in nature, without intervention from living things. Sometimes they happen fast. Other times they happen across an exceptionally long span. Some events that occur quickly include forest fires, earthquakes, and hurricanes. An example of something that takes longer would be weathering.

The effects of a forest fire can devastate a community. A forest fire can destroy shelter for animals, burn and destroy vegetation, and disrupt generations of development. However, it might also have some positive effects. Some kinds of trees make seeds that can only grow after they've been burned. A forest fire can also clear overpopulated communities as well, which can help the system rebuild free of disease.

An earthquake is another nonliving cause of environmental change. An earthquake can change the landscape completely in a matter of seconds. Sometimes the land slides, which causes it to rise. Other times the land might separate. This can disrupt vegetation in the area and cause it to die. This can lead to a chain effect in which the local animal life that depends on vegetation for food will die or relocate. Earthquakes can also have benefits, however. An earthquake might cause the development of a natural basin for storing water. It might also make a rock formation that can be used for shelter.

A hurricane can also change an environment quite quickly. The most powerful hurricanes can tear apart vast areas across the globe. A hurricane usually leads to flooding as well, so the effects of the hurricane can last much longer than those of other natural events. Conversely to forest fires, hurricanes can bring enormous amounts of water to areas in drought. They can also refill underground aquifers. Depending on the situation, a hurricane can destroy an environment or save it.

One of the least noticeable nonliving environmental changes is weathering. Weathering describes the breaking down of rock through forced contact with air and water. The change happens over vast periods of time. With technology and repeated observation, though, scientists have been able to show entire mountains disappearing from weathering. This natural change can cause avalanches in snowy regions. It can force natural dams to cave in, releasing massive amounts of water. It can even make cliff tops crumble under their own weight.

Many other nonliving causes of change in the environment happen naturally. Some of these changes can be very negative, but those same changes may have benefits as well. Many naturally occurring changes in the environment help to keep balance, even if it seems like chaos.

While quite a few nonliving factors can cause environmental change, there are equally as many living factors that cause it as well. Just like nonliving factors, the living ones can make changes that are both harmful and helpful, depending on one's perspective. From the smallest bacteria to the most fearsome lions, all living things within an environment have an effect on each other. Some can even have an effect from far away.

Some bacteria can be difficult to see with the naked eye. However, bacteria can completely destroy an environment. In other cases, they can be a cornerstone in the success of a system of life. Certain kinds of bacteria are very harmful. If breathed in, they can cause death to a more complex organism. Other bacteria are helpful. For example, take the bacteria found inside some animals' mouths. Those bacteria can help break down the food that gets stuck in animals' teeth. If those bacteria did not exist, that food would stay stuck in the animals' teeth, causing tooth decay and problems with their gums. If an animal loses its teeth, it might not be able to survive. Carnivores in the wild cannot survive without their sharp teeth. So, carnivores and the bacteria in their mouths have what is called a symbiotic relationship. The carnivore needs its teeth to be cleaned, and the bacteria in its mouth need the food in the carnivore's teeth.

Another small—but more easily seen—living thing that has an effect on its environment is grass. Did you know that every single blade of grass is its own plant with roots? There are many different kinds of grass in different environments. Places that have more rain and are close to sea level have thicker grass that can soak up more ground water. More mountainous areas have thinner grass. This grass is more flexible in the wind and doesn't need as much water. The thinner grass is also more easily digested by animals that eat it. Imagine switching those two kinds of grass. If switched, the more watery area would be mostly puddles and ponds because the thin grass could not soak up enough water. As a result, all of the other plants and animals would have to deal with the extra water. In the mountainous region, the thick grass would not receive enough water to survive. It would likely die. Then the animals that eat the grass would lose their food source and die. The larger animals that eat them would lose their food source and die. The entire ecosystem would be destroyed.

Lions are typically found in mountains all over the world or in the savannah lands of Africa. As the top natural predator in the wild, it would be easy for the lioness to kill all of its prey quickly and eat banquet style with its family. This is not the case. Lions are part of a larger environment that requires them to ration their food. If they overeat, they will run out of food before their prey can reproduce. If any food source becomes endangered in their area, the lions will have to move or they will not survive. Another reason lions do not kill prey and stockpile it for later is because of harmful bacteria. When an animal decays, bacteria and other organisms are breaking it down. If a lion eats these bacteria, it can become very sick or even die. Even the king of the jungle can be taken down by something too small to see!

The living factors of the environment can have vast consequences when changed. But they can also have exceptional benefits. When the changes in the environment are expected, then the environment can benefit and all of the organisms living there thrive. If the change is unexpected, or too much changes at once, the entire environment can be destroyed.

Humans can affect their environment in ways equal to, or sometimes even greater than, nature itself. The effects of humans on the nonliving environment can be both harmful and beneficial. Changing the landscape, mining for resources, and disposing waste are just a few ways humans impact the nonliving environment. The effects can be frightening when they go unchecked, but there are some people who try to keep balance.

One major change that humans cause is the building of communities and cities in natural areas. The heightened activity in a habitat—a place where a living thing usually lives—can cause many problems with the wildlife, but nonliving things are affected too. Large portions of land are built up or broken down to be made level and easy to place buildings upon. This can change weather patterns over time if the area is large enough. It also changes how the land is able to provide nutrients for plants to grow without help. Some people work to protect landscapes. They section off parts of the natural landscape by making it illegal to build there. In the United States, these places are called "preserves." They are areas where the nonliving and living elements of the environment are undisturbed by people who would change the natural state.

When humans mine for resources, they also have an effect on the nonliving environment. For example, humans currently need coal and oil for energy. These are located underground, so digging or drilling is necessary to get to them. The digging and drilling can be disruptive to the natural environment because coal and oil would not naturally come to the surface most of the time. Oil can poison water sources, which would affect many living organisms. This poisoning is called pollution. Many people work to clean up any mistakes, though. Individuals and large groups of people clean up oil spills, make laws against polluting certain areas, and even make it so that some areas are not allowed to be mined at all.

Human waste, or trash, is another significant factor that changes the nonliving environment. Because humans produce so much waste, much of it that does not decompose must be placed in landfills. These are places where trash accumulates away from people. However, they still affect the rest of the environment. Even if handled properly, trash can still pollute soil and water. Many people try to fight this problem. At the very least, all people agree that recycling, which is the act of reusing certain kinds of waste, is a good idea. Plastic, metal cans, glass, and paper can be recycled, which cuts down on waste. Recycling paper is especially helpful. Doing so decreases the need to cut down trees, which are needed for oxygen.

The human impact on the nonliving environment is scary when it is ignored. Some humans do not see the need to protect the environment. Some do not think the human impact is significant enough to warrant changes. Others work very hard to conserve every day by recycling or helping clean up pollution. One thing is for sure: the impact humans have on the nonliving environment can have major effects on the living.

The human impact on other living organisms in an environment can be both harmful and beneficial. From cutting down entire forests to planting thousands of trees, humans make a big difference on plant life. They also impact animals and bacteria as well. Some changes are meant to intentionally destroy forms of life. Others are meant to save life forms from extinction.

Human actions can have complex effects on other life forms. For example, some bacteria will cause sickness and even death to humans. To fight these bacteria, humans created antibacterial creams and sanitizers. While this is a good change to the environment for humans, it has had negative effects for humans as well. Penicillin, the first antibiotic medicine for killing bacteria, only killed most kinds of bacteria. Some bacteria were not affected. As a result, those tough bacteria are the ones that reproduced most. Scientists and researchers continue to develop more antibacterial medicines, but each time, some bacteria manage to survive. As a result, these "super bacteria" are difficult to kill. Now humans must continue to find new ways to deal with the effects they have caused.

Humans have impacted plant life in significant ways. The most significant has been deforestation. The removal of trees for human use can impact entire ecosystems to the point of total devastation. Soil turns rotten, animals lose homes and food, and trees become unable to return. Luckily, some have realized the danger of deforestation. They have decided to deal with its effects and protect the forests as well as themselves. Since trees need to reproduce to be renewable, some countries have passed laws that require individuals and companies to plant a new tree for every tree they cut down. This kind of planning allows humans to benefit from the trees while ensuring that the ecosystem continues to survive.

Humans have a significant impact on animals, too. Since humans like to keep some animals as pets, many animals are born in captivity or taken directly from the wild. Humans are more able to adapt to different environments, so some animals are taken out of their natural environments and brought to places where they may not belong. For example, giant pythons, which are extremely large snakes, are sometimes taken as pets. Humans often quickly find out that they may not be able to take care of such large animals. In the United States, people have released giant pythons into the wild in near-tropical environments like the Everglades in Florida. This action has changed the entire ecosystem because it introduced a large predator that requires lots of food. Other animals must struggle to compete with them for food. Even crocodiles and alligators struggle because they are so big. This seemingly small action has had a huge effect.

Humans impact the living organisms in the environment in positive and negative ways. There is a very fine line between the effects that are good for all living things and those that are bad for them. Some negative effects could not be known in advance. Some of the changes are meant to intentionally destroy life in order to enhance the lives of other organisms. One thing is for sure: for better or worse, humans have a significant impact on the living organisms around them.

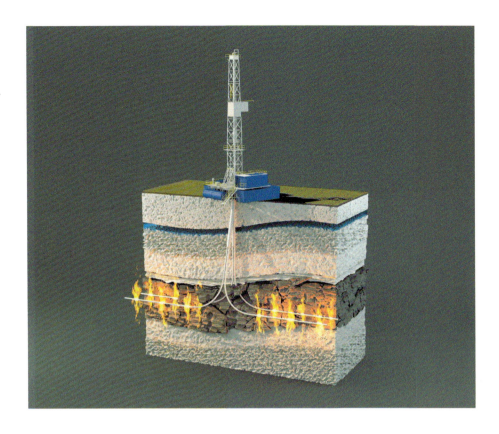

Editorial Note: *This piece has been written to demonstrate an example of a persuasive speech. It is not presented as neutral fact.*

The Dangers of Fracking: A Speech

written by Summer York

Good afternoon. Radium, lead, mercury, formaldehyde, methane, carcinogens: All of these are toxic chemicals, and all are used in fracking. Today I'm going to tell you about the dangers of fracking. Fracking is the common term for hydraulic fracturing. This is a method of drilling deep underground to reach stores of oil and natural gas. In fracking, water is mixed with sand and toxic chemicals to create fracking fluid. The fluid is forcefully pumped into a well in order to fracture the underground rocks holding oil and natural gas. The oil or gas is then released into the well and can be extracted. This may sound simple, but fracking is highly controversial. Supporters of fracking claim the process is safe and that it provides jobs and energy resources. This may be true, but at what cost? There are many dangers associated with fracking. Three major dangers are health risks, environmental damage, and worksite hazards. For these three reasons, fracking should be banned until the process is made less harmful to people and the environment.

First, the toxic chemicals used in fracking pose many health risks for humans. When fracking fluid is pumped into a well, some of the fluid can leak out of the underground pipeline. Thus, drinking water from groundwater sources is contaminated with harmful chemicals. According to *DangersofFracking.org*, methane levels are seventeen times higher in drinking water wells near fracking sites than in normal wells. When people drink water from the contaminated water sources, they ingest the toxic chemicals. That's not all. Toxic fumes are also harmful to people near fracking sites. The article "Fracking Opponents in Pennsylvania Dealt Rare Victory by State Court" cites a report claiming that "a dozen chemicals used regularly in fracking are suspected of being endocrine disrupting chemicals, or EDCs…that have been linked to heightened risks of cancer." Health concerns have prompted some cities to pass laws banning fracking near communities. Fracking should be stopped until its health risks are better understood.

Second, fracking damages the environment. Fracking fluid can leak from the well pipeline during the fracking process. Also, if the fracking fluid is not retrieved from the well, it can seep into the ground or evaporate. This toxic fluid pollutes the soil, water, and air near the fracking area. According to the article "Fracking Opponents," "Researchers found high levels of radioactivity, salts, and metals in water and sediment located downstream from a treatment facility which processes fracking wastewater from oil and gas production sites in Pennsylvania's Marcellus shale formation." Such pollution damages the natural environment. Fracking should stop until the industry uses stricter practices to protect the environment.

Third, fracking has resulted in numerous accidents. This calls into question how safe fracking is for workers. Lohan cites Schneider and Geewax as saying, "Last year, 138 [fracking] workers were killed on the job—an increase of more than 100 percent since 2009." In the past few years, there have been several explosions and spills on fracking sites. There have also been numerous truck crashes and train derailments of vehicles carrying crude oil from fracking sites, which can be toxic. Due to such alarming facts, some fracking companies have been cited for their negligence. In Lohan's article, Vaidyanathan reports that Jay-Bee Oil & Gas has received thirty-eight worker safety violations by the federal Occupational Safety and Health Administration. The U.S. Department of Labor is also concerned with worker exposure to fracking chemicals. It is clear that fracking activities should halt until companies make conditions safer for workers.

Today I have told you about the dangers of fracking, including health risks, environmental damage, and worksite hazards. The evidence is staggering. Fracking companies cannot be allowed to conduct their business while harming people and the environment. These companies must be held accountable. Currently, the costs of fracking are just too high, especially with the promise of cleaner energies like solar and wind power. Fortunately, you have a voice. Contact your local government officials. Urge them to stop fracking until the practice is made safer for all. Thank you.

Expository Essay Outline

I. Introduction
- A. Hook Sentence
    1. Begin your essay with a general statement about your topic that grabs the reader's attention.
    2. Examples include a relevant quotation, a question, an anecdote (short story), a fascinating fact, a definition, an analogy, or a problem that needs a solution.
- B. Context
    1. The following three to four sentences should provide the context, or background information.
    2. This allows the reader to fully understand the topic.
- C. Thesis Statement
    1. State the main idea or message of your essay.
    2. Ensure your ability to support it with evidence in the body paragraphs.

II. Each of Three Body Paragraphs
- A. Topic Sentence
    1. Provide the main idea of the paragraph.
- B. Supporting Details
    1. Include supporting details to further describe, explain, or define this idea. These details should provide evidence to support your thesis statement.
    2. This evidence can come from a text (quotes, paraphrases, a summary, etc.) or from other sources (first-person interviews, your personal experiences, etc.).
- C. Analysis of Evidence
    1. Explain the significance of the evidence you have provided.
    2. Ask yourself why you chose it. How does this evidence support your thesis?
- D. Closing Sentence
    1. The paragraph may end with a concluding thought about the topic.
    2. It may also end with a transition sentence that leads into the next idea and demonstrates how these ideas work together to support your thesis.

III. Conclusion
- A. Overview
    1. Restate your thesis in words different from those in the introduction.
    2. Provide the reader with an overview of the main ideas discussed in your essay.
- B. Final Thought
    1. Leave your reader with a final thought on the topic to provide a lasting impression and encourage your reader to think further about the topic.
    2. Offer a solution, a prediction, next steps, or new questions that your essay generated.

Editorial Note: *This piece has been written to demonstrate an example of a persuasive speech outline. It is not presented as neutral fact.*

The Dangers of Fracking: Outline

written by Summer York

I. Introduction
    A. Attention-grabbing statement
        1. Toxic chemicals in fracking: radium, lead, mercury, formaldehyde, methane, carcinogens
        2. Dangers of fracking
    B. Background information
        1. What it is
            a. Common term for hydraulic fracturing
            b. Method of drilling deep underground for oil and natural gas
        2. How it works
            a. Water mixed with sand and toxic chemicals to make fracking fluid
            b. Fluid pumped into a well to fracture underground shale rocks; oil or gas released and extracted
        3. Controversy
            a. Fracking highly controversial
            b. Supporters claim:
                i. Safe process
                ii. Provides jobs and energy resources
            c. Might have positives, but at what cost?
    C. Preview
        1. Three dangers associated with fracking
            a. Health risks
            b. Environmental damage
            c. Worksite accidents
        2. Argument: should be banned until process is made less harmful to people and the environment

II. Health risks
    A. Toxic chemicals: health risks for humans
    B. When fracking fluid is pumped into a well
        1. Fluid can leak out of the underground pipeline.
        2. Drinking water from groundwater sources contaminated
    C. Support from DangersofFracking.org
        1. Methane levels seventeen times higher in drinking water near fracking sites
        2. People drink contaminated water, ingest toxic chemicals
    D. Toxic fumes harmful to people
        1. Article "Fracking Opponents in Pennsylvania Dealt Rare Victory by State Court" cites Endocrinology report: "a dozen chemicals used regularly in fracking are suspected of being endocrine disrupting chemicals, or EDCs…that have been linked to heightened risks of cancer"
        2. Fracking banned in some cities
    E. Should be stopped until health risks are better understood

III. Environmental damage
   A. Damages the environment
   B. Damages in the fracking process
      1. Fluid can leak from well pipeline
      2. If fracking fluid not retrieved from well, can seep into the ground or evaporate
      3. Toxic fluid pollutes soil, water, and air
      4. "Fracking Opponents" quote: "researchers found high levels of radioactivity, salts, and metals in water and sediment located downstream from a treatment facility which processes fracking wastewater from oil and gas production sites in Pennsylvania's Marcellus shale formation"
      5. Such pollution damages the environment.
   C. Should stop until industry uses stricter practices to protect environment

IV. Worker safety
   A. Has resulted in numerous accidents
   B. Dangers for fracking workers
      1. Lohan cites Schneider and Geewax: "Last year, 138 [fracking] workers were killed on the job—an increase of more than 100 percent since 2009."
      2. Fracking accidents in past few years
         a. Several explosions and spills
         b. Numerous truck crashes/train derailments of vehicles carrying crude oil from fracking sites
   C. Some companies cited for neglect
      1. In Lohan: Jay-Bee Oil & Gas has received thirty-eight worker safety violations by federal Occupational Safety and Health Administration.
      2. U.S. Department of Labor concerned with worker exposure to fracking chemicals
   D. Activities should halt until companies make conditions safer for workers.

V. Conclusion
   A. Review of fracking dangers
      1. Health risks
      2. Environmental damage
      3. Worksite accidents
   B. Persuade
      1. Staggering evidence
      2. Fracking companies cannot be allowed to conduct business while harming people and the environment.
      3. Costs of fracking too high, especially compared with cleaner energies like solar/wind power
   C. Call to action
      1. You have a voice.
      2. Contact local government officials
      3. Urge officials to stop fracking until practice is made safer

We Need a Playground!

written by Vincent J. Scotto
illustrated by Brian Cibelli

Friends and neighbors, an important part of life is making sure one receives enough play time. No matter what age, every person can benefit from time to unwind and play in a safe place. Some will play with others. Some may play alone. But one thing is for sure: everyone can use a little bit of play! It is this writer's opinion that, in order to improve the amount of safe play children are naturally getting, we need to build a playground in the neighborhood.

The first playgrounds were actually built in connection with schools. This means that learning institutions, designed to help children become better equipped to enter the world as adults, thought that playgrounds were necessary. According to research on child development, children need free play to help brain development as well as burn off excess energy. This can lead to higher attention in settings where sitting still may be required. We need a playground nearby to give the children in our community a chance to burn some energy and have stronger brains!

In 1907, President Theodore Roosevelt made it his mission to make playgrounds available in cities. You may be wondering why the president of the United States thought that playing was important. He said:

"City streets are unsatisfactory playgrounds for children because of the danger, because most good games are against the law, because they are too hot in summer, and because in crowded sections of the city they are apt to be schools of crime."

Roosevelt was right! According to statistics in 2012, more than one hundred years later, neighborhoods with no working playgrounds had more juvenile crime cases and accidental deaths than neighborhoods with usable playgrounds. Our neighborhood needs a playground—by order of the president!

Another benefit to having a playground in the neighborhood is that it brings people together. Even if the children are the ones playing, it brings their parents there to watch them as well. This way, more parents will meet each other. Maybe they will schedule playdates and help their children make more friends! According to the Department of Health (2004), when children and families come together in places like playgrounds, it enhances the community's ability to keep an eye on everyone's children and help with their social development. It's kind of like being on a team with lots of coaches to help everyone instead of just one or two coaches. Our neighborhood needs this playground!

Sometimes playing alone can make kids think they aren't important to anyone. Sometimes children think they don't have any friends. Research has shown evidence that the use of playgrounds improves children's self-esteem because they provide lots of choices for fun and plenty of chances to play with others. Our neighborhood needs to get together and just have fun so that everyone can feel good about themselves. With a playground, all of the children can come together and play with one another. Our community needs this playground!

Some dissenters might worry about the safety of our children on playground equipment. Safety is definitely important to this writer. While accidental injury is a concern, recently developed equipment for playgrounds is much safer than when playgrounds were first made from all metal with gravel floors. Now there are playgrounds covered with rubber padding so that children can trip and still be all right. Many of the toys on the grounds are fastened to the floor so that they cannot be removed. The more physically demanding structures and toys have resistors so that younger, less-developed children are not strong enough to move them and hurt themselves. If safety is a concern, our goal should be to select the appropriate equipment in advance, not stop a playground from happening at all. We need this playground in our neighborhood!

This writer urges the reader to advocate for a playground in our neighborhood. If you are an adult who has the voting power, just remember the facts. This will cut down on crime, decrease accidental death, and improve the social development of our neighborhood's children. If you are a child reading this essay, state those facts to your parents! Make sure they know how good this will be for you and them. If you need to, use the broken record technique and keep asking if they've voted yet. We can get this playground in our neighborhood and we will all benefit from it, but you need to go out and make it happen!

Editorial: Vote Peter Ash for Student Council President

written by Jennifer Tkocs

OPINION

STAFF EDITORIAL

STUDENT COUNCIL elections are just around the corner, and the races are heating up. Daniel Haskins is running unopposed for vice president. However, the presidential race is an exciting one. This year, the office of president will go to either Peter Ash or Kevin Murphy. Peter Ash is new to student government. Kevin Murphy, as you know, is running for reelection.

We of the editorial staff will now explain to the readers of the *Bowhouse Elementary Gazette* why re-electing Kevin Murphy is the wrong choice.

Last year, Kevin Murphy took office with many big plans. His campaign promised to be unlike any other. Kevin promised many changes. Ask yourselves, readers: Has Kevin followed through on any of his promises?

Kevin Murphy promised that as president, he would arrange for the PA system to play music in the halls between classes. Surely, you remember his pamphlets. He promised that each week of the month would have a different musical theme. One week would have rock music, one week would have country, and so on. Yet, each day, the PA system plays only announcements from the front office.

Kevin Murphy also promised that we would get beanbag chairs for the library. Surely, you remember his campaign flyers from last year. They featured glossy photos of these beanbags. He assured us all that we could relax in beanbags while reading at recess. As of today, there are still only hard chairs and that smelly old couch in the library.

A history of unkept promises

Kevin Murphy's most appalling failure relates to our school lunches. He promised that if we elected him president, we would have tater tots every day at lunch. Surely, you remember his tater tot petition. The support for this cause was overwhelming. However, Kevin never even presented the petition to our superintendent, Dr. Steele. As a result, we still only have tater tots on Thursdays.

Consider these failures when you vote next week, readers. Do you want a fresh, new president in office? Peter Ash will be that president. Please do your part as a Bowhouse Elementary citizen. Vote Kevin Murphy out of office. Vote against his broken promises of beanbag chairs and tater tots.

Benefits of Children Learning a Musical Instrument

written by Katie Catanzarite

What thing do movies, TV shows, and musicals almost always have in common? That common thing is music. Music can be subtle. Sometimes, TV shows need a small melody to pair with a dramatic scene. Music can also be grand. A musical often features one big song right before the intermission. Including music in entertainment offers many benefits. There are even more advantages when you can play an instrument yourself. When young children learn how to play a musical instrument, it can improve their work ethic, teach them how to pay attention to detail, and open different doors of opportunity.

Learning how to play a musical instrument can improve your work ethic. Many musicians begin their careers at a young age. A majority of instruments, such as the piano and guitar, involve using both hands. They call for the musician to be able to read notes. Think of your favorite singer. He or she probably knows how to read music on some level. How long does it take a person to learn an instrument well enough to play in front of an audience? The work usually must begin early. At the age of eight, a child may learn scales and chords. By the age of eighteen, the child may have grown into an adult who is able to play Beethoven. You gain an understanding of your chosen instrument, but you also learn discipline and the value of practice. You can apply these strategies to schoolwork or sports. Learning a musical instrument teaches you that hard work will pay off.

Learning a musical instrument also teaches you how to pay attention to detail. When learning any instrument, musicians must keep many tiny details in mind. Musicians must learn how to position their fingers. They must learn how to make different kinds of sounds. They must learn how to control their volume. If you can learn all the details of an instrument, then you can understand how to view a problem from multiple angles. You will know how to tweak something just enough to make an overall improvement.

Learning a musical instrument offers many new opportunities. Not all musicians go on to play in the symphony. However, they may earn a living by writing music—maybe for one of those TV shows or movies they love. They may also be special librarians who recommend music instead of books. They may even become music therapists. Music therapists help the ill through music. If you learn how to play an instrument early on, you may have an advantage in the future.

Of course, not everyone will go on to be the next Mozart. Even so, musical instruments teach skills that are hard to gain otherwise. Learning a musical instrument at a young age improves your work ethic. It also teaches you how to pay attention to detail. Finally, it opens different doors of opportunity. Playing an instrument is not easy, but there is nothing sweeter than seeing all of your practice pay off.

Mummies in Ancient Egypt

written by Jennifer Tkocs
illustrated by David Rushbrook

On November 5, 1922, after more than thirty years of excavations and on the brink of abandoning the search, British archaeologist Howard Carter discovered a set of stairs that would change his life. Since age seventeen, Carter had worked in Egypt. He had progressed through the ranks of archaeology, from copying inscriptions to eventually leading excavations. The discovery at the heart of his search was the lost tomb of a boy pharaoh. The pharaoh's name was King Tutankhamun, or King Tut.

Many had searched for King Tut's tomb. Carter was the first person to be successful. He based the location of his excavation, or dig, on clues from random artifacts that had been found bearing Tutankhamun's name. The clues led him to a place now known as the Valley of the Kings. This area is home to at least sixty-three tombs of pharaohs and nobles from the eighteenth to twentieth dynasties of Egypt.

After fourteen months, Carter and his team discovered the body of King Tut within the tomb on January 3, 1924. It immediately caused a worldwide stir. People on every continent became fascinated with the long-dead pharaoh and Egyptology in general. The public had many questions: How did King Tut die? How old was he? What was the meaning of all of the art inside his tomb? Why were the tombs of ancient Egyptians filled with so many treasures? And why was mummification such an important part of their burial process?

While mummies have been found all over the world, the ones that seem to offer the most intrigue are those of Egypt. In the late 1800s and early 1900s, much of the interest was among wealthy Europeans and Americans like Howard Carter and his financial sponsor, Lord Carnarvon. These men hungered for the treasure found within the tombs and the fame that would accompany their discoveries. Thieves and grave robbers similarly sought the financial gains of the gold and riches within the tombs. But today, archaeologists and historians find mummies fascinating for more than their fortunes. Researching mummies is a unique opportunity to travel into the past and understand the customs, beliefs, and practices of an ancient civilization.

Through analysis of the texts and art found in archaeological excavations, as well as inspection of the bodies of the mummified Egyptians that have been found, much has been revealed about life and death in ancient Egypt. Perhaps most interesting are their practices relating to death and the afterlife. Wealthy Egyptians were buried in ornate tombs, which held extensive inventories of riches. Egyptian nobles and the rich also endured a lengthy embalming process following their deaths. All of this was part of an elaborate transition from this planet to the afterlife.

The process was rooted in the religious beliefs of ancient Egypt. Ancient Egyptians believed that the soul continued on to another realm after death. In Aaru, or "The Field of Reeds," Egyptians would enjoy an idyllic life, free from worry and negativity. Although they would continue to perform work, such as farming and hunting, the afterlife was enjoyable and free from stress. The wealthy or powerful believed they could become one with the gods. However, to ensure this magnificent afterlife occurred, many critical steps had to be taken following a person's death to prepare the body and soul.

The Egyptians believed that the soul was made up of five parts. The two most important parts were called the Ba and the Ka. Combined, the Ba and Ka were referred to as the Akh, which was the soul of each person.

The Ba, usually depicted as a bird with a human head, was the part of the soul that could remain in the land of the living. During the day, the Ba was thought to travel to friends and family of the deceased and watch over them. The Ka, on the other hand, was the life force of each person. In death, the Ka would spend each day in the Field of Reeds. At night, Egyptians believed that both the Ba and the Ka would reunite in the body within the tomb.

In order for the Ba and Ka to exist and find their way home to rest each night, a person's body had to remain a well-maintained vessel after death. Since the Ka was the life force, it required food just as a living human would. Tombs were stocked with food, wine, and beer at the burial. Later, offerings of food were often made to the tomb. This was to ensure that the people in each tomb received the nourishment they needed in the afterlife. The parts of the soul required sleep as well, which was one of the reasons the Ba and Ka needed to return to the body each night.

To preserve the body so it could serve as an effective home for the spirit, embalmers followed a lengthy procedure. Although some of the styles and techniques varied through different eras, much of the process was the same.

The body would be taken to the ibu, or "place of purification." This was where the embalming and preservation process was carried out. The chief embalmer would sometimes wear a mask with the head of Anubis, the god of embalming, during the procedure. Anubis was believed to watch over the entire embalming process.

First, the embalmers washed the person's body and anointed it with sacred oils. Next, the embalmers made a large incision in the side of the body to remove the internal organs. Practically, this made sense because the organs would be the first to decompose. But there were spiritual reasons behind this step as well. The organs were placed into vessels called canopic jars. Each jar was decorated with the head of one of four minor gods, known as the Four Sons of Horus.

Hapy, the baboon, guarded the lungs. Duamutef, the jackal, guarded the stomach and upper intestines. Qebehsenuef, the falcon, guarded the lower intestines. And Imsety, the human, guarded the liver. First, the organs were packed in natron, a natural salt, which dried them out and preserved them. Then they were deposited into the canopic jars. The jars were placed inside the tomb next to the sarcophagus, or coffin. They were left close by so that the deceased could have access to them in the afterlife.

Ancient Egyptians did not believe the brain had much purpose, so it was removed and discarded. The embalmer inserted a long hook through the deceased's nose and used it to break apart and pull the brain out of the head.

However, the most important organ in ancient Egyptian belief was the heart. The heart remained in the person's body. It was thought to be part of an essential ceremony early in the afterlife known as the Weighing of the Heart. The heart was weighed on scales against the Feather of Ma'at. Ma'at had the wings of a vulture and a majestic feathered headdress. She was the goddess of truth, justice, and balance. Osiris (the Lord of the Dead) and a panel of judges would weigh the deceased's heart on the Scales of Justice opposite a feather from Ma'at's headdress. If the person had done good deeds, the heart would weigh as light as Ma'at's feather. If the person had done evil deeds, it would be heavier. Only with a heart as light as Ma'at's feather could one enter the Field of Reeds.

After all of the other organs had been removed from the body, the embalmers covered and stuffed the body with natron. The body sat for forty days, during which time it dried and became preserved. At the end of the forty days, the embalmers would again wash the body and stuff it with sawdust and linen. These helped the body retain its shape in the absence of normal fluids and organs.

The embalmers covered the body in sacred oils a final time. Afterward, they would begin to wrap the body. Between the layers of linen wrappings, they placed amulets. These were charms or trinkets that were thought to protect the person during his or her journey to the Field of Reeds. While the embalmers wrapped the body, priests would come to the ibu and read spells for additional protection.

Before the mummy was placed into the coffin, it would be given a scroll with spells from the Book of the Dead to hold. The Lord of the Dead, Osiris, was painted on a cloth and wrapped around the mummy. Finally, the mummy was placed inside a coffin, which was lowered into another coffin. Many mummies have been found within a series of three to four coffins. King Tut was buried in eight coffins.

After the end of this process, the family and friends hosted the funeral and mourned the deceased. Funerary priests performed the Opening of the Mouth Ceremony. Because ancient Egyptians believed the spirit needed to eat and drink in the afterlife, the priests would hold amulets and charms over the mummy's mouth. This was supposed to open the airways before the deceased began the journey to the Field of Reeds.

Ancient Egyptians believed that between burial and the weighing of the deceased's heart on the Scales of Justice, the spirit had to take a journey. This journey passed through twelve gates guarded by demons in Duat, the Egyptian underworld. To pass through each gate, he or she needed to give the correct name of the demon guarding it. The twelve gates represented the twelve hours of the night; the deceased's spirit would begin the journey at nightfall and arrive in the Hall of Judgment at dawn. At the Hall of Judgment, Osiris would oversee the Weighing of the Heart.

At last, following Osiris's judgment, the deceased could enter the Field of Reeds and begin to enjoy the afterlife.

Even with as much as is currently known about ancient Egyptian culture, there are many things that are still to be discovered. Although King Tut's mummy was found in the 1920s, it is still being researched to this day. Modern science allows for much more in-depth exploration of mummies. King Tut's body has been examined on x-ray machines and through CT scans. Yet, even with this technology, many questions remain unanswered. How did he die? Was it plague, murder, or injury? Recent research revealed a large hole in his chest and an absent breastbone. This suggests his death may even have been caused by a fatal hippopotamus bite sustained during a hunt.

Mummies from ancient Egypt provide a wealth of information into the past. They are unlike almost any other type of artifact. But even with each bit of knowledge that comes to light, it seems a dozen new questions are formed as well. The fascination that started with Howard Carter's monumental discovery in 1922 may never disappear.

Energy Issues

written by Mark Weimer

Within the next century, climate change could cause flooding that will put Florida under water. A big cause of climate change is the heavy use of fossil fuels. Earth can no longer sustain a normal climate. Humans are destroying biomes by mining for fossil fuels. We must find a way to replace the energy that fossil fuels provide. There are other fuels available that we can use today. We must quickly reduce the pollution caused by fossil fuels. If we do not, natural disasters will get worse.

Oil and gas drilling cause climate change. Using fossil fuels also causes climate change. Both result in pollution and environmental damage. As Earth's oceans warm and the ice caps melt, Earth absorbs more of the Sun's energy. Warmer oceans cause many problems worldwide. Each year, storms are more violent. Floods are larger. Droughts are more severe. Human beings are not the only ones who feel the impact. Wherever humans mine for fossil fuels, they destroy the natural environment. Fracking for gas near the faultlines (the cracks in Earth's surface) has caused earthquakes. Fracking chemicals have poisoned water wells near drilling sites. By improving wind, solar, hydroelectric, and nuclear technologies, we do not need to dig for fossil fuels.

Wind provides stable power. Wind farms are slowly expanding across America. Solar technology has gotten much better in recent years. It could easily provide all the power the world would ever need. Nuclear technology has always been a huge producer of energy. New reactor technology is safer than ever before. It can create massive amounts of power with very little waste. We can use these technologies today. In the near future, scientists will be able to generate power from the tides of the ocean as well.

George the Great and Powerful

written by Jennifer Tkocs

I didn't always want to be a magician. In fact, I spent most of my early years hoping to be president of a successful company, like my dad. But everything changed one day when I was nine years old.

Each autumn, the circus came to our town. It stayed for two weeks, and each year, my siblings and I tried to see as many of the exhibits as we could. My twelve-year-old sister, Lindsay, loved the elephants. She hoped someday to be a veterinarian. My eldest brother, Michael, loved the daredevil acts. He was trying to restore a rusty old motorcycle in our garage, now that he was old enough to ride one.

My favorite part of the circus was the magic show. Each time the circus visited, the famous magician, Anthony Marvel, held daily magic shows in his own tent. As soon as school ended each day, I rushed to the fairgrounds to watch.

Although I loved Anthony Marvel's shows, I never dreamed that I, too, could be a magician. His tricks were phenomenal. I asked Michael once how he thought Anthony Marvel made doves appear out of thin air.

"Some people are just born with magic in their blood," Michael told me.

I wished that I had been born that way. I'd been born so ordinary. I was as ordinary as a stale box of crackers. I could barely get bread to toast without burning it. There was no way I could ever do the awesome tricks that Anthony Marvel did.

Year after year, I sat in the front row of Anthony Marvel's shows, watching. I watched him saw his assistant in half dozens of times. Each time, she emerged in one piece. She never even flinched when the saw cut through her like a knife cutting through

butter. I didn't know how it worked every time. It was just magic, I guessed. That's all there was to it.

One day, I met up with Lindsay after the magic show. "George, guess what?" she said. "I met the elephant trainer. She noticed me spending so much time around their pen every day. And guess what else?"

"She thinks you look like an elephant and would fit right in with them?" I said.

Lindsay crossed her arms. "Not at all! You're so rude! She said that I could help her give the elephants baths. And she will teach me more about them. I'll be a master elephant trainer in no time!"

I scowled. That wasn't fair. How did Lindsay get to make friends with her idol? I was just a perpetual audience member. Anthony Marvel didn't even know I existed. *He must know I don't have any magic in my blood*, I thought.

The next day, I thought about skipping the magic show. I felt as low as a beetle after learning that Lindsay was going to be the elephant trainer's apprentice.

Michael was probably going to finish his motorcycle before winter. They were both going to run off to join the circus, and I was still going to be the same old George, boring as plain oatmeal, stuck at home.

But something at the last minute convinced me to go. What if Anthony Marvel debuted a fantastic new trick and I missed it? Even worse, what if Lindsay went and I didn't, and then Anthony Marvel asked her to be his new assistant? I couldn't risk it.

Even though I was feeling bad, I dragged myself to the magic show. I got my usual spot in the front row and settled in. What magic would Anthony Marvel show us today?

He breezed through a few of his regular tricks; flowers jumped out of nowhere, and rabbits seemed to replicate before our very eyes. Then, he called out into the crowd for a volunteer. My hand shot up into the air. "Ah, yes, the young gentleman in the front row," Anthony Marvel said.

I couldn't believe he picked me! Out of all the times I'd volunteered at one of his shows, he had never chosen me to go on stage. My feet were cement blocks as I made my way up the wooden steps. My heart was a prisoner trying to leap out of its cage.

"Now I am going to do a card trick," he said. "This is a very complicated trick, and it requires you to focus. Can you promise you will focus as hard as you can?"

"I'm a laser beam," I assured Anthony Marvel. "I'm perfectly focused!"

"Excellent. I am going to hold out these cards, and I'll need you to choose one." He fanned the cards out in front of me, and I picked one from the middle. "Remember what your card is," he told me. "You can hold the card out to the audience and show them. I will look away."

I looked down at the card in my hand. It was the ace of spades. I did my best to conceal it from Anthony Marvel. Carefully, I turned to face the audience and showed them my card, keeping it hidden from the magician behind me.

As I held the card up, though, I noticed something on the back. There, woven into the design on the card, was a little notch. It was barely noticeable, but the light caught it in just a way that I could see it. I wondered what it meant. Maybe it was just a misprint.

"All right, son, please place your card back into this deck," Anthony Marvel said. I slid the card into a different space in the deck. As I did, the cards on either side slid apart from each other, and I noticed that they, too, had notches in the back. They were in different locations than the notch on my card.

"I will shuffle this deck three times," Anthony Marvel said. "I will then place the deck beneath my trusty rabbit. A magical rabbit like that only increases the magic in the deck of cards."

I watched as Anthony Marvel did his showmanship bit. The cards danced between his hands, but I was only half-paying attention. *What was the meaning of those notches on the cards?* I wondered. I barely heard as Anthony Marvel plucked my card out from under the rabbit. "Mister Nibbles was sitting on top of an ace of spades. Was that your card?"

"It was," I said. "Thank you."

The crowd burst into applause, but I was a hundred miles away, lost in thought. *It wasn't magic at all*, I realized. The different notches in the card design—they had to mean something. I had to get ahold of that deck.

Later that evening, after the magic show ended, I went to visit Lindsay at the elephant pen. "I need your help," I told her. I knew she would stay late after the other circus staff had gone home. "Let me stay here with you when you put the elephants to bed."

Lindsay was suspicious, but she agreed. "If you get me into trouble," she warned, "you're dead meat!"

"I won't," I promised.

I waited around with her, watching the other circus members leave for the day. At last, Anthony Marvel walked out. He was not carrying anything with him. Perfect; this meant he had left his deck of cards.

I slipped quietly into the magic tent. There was no one around to notice me, but I crept as quietly as one of Anthony Marvel's rabbits, just in case. Backstage, tables were set up with the magician's props. There, at the end of the table, was the deck of cards. Checking one last time to make sure no one was around, I snatched it up and put it in my pocket.

That night at home, I studied the cards. It only took a few minutes to unlock the secret the playing cards were keeping. Spades had markings in the bottom left corner, clubs had markings in the top left corner, and hearts and diamonds had markings on the right side. The marks were placed inside a circle, like hands on a clock with thirteen numbers.

That's it, I thought. *He can see the back of the card. He can read the placement of the notch, and that's how he can tell which card you've pulled, even without seeing the front!*

I realized that there was no magic involved. It was just skill and careful attention to detail. What if every trick was like this? What if all magic was just sleight of hand or a quickly performed illusion?

As I sat in my room that night with Anthony Marvel's trick deck of cards, I realized that my brother had been wrong. You weren't born with magic in your blood. You were born with the desire to entertain. You had to learn the magic to reach this goal. My life was never going to be the same.

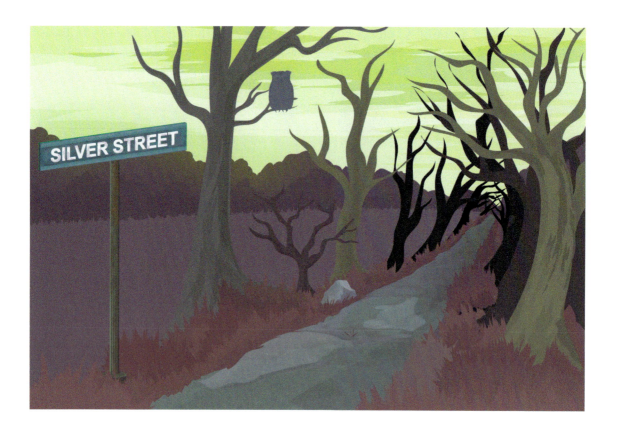

That House at the End of Silver Street

written by Steve Karscig
illustrated by Walter Sattazahn

That scary house at the end of Silver Street:
Like a bad mark on a report card,
it's every kid's worst fear.
Nothing good will ever come of it.

That gloomy house at the end of Silver Street:
Its windows are drooping eyes that watch,
with out-of-place shingles for hair and an open door
like a mouth that swallows courage.

That wicked house at the end of Silver Street:
Its lawn is dry as desert sands;
its bushes and trees are crooked characters.
Frozen from fright, it takes us an hour just to walk by!

The Basement

written by Vincent J. Scotto
illustrated by Mallory Senich

Most kids my age aren't afraid of things like the monster under the bed or the ghost in the attic. That's mainly because those things don't exist. I don't believe in them either, but there is definitely something in my basement. It attacked me one night last summer.

My mother sent me down to change the laundry that fateful night. When I opened the door, the basement exhaled a cold breath of air across my face and down my spine; it was unusually cold for a summer night. I scampered down the stairs like a mouse, quick and light-footed. When I reached the bottom, an odor that smelled like a rotting animal carcass invaded my nostrils. It was as if the room had waited for my arrival before unleashing the foul scent. I was as stiff as a board and fraught with uncertainty.

I worked my way through the darkness to find the pull string to the light bulb near the middle of the room. Suddenly, a basket on the floor grabbed my leg and tripped me. I crashed to the ground and found myself face to face with a set of large yellow eyes. I unexpectedly became a screeching bird, wailing for my life. I sped back up the stairs as quick as a racecar and slammed the door behind me.

I don't scare easily, but no one will be convincing me to return to my basement any time soon. My mother asks me to do the laundry, but I refuse to allow myself to be eaten by the creature in the basement. Perhaps I'll be a roaring lion someday, but for now, I'm just a cowering little kitten.

Mrs. Drummond's Secret

written by Jennifer Tkocs
illustrated by Sean Kennedy

Mrs. Drummond was a strange bird. That's what my mom would whisper when we stared too much, and what she meant was "so stop looking at her." But it was so hard to stop staring.

The fact was this: Mrs. Drummond actually looked like a strange bird. She was small and slightly puffy around the shoulders, sort of like a flustered owl who'd just been woken up. And her hats! She always wore the silliest hats, grand purple things with ostrich feathers and peacock plumes and sequins.

She was a mystery who had lived next door to us since forever. My brother and I had always been fascinated with her fashion and her odd, excited way of talking. When my mother wasn't paying attention, we would practice our impressions. "Oh my gracious!" was a favorite of ours. Mrs. Drummond put the accent on the *a-c-i* part of the word and held her hand to her heart like a drum that needed to be silenced.

But aside from her silly hats and over-exaggerated expressions, we didn't know much about Mrs. Drummond. She lived alone, and we hadn't ever seen any of her family. Mostly she kept to herself and we only saw her in passing.

And then, one night in April, I heard my brother's footsteps in the hallway long after we were supposed to be asleep. "Annie!" I heard his whisper in the dark as quiet as leaves in a breeze.

"Shhh!" I whispered back. "You'll wake Mom!"

"It's important!" he hissed from my doorway. "Come on, hurry!"

We crept down the hallway like a pair of mice until we reached his room. The windows in Toby's room overlooked Mrs. Drummond's backyard. "Look," he said, pointing out the window.

The moon was a bright lamp that night, and we could see clearly into Mrs. Drummond's yard. And there she was, hustling between the backdoor and the orchard past the edge of her yard. Instead of her usual bright colors, she wore an outfit as black as nighttime shadows.

"What do you think she's doing?" Toby whispered to me.

"I have no idea," I said. "Let's keep watching."

But even though the moon was so bright overhead, we couldn't see where Mrs. Drummond was going once she passed the trees at the edge of her lawn. She was a little dark blur darting between the backdoor and the trees, carrying something that we couldn't quite see.

A voice startled us from our spying. "Children! It is well past your bedtime!" Our mother stood in the doorway, hands on her hips. Even in the dark I could see the disproving scowl on her face. "Annie, go to your room. And Toby, shut those curtains and get into bed."

"Yes, Mom," we said, out-of-bed-too-late criminals who had been caught red-handed. I went back to my room, but sleep was far off. My mind raced, trying to figure out what Mrs. Drummond could have been doing out there.

The next morning, the rain was cats and dogs. I could tell it had put Toby in a sour mood as soon as I sat down at the breakfast table. "Now we have to wait another day," he said without even saying hello.

"Wait another day for what?" I asked.

"To find out you-know-what," he said with gritted teeth.

I realized what he meant. "Ohhhhh! Mrs. Drummond!" I mouthed at him across the table, and he nodded. I guess I hadn't thought that we would actually ever find out what she was doing.

"Tomorrow it will be, then," Toby said. He crossed his arms and sat back in his chair. "Tomorrow we discover the truth."

"The truth about what?" asked our mom, coming into the room.

"Whether or not it's going to pour like a monsoon for two days straight," I said quickly. We would never get away with any plan if Mom was onto us.

"Weatherman says it'll dry up before we know it," she said.

Toby and I both sighed. We were safe from being found out so far.

We spent the rest of the day speculating about Mrs. Drummond. "What if she's a spy?" Toby suggested.

"Spying for whom?" I asked.

Toby shrugged. "The government, I guess. Or the mob. Who else hires spies?"

"Maybe there's a secret portal to another world back there," I said.

Toby liked this idea. "I hope that's what it is. And if so, we are definitely sneaking back there. Can you imagine how awesome a secret portal would be?"

Maybe there was a hidden land back there, I thought. "What if the portal goes to a secret world? And what if we go to the secret land and they make us king and queen?"

Toby thought for a minute. "Then I'm going to wear a crown—a crown as tall as a water pitcher. And I'm going to get a stack of pancakes that's even taller than that every morning for breakfast!"

I rolled my eyes. "You'd be king of a secret land, and all you'd do is eat pancakes and wear a big crown?"

"And have a pet unicorn, probably," he said. With that idea, I could not argue.

We sat by the window in Toby's room, waiting to see if Mrs. Drummond would resume her strange behavior during the day. But though we watched for over an hour, the closest she came to her backyard was the window in her kitchen above her sink.

That night, we waited until just after dark and crept back to the window, hoping our mother wouldn't see us. The rain had finally stopped in the late afternoon, but our yards were muddy marshes. I worried that maybe the sloppy grass would keep Mrs. Drummond in her house that night.

But it was only fifteen minutes into our watch when she emerged from the backdoor. She was wearing bright purple galoshes that were illuminated by her flashlight—there was no moon that night to light her path. We squinted into the darkness, trying to see what she was carrying, but all we could make out was the flashlight and a dark bag.

"She can't be a spy in purple galoshes!" said Toby.

"She could if she's trying to go undercover," I reminded him. "Maybe 'crazy old lady' is just her undercover uniform!"

"Tomorrow night," said Toby. "Tomorrow night we will learn the truth."

The next morning, the rain had passed by completely and the sun was shining like a blinding jewel. It was hard to be patient; every minute was like an hour. Most importantly we had to keep our plans from our mom, who'd surely not let us get away with them.

At last, it was night. We waited in Toby's room by the window until we saw Mrs. Drummond leave the house. "Now's our chance!" Toby said.

Now we were the secret agents, creeping stealthily down the stairs. I pushed the backdoor open as carefully as I could so that it wouldn't make a sound. Toby and I snuck out, and I delicately pushed the door shut behind us. We inched toward the edge of our lawn, waiting for Mrs. Drummond to pass by again.

Finally, she darted past us and into her backdoor. "Now!" whispered Toby. We hurried through the shadows to the edge of the lawn. Once we were through the orchard we could finally see it: there, just beyond the trees, was a little brick building that resembled a chicken coop.

"Chickens?" I said out loud. "She's raising chickens?"

Toby shook his head. "No way we've been spying on her every night just to find out that she's a farmer!"

And then we heard a voice behind us through the trees. "Oh my *gracious*, you two gave me a fright!"

Toby and I both froze in our tracks. We'd been caught—not by our mother as we'd worried, but by Mrs. Drummond herself! Toby's voice had abandoned him, so I had to speak for both of us. "Hi, Mrs. Drummond, we were just…" My voice trailed off. I had no words.

"Coming to give me a hand, I would hope!" she said. "Here, carry this." She shoved a handful of baby bottles into my arms. "Come on now, they won't wait all night!" she said, ushering us into the little brick building.

"Who won't wait—" I started to say, but stopped as my eyes adjusted to the darkness. Inside the little building were a dozen hungry eyes and half as many tiny, round black sniffing noses. "Oh!" I exclaimed. "Who are they?"

"Baby raccoons, of course," Mrs. Drummond said. "Now come on, help me feed them!"

Bewildered, I handed some of the bottles to my brother and Mrs. Drummond. We followed her lead and fed the baby raccoons from the bottles, going down the line until each had drunk his or her fill. "What happened to them?" I asked.

"Their mother was injured in a hunter's trap," she explained. "Don't fret children, she's on the mend, but the wildlife in our forest knows they can count on old Mrs. Drummond when they fall on hard times."

I shot my brother a skeptical look, but he shrugged and continued feeding the raccoon kit in front of him as if he'd been doing it all his life. "So you… do this often?" I asked Mrs. Drummond.

"Oh, of course, my dear! If they didn't have me, who would they have?"

I didn't have an answer.

"I'm the keeper of these woods, my dear," she continued. "Animals know they can come to me to receive care and loving attention in their times of need. When these kits are old enough and their mother is healthy enough, they'll go back to the wild. But for now, they know they have sanctuary here."

My eyes must have been as wide as saucers then, because Mrs. Drummond patted my arm. "Surely you knew all of this before?"

I shook my head. "We thought…"

"We thought you were a ninja!" Toby interjected, finally finding his voice.

Mrs. Drummond laughed. "Oh my gracious, no! That would just be silly! I'm just the caretaker of the animals here."

"And you're out at night right now because the raccoon kits are nocturnal," I said.

"Exactly, my dear. I adjust my schedule to the needs of my current residents."

I watched as the raccoon kits yawned, curled up, and became tiny little balls next to each other to sleep. They were so sweet and tiny. Mrs. Drummond definitely had the best job of any grown-up I knew.

"How would you two like to be my special assistants?" she asked.

"Us? Really?" Toby said.

"Of course. Look, you're naturals! The kits love you! Look how content they all are," she said, pointing to the smiling little faces. "I'll of course have to ask your mother's permission, but I could definitely use some assistants to help me. I'm a busy bee caring for all of these animals myself!"

"We would love it!" I said. "I mean, as long as our mom is okay with it."

"Then I'll speak to her in the morning, and we'll get it all worked out," Mrs. Drummond said. "For now though, it's getting late and she's going to notice you two are missing. Go back home, and we'll talk in the morning."

We said goodbye to the raccoon kits and went back to our house, sneaking in as carefully as before so that we didn't alarm our mother. We were both so excited to begin our jobs as Mrs. Drummond's helpers.

"So who knew," Toby said as we climbed the stairs to our bedrooms. "Mrs. Drummond isn't the kind of crazy we thought she was at all."

"Very true," I said. "She's the best kind of crazy I know. And I was right all along—there really is a secret world beyond those trees!"

"In that case," Toby said, "I hope those raccoons won't mind if I show up tomorrow night in my crown!"

A Place I Cannot Go

written by Summer York
illustrated by Sean Ricciardi

There is a place I know,
Somewhere I long to get.
You are there right now, although
I cannot follow yet;
It's not my time to leave, and so
I'll stay here with regret.

I felt so sad upon the day
You went to find your grace,
Though *sad* does not convey
The depth of loss that I now face.
My heart is cold and grey
As stone in this dark, quiet place.

How do I say goodbye
To you, one whom I loved so dear?
I have not strength to try
For you're no longer here.
I'll wait to catch your eye
And dream that you are near
Until the day that I
May see that place you went appear.

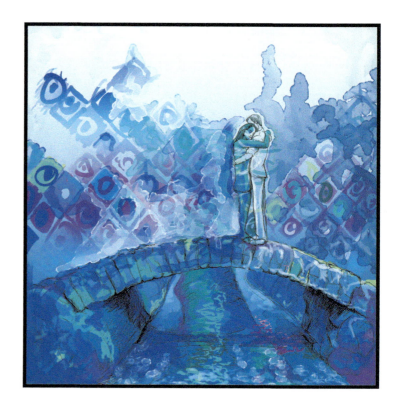

The Sparrow

written by Summer York
illustrated by David Rushbrook

A small sparrow alit at my window one day
For a rest from his journey to lands far away.
I asked where he would go and where he had been.
Who could guess which exotic locations he'd seen?

From the highest of mountains and tallest of trees
To the lowest green valleys and deepest blue seas?
Maybe deserts that shine like the sun, gleaming bright!
I could barely imagine each glorious sight.

Of all great destinations that sparrow could go,
Why he came to my dreary abode, I don't know.
There is only much wretchedness, here only strife—
No escape from the woe and the gloom of this life.

As I yearned for the places that little bird flew,
I would never see most of them, sadly, I knew.
And then freedom was Sparrow's; he took to the sky.
He was destined for places far better than I.

Lady Liberty

written by Summer York
illustrated by Sean Kennedy

In fine America,
Rich land across the sea,
Reign freedom and goodwill
And opportunity.

To this most blessèd land,
I slowly journeyed on
Across the bleak, blue ocean
From dawn to dusk to dawn.

Then over the horizon,
Sun rising in the sky,
She stood alone, aglow,
Her blazing torch held high.

Her noble features gleamed
As she waited for me,
A beacon in the morning:
My Lady Liberty!

I watched her face with wonder.
My past, it slipped away.
And standing in her presence,
A new life starts today.

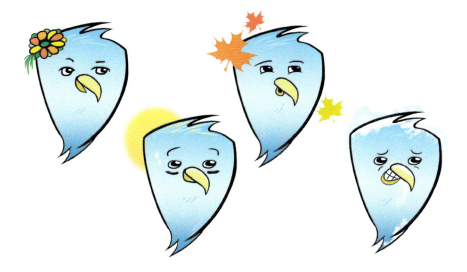

My Favorite Season

by Vincent J. Scotto
illustrated by Brian Cibelli

Perhaps my favorite season is spring,
with sprouting buds and birds that sing
and games of jumping and skipping.
But then I feel the first bee sting.
Another season might be more my thing.

Perhaps my favorite season is summer.
There's swimming everywhere in deep blue water.
But even then it may be much hotter,
and in the nighttime my sleep shall suffer!
Enough of that season; I'll think of another.

Perhaps my favorite season is fall,
with backyard sports like flag football.
But all of the plants, they're growing so small.
Cold rain and wet leaves will cover up all.
I'll dream of the last season I can recall.

Perhaps my favorite season is winter,
with lakes frozen over without a splinter…
and wind that bites my skin, so bitter.
The best season can't be one where I'll shiver.
But what of the spring? Perhaps it can deliver.

Visit Pittsburgh

written by Summer York
illustrated by Sean Ricciardi

Are you looking for your next travel destination? Consider visiting Pittsburgh, Pennsylvania, on your next getaway. Pittsburgh earned a reputation as a soot-covered, industrial steel town. While this was true during and after the Industrial Revolution, Pittsburgh has since transformed into a bustling metropolis filled with attractions for residents and visitors alike. Visit Pittsburgh to see its thriving cultural districts, state-of-the-art professional sporting venues, and historical landmarks.

Pittsburgh's cultural scene is flourishing with theatre, arts, and entertainment. For example, you can catch a live performance at one of the downtown theaters, such as the Benedum Center, Heinz Hall, and the O'Reilly Theater; each hosts national tours and local productions. View stunning exhibits at one of many noteworthy museums, like the Carnegie Museum of Natural History, the Andy Warhol Museum, the Heinz History Center, and Phipps Conservatory. Visit during the Pittsburgh Arts Festival to sample famous Pittsburgh cuisine and see handcrafted works made by local artisans. This city's cultural offerings are numerous and growing all the time.

On the other hand, if cultural attractions do not interest you, you may love the many sporting venues that Pittsburgh offers. Experience the excitement of Pittsburgh's black and gold professional sports teams. The Steelers football team plays at Heinz Field, and the Pirates baseball team plays at PNC Park, both of which opened in 2001. The Penguins ice hockey team plays at the Consol Energy Center, completed in 2010. Pittsburgh is also home to the Riverhounds professional soccer team, which plays at Highmark Stadium, and the University of Pittsburgh Panthers collegiate sports teams. Cheer on your favorite team with thousands of other Pittsburgh fans.

Additionally, visit Pittsburgh's several historical landmarks, some of which date back prior to the birth of our nation. Pittsburgh's three rivers meet at a point in the city called Point State Park, which was once the site of Fort Pitt, a British stronghold during the French and Indian War. Fort Pitt's blockhouse is now preserved as a museum that houses relics from this period. Take a ride up Mount Washington in one of two working inclines—cable cars that glide up and down the side of the mountain—to take in the breathtaking view of the city from one of Mount Washington's overlooks. Tour Clayton, the preserved mansion owned by the famed Henry Clay Frick, and its lush grounds and elegant carriages. You may also want to tour the area's many manufacturing sites at the Rivers of Steel National Heritage Area, a museum dedicated to preserving Pittsburgh's legacy in the steel industry. Furthermore, many of Pittsburgh's bridges and buildings themselves are historical landmarks, such as the Roberto Clemente Bridge, the Rachel Carson Bridge, the Allegheny Observatory, the Cathedral of Learning, the Pennsylvania Railroad Station, and the Allegheny County Courthouse. Pittsburgh values its rich history and has preserved it for everyone to treasure.

In conclusion, consider visiting Pittsburgh for its growing cultural scene, its vibrant sports life, and its vast historical legacy. Whether you see an exhibit at the Mattress Factory contemporary art museum, watch a Pitt Panthers basketball game at the Peterson Events Center, or tour the USS *Requin* submarine from World War II at the Carnegie Science Center, you are sure to find many interesting attractions in and around Pittsburgh. Consult a travel agent or research online and plan a visit to this fabulous city for your next getaway.

Persuasive Essay Outline

I. Introduction
- A. Hook Sentence
    1. Begin your essay with a general statement about your topic that grabs the reader's attention.
    2. An interesting fact, a statistic, a famous quotation, or a question provides an excellent hook statement for a persuasive essay.
- B. Introduce the Topic
    1. It is important to provide one to two sentences letting the reader know why this is an important issue.
    2. The reader should clearly understand why the topic matters and why it is worthy of concern.
- C. Context
    1. The following three to four sentences should provide the context or background information that the reader needs in order to fully understand the topic.
    2. These sentences should build toward the thesis statement.
- D. Thesis Statement
    1. This statement presents the central argument or defining position of the essay.
    2. It should suggest how the argument will be supported with evidence provided in the body paragraphs.

II. Each of Three Body Paragraphs
- A. Topic Sentence
    1. The first sentence of each body paragraph should be a topic sentence that states one main reason for supporting the claim expressed in the thesis statement.
- B. Supporting Details
    1. Include supporting details to further describe, explain, or prove the topic sentence. These details should provide evidence to support your thesis statement.
    2. This evidence can come from a text (quotes, paraphrases, a summary, etc.) or from other sources (first-person interviews, your personal experiences, etc.).
- C. Analysis of Evidence
    1. Explain the significance of the evidence you have provided.
    2. Why did you choose it? How does this evidence support your thesis?
- D. Closing Sentence
    1. The paragraph may end with a concluding thought regarding the topic.
    2. The paragraph may also end with a transition sentence that leads into the next reason and emonstrates how these ideas work together to support the thesis.

III. Conclusion
- A. Overview
    1. Restate your thesis in words different from those used in the introduction.
    2. Provide the reader with an overview of the reasons you gave to support the claim you made in your thesis.
- B. Final Thought
    1. A good conclusion should end with a powerful final thought or concluding statement. This concluding statement is your last chance to persuade your reader.
    2. Your final thought should leave the reader with something to contemplate even after reading your essay. For example, you might write a call to action or make a final plea to your reader to take action in support of your proposal.

Essay Structure Map

Introduction

Children benefit from learning to play a musical instrument.

Main Idea 1

Learning how to play a musical instrument can improve your work ethic.

Main Idea 2

Learning how to play a musical instrument teaches you attention to detail.

Main Idea 3

Learning how to play a musical instrument offers many new opportunities.

Supporting Detail

You must learn how to read music.

Supporting Detail

Musicians must learn how to position their fingers.

Supporting Detail:

Musicians can earn a living by writing music.

Supporting Detail

Learning to play an instrument helps you learn discipline and the value of practice.

Supporting Detail

Musicians must learn how to make different kinds of sounds with their instruments.

Supporting Detail

Musicians can be librarians who specialize in music instead of books.

Supporting Detail

You can apply these strategies to school work and sports.

Supporting Detail

Musicians must learn how to control the volume of the sounds they produce on their instruments.

Supporting Detail

Musicians can become music therapists, or professionals who help the ill or injured through music.

Conclusion

Playing a musical instrument is not easy, but there is nothing sweeter than seeing all your practice pay off.

Steven and the Turtles

written by Summer York
illustrated by Mallory Senich

October 5, 2011

Commissioner Henry Parnell
Massachusetts Department of Environmental Protection
One Winter Street
Boston, Massachusetts 02108

Dear Commissioner Parnell,

My name is Steven Brown, and I am a fourth-grader at Hillsboro Elementary School. I am writing to you because yesterday I found pollution near the forest by my house. Pollution is very bad for the environment, plants, animals, and people. I learned in science class that all living things depend on clean air to breathe and clean water to drink. But pollution makes the air and water dirty. I am afraid that the pollution I found will destroy my favorite part of the forest. It could make the plants and animals sick. I need your help!

My family lives on a small farm at the edge of Myles Standish State Forest in Plymouth County, Massachusetts. I like to explore the forest looking for cool plants and animals. I don't go too far when I'm by myself, though, because I'm not allowed. Yesterday, after school, my mom said that I could walk down to the pond. It is right inside the forest. The pond is my favorite place to go because there are turtles living near it. I like to watch them swim in the water and lie in the sun.

But when I got to the pond, I noticed a weird smell. It smelled like the stuff my mom uses to mop the floor. I didn't know where it was coming from. After looking around for a while, I didn't see anything near the pond, so I walked farther along the forest edge. I passed the line where our property ends and the next farm begins. This farm has been abandoned for as long as I can remember. I climbed the steep hill leading up to where the old farmhouse used to be. I thought I might be able to get a better look into the forest from high up. But as I climbed the hill, the smell got stronger. Soon it was stinging my nose. At the top of the hill, I couldn't believe what I saw! There were all these barrels lying on their sides, and there was green liquid everywhere. The smell was awful! Someone must have dumped those barrels on the abandoned farmland, thinking that no one would find them.

I knew right away that this was pollution because we are learning about it in school. My teacher, Mrs. Jones, said that pollution is very harmful to the plants and animals living in an area. She also said that it is our job to take care of the environment and all living things. I was very angry. Who could do such a terrible thing?

Suddenly, I remembered the turtles that live near the pond. If those smelly chemicals leaked down the hill into the forest, the turtles could die! I had looked those turtles up on the Internet a few days before. They are Plymouth red-bellied turtles. They are on the endangered species list! They only live here in Massachusetts and in a few other New England states. In fact, there are only about three hundred of those turtles on the whole earth! I knew I had to rescue the turtles before they got sick, but I was afraid I might already be too late.

I ran back down the hill into the forest. Then, all of a sudden, I heard a quad driving by. It was a park ranger! So, I ran over, waving my arms and yelling for him to stop. The park ranger said his name was Josh and asked me what was wrong.

I told Josh about the barrels leaking the gooey green chemicals on the abandoned farm. I said that I was afraid the chemicals might leak into the forest. Then, I explained that I knew the turtles living near the pond were Plymouth red-bellied turtles, an endangered species. Josh asked me to show him where I found the barrels. I took him out of the forest and up the hill. When he saw the mess, he looked very sad and very angry. He was just as angry as I was! He promised to report the chemical spill immediately and that he would take care of the turtles and all the other wildlife that lived near the forest edge. Then, he told me to go home because he didn't want me to get sick from the chemical fumes.

When I got home, I told my mom about how someone had dumped chemicals up on the hill on the abandoned farm. I was very sad to think that the turtles and the other plants and animals in the forest could die because someone had polluted the area. I was also sad because I felt like there was nothing I could do to help. My mom suggested that I write a letter to the Massachusetts Department of Environmental Protection. She said that the organization works to protect wildlife in our area. That's why I'm writing to you. I am hoping that since you are the commissioner, this letter will convince you and your organization to save the turtles and other living things in the forest by helping to clean up the chemical spill.

It is bad enough that the chemicals polluted the land on the farm. But if the harmful chemicals run down the hill from the farm and into the forest, all the living things near the forest edge would be lost. The smell from the chemicals could drive the animals away or make them sick. If it rains, the rain might wash the chemicals down the hill and into the pond. If any animals drink the toxic water, they will die. The chemicals might also get into the dirt in the forest, killing the trees that some animals live in and the plants they eat. I am especially worried about the turtles because, if the chemicals hurt them, the species will be even closer to extinction. Please save the turtles and the other wildlife in the forest.

I am also asking you to make sure that no one else can dump chemicals near Myles Standish State Forest. You should ask the Massachusetts government to hire more park rangers like Josh to patrol near the edges of the forest. You should also ask the government to make stricter laws against pollution. The stricter laws might make someone think twice before polluting the environment. Last, you should give educational classes at the Plymouth Community Center to teach people that littering and dumping chemicals is bad. Maybe if more people knew how bad pollution is for the earth, not as many people would do it. Please help to keep the forest and earth clean for all living things.

Sincerely,

Steven Brown

Green or Orange on St. Patrick's Day?

(errors version)
written by Summer York

The current Irish flag was officially recognized in 1937. It has three equal columns of color: green, white, and orange. The green symbolizes the Irish Catholics, the orange represents the Irish Protestants, and the white in the middle is for the peace between the two religious groups. These colors symbolize Ireland's difficult struggle for harmony. Thus, not everyone wears green on St. Patrick's Day. What color do u wear?

St. Patrick is the patron saint of Ireland. In early times, the people of Ireland were mostly pagan, meaning they worshiped several gods. St. Patrick went to Ireland in AD 432 to teach Catholicism. It is said that St. Patrick used the green three-leaf clover to teach the Irish about the Catholic trinity. All u should know that green is the predominant color of St. Patrick's Day.

For many centuries, Catholicism was the main religion of Ireland. However, in 1541, British King Henry VIII became ruler of Ireland. King Henry opposed Catholicism, which began a tradition of Catholic oppression in Ireland. In 1608, British Catholic King James I sent thousands of English Protestants to Northern Ireland to take over Irish lands, which wasn't cool at all with those Irish. In 1689, William III of Orange became king of England, Scotland, and Ireland. William of Orange was Protestant, and he spread his faith throughout these countries.

 I'm Catholic, but I don't think I'm Irish. Irish Catholics continued to be oppressed by British rule until 1921, when Britain gave up control of most of Ireland. But it retained Northern Ireland, which is still part of the United Kingdom. The free part of Ireland became the independent Irish Republic in 1949. After

many more years of fighting, the political and religious groups in Northern Ireland reached the Good Friday Agreement in 1998. This agreement was a step toward establishing peace in the region.

In the United States, most people wear green on St. Patrick's Day whether they are Irish or not. IDK what I'm gonna wear this year yet. In fact, the Irish have a saying that "Everyone is Irish on St. Patrick's Day." But some still honor the struggle for peace in Ireland by wearing the color of their religion. Irish Catholics wear green to pay tribute to the Catholic tradition of their homeland while Irish Protestants wear orange in remembrance of William of Orange. No matter which color one wears, though, the flag is a reminder that green and orange are both Irish.

The Griffin

(also known as **griffon** or **gryphon**)

- **Type:** *mythical creature*
- **Height:** *2 m (avg.)*
- **Weight:** *225 kg (avg.)*
- **Wingspan:** *7.62 m (avg.)*
- **Similar Species:** *opinicus, hippogrypf, sphinx, Anzû, lamassu*

griffins in heraldry

lion-like, posterior, hind legs, and tail

eagle-like head, wings, and talons

human male 1.8 meters (5'10")

The Griffin

written by Vincent J. Scotto
illustrated by Matthew Casper

In most old stories, the griffin has a lion's body, hind legs, and tail, with an eagle's head, wings, and talons. The lion was considered king of the beasts, and the eagle was considered king of the birds. Thus, the griffin was regarded as a notably powerful and regal creature. Griffins commonly appear in the art and lore of Ancient Greece. However, representations of griffins in Ancient Persian and Ancient Egyptian art date even further back. According to legend, griffins guarded treasures and priceless possessions. In one widely shared story, a griffin's claw healed the sick, and one of its feathers enabled the blind to see. These attributes of the griffin in storytelling led many to use its resemblance for war, sports, and statues, representing protection, military strength, or courage.

The Land Remains

written by Summer York
illustrated by Doyle Daigle II

I pause in my labors to wipe
the day's work from my face in
streaks, to survey
the land I been toilin over;
this here sweep of red
Georgia clay, and those over yonder,
jus' sproutin the first promises of green,
stir up within these weary bones a pride
bought only with yer own sweat an blood.

I stoop to crumble the red earth
tween my fingers, breathe in its
riches. I hold in my fist the histories
of generations long gone by.
Paw, and Granddaddy,
and his afore him
walk longside me, tillin and troddin the same
soil that now stains my hands that
in-the-blood Georgia red.

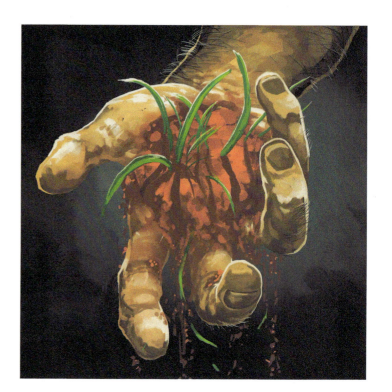

There, too, wait the unfamiliar
specters not yet walked—
my boy's boys, and
their youngins, and ten generations
hence—who gon inherit
this land? Love it;
work it;
tend it and give they hearts to the red
Georgia earth as their ancestors did.

I see em. They all wavin, a jubilee
that beckons to me
cross that haze of time.
And then in a blink they're gone, swept
into oblivion. Dusty clay scratched up
in a dry spell. But the red Georgia soil, that
soul neath my feet, the legacy gave upon
me an I'll give upon them, will endure
til time's end. The land remains.

The Strange Case of Dr. Jekyll and Mr. Hyde

adapted by Vincent J. Scotto
illustrated by Sean Ricciardi

<u>Cast</u>

DR. HENRY JEKYLL	late 20s; wealthy, intelligent physician
MR. EDWARD HYDE	late 20s; mysterious, dark, evil
MR. GABRIEL JOHN UTTERSON	40s; wealthy, respected, rational lawyer
DR. HASTIE LANYON	30s; wealthy, respected physician
MR. POOLE	50s; Jekyll's butler
MR. ENFIELD	40s; Utterson's less-privileged cousin
SIR DANVERS CAREW	50s; wealthy, well-respected member of Parliament
POLICEMAN 1	late 20s
POLICEMAN 2	late 20s

<u>Setting</u>

London, England. Locations around the city, including Jekyll's house, streets, and offices.

<u>ACT I</u>

<u>SCENE ONE</u>

Scene: *A particularly prosperous London street. The cellar entrance to one building is seen, though, which appears to be unkempt and neglected.*

Enter UTTERSON and ENFIELD. UTTERSON, a wealthy, well-respected lawyer, is dressed in a fine suit with a top hat. ENFIELD, cousin of UTTERSON and a respectable gentleman, is also dressed in a fine suit with a top hat. The two walk side by side.

UTTERSON: Quite a nice part of town. Wouldn't you say, Mr. Enfield?

ENFIELD: Indeed it is, Mr. Utterson. I do say: I enjoy our walks together, cousin. It gives us a chance to see more of the prosperity of the city together.

UTTERSON: Indeed it does, cousin. [*points to the neglected house*] What of this place?

ENFIELD [*excited*]: I was actually down this way not too long ago, late one night, and saw a peculiar affair.

UTTERSON: While I am not one for gossip, you have tickled my interest.

ENFIELD: Well, it was right outside this house here. I was walking down this street when I saw a man barrel right into a young woman!

UTTERSON: Astonishing!

ENFIELD [*moving about*]: Naturally, I went after the man and was able to catch him right here, outside this house.

UTTERSON: What came of it, Enfield?

ENFIELD: A small crowd had formed, demanding that he make amends. Oh, did they despise him!

UTTERSON: Surely, it could not have been that terrible.

ENFIELD: You would only believe me if you saw him. He was such a horrific sight.

UTTERSON: I'm not sure what you mean.

ENFIELD: His face was [*pauses*] indescribable. I can see it clear as day in my mind, but I cannot explain how [*pauses*] awful he looked.

UTTERSON: Well, then, did he make amends?

ENFIELD: This is the most peculiar part. He dashed into this seemingly abandoned house and came back out with a check for one hundred pounds!

UTTERSON: The check must have been a fake, Enfield.

ENFIELD: I had my suspicions. Even more strange is the signature on the check. A well-established, respectable man of the city had signed it. A doctor, no less!

UTTERSON: As I said, it must have been a forgery.

ENFIELD: I recognized the signature. It was authentic.

UTTERSON: Well, the signer must have been blackmailed. If this man is so outlandish that must be the only possibility. Who was this reviled man?

ENFIELD: His name is Mr. Hyde.

UTTERSON: I know this name. I believe I know who signed the check.

ENFIELD: I've never seen a man so despised, and yet I can't explain why. He must have a deformity, but I can't explain at which point.

UTTERSON: Let us remember that a respectable man is involved. Minding one's own business is a virtue, so let us never speak of this again.

ENFIELD: Surely, Mr. Utterson.

Exit UTTERSON and ENFIELD.

SCENE TWO

Scene: *UTTERSON's house. It contains a bed on one side with a night table and candelabra, a dining area with a table and chairs in the center of the set, and, on the opposite side, a desk with a chair and shelving filled with files and books. UTTERSON sits at the dining table, looking over a document.*

LANYON [*off stage*]: Hello? Mr. Utterson?

UTTERSON: Come in, Dr. Lanyon.

LANYON enters and stands at the dining table. LANYON is a well-dressed, respected individual. He is in casual attire, but is clearly a wealthy man.

LANYON: Good evening, Mr. Utterson.

UTTERSON [*getting up and shaking hands*]: Good evening to you as well, doctor. Thank you for coming over. Have a seat. May I offer you some tea?

LANYON [*sits*]: That's all right. I'm only able to stay a short while. You understand, I'm sure.

UTTERSON: Of course. I'll get right to the point then. I've been thinking of our mutual friend, Dr. Jekyll.

LANYON: Ah, yes. Dr. Jekyll. What about him?

UTTERSON: I've been reviewing some of my documents concerning his will. As his lawyer, I recently executed an update to his will that was somewhat peculiar.

LANYON: What exactly does his will have to do with me? Has he left me something?

UTTERSON [*passing a piece of paper to LANYON*]: I wonder if you might take a look at the will.

LANYON looks at the document, while JEKYLL speaks off stage.

JEKYLL [*off stage*]: Upon my death or disappearance, I, Dr. Henry Jekyll, do hereby leave all of my property and assets to Mr. Edward Hyde.

LANYON: This looks like a fairly standard will of rights, but I don't see how I may be of help. What is the question?

UTTERSON: As a close friend of Dr. Jekyll, I thought you might be able to give me some more information about Mr. Hyde. I've never met Hyde, and as Dr. Jekyll's lawyer, I think it right that I know something of the man.

LANYON [*sighs*]: To be quite honest, Dr. Jekyll and I are not as close as we once were.

UTTERSON: Oh?

LANYON: We fell upon some…differences. His most recent work isn't scientific in nature.

UTTERSON: Is that so?

LANYON [*nods*]: A bunch of nonsense, really. His experiments are all a bunch of balderdash. As a result, we've not spoken more than a few words in quite some time.

UTTERSON: And this Hyde fellow?

LANYON: I can't say I've heard of him.

LANYON passes the document back to UTTERSON.

UTTERSON: Thank you for your time, doctor.

LANYON: Not a problem. We should schedule another time where we might go for a stroll.

UTTERSON: That would be nice. You'll see your way out then, Dr. Lanyon?

LANYON: Yes. Good night, Utterson.

LANYON exits. UTTERSON returns the document to his desk in the study and goes to the bedroom.

UTTERSON [*changing into night robes, talking to himself*]: I cannot fathom any reason for Jekyll to give his entire fortune to a man like Hyde. Jekyll is a respected, established man. He wouldn't have anything to do with such a person. [*pauses*] What if Hyde has blackmailed him? I wonder what Hyde would be able to hold over him. Perhaps Hyde is somehow involved in Jekyll's experiments of which Lanyon spoke.

UTTERSON lies down in the bed and falls asleep. Lights dim and two silhouettes appear on stage. Their figures can be seen, but their identities are a mystery. They appear to be pushing and shoving. Thunder crashes.

HYDE [*yelling off stage*]: You'll do as I say, Jekyll!

JEKYLL [*off stage*]: Please don't hurt me. I'll do whatever you want, Hyde!

The two silhouettes quickly exit. UTTERSON sits up and yelps.

UTTERSON [*awakes and sits up*]: No!

Fade to black. End scene.

SCENE THREE

Scene: *Outside the neglected cellar entrance. UTTERSON observes the entrance from afar.*

UTTERSON: I'm sure if I wait here long enough, I'll see him.

Enter HYDE. HYDE is a small, hunched young man who wears a large overcoat with a top hat and carries a cane. His face is well hidden for the majority of the scene. HYDE approaches the cellar door, but is stopped by UTTERSON.

UTTERSON: Good day, sir! Are you Mr. Hyde?

HYDE [*grumbles*]: Who wants to know?

UTTERSON [*clearing his throat*]: I'm Gabriel Utterson, Dr. Henry Jekyll's lawyer and friend.

HYDE [*more excited*]: Ah! Yes. Mr. Utterson. Edward Hyde is my name. What can I do for you?

UTTERSON: I thought that I might introduce myself since I am to execute Dr. Jekyll's will to you in the event of his passing [*pauses*] or disappearance.

Silence falls as UTTERSON tries to see HYDE's face.

HYDE: Of course. Let me give you my personal address.

HYDE reaches for a card and hands it to UTTERSON.

UTTERSON: Thank you, Mr. Hyde. I don't suppose you might let me take a look at you. I'm feeling quite uneasy that I can't see your face.

HYDE shows his face more clearly. He looks somewhat subhuman, almost apelike. UTTERSON shows his discomfort with HYDE's look.

HYDE: Just be sure you get in touch with me when Dr. Jekyll *turns*.

UTTERSON walks off stage backward, staring at HYDE. HYDE smirks and turns to the cellar door. Fade to black. End scene.

SCENE FOUR

Scene: *JEKYLL's townhouse. It is extremely well-kept. MR. POOLE, JEKYLL's butler, is performing some light dusting.*

Knocking sounds at the door. MR. POOLE walks over to open the door.

MR. POOLE: Hello, Mr. Utterson!

UTTERSON: Good day, Mr. Poole. Is Dr. Jekyll available?

MR. POOLE: I'm afraid not, sir. He may yet return soon. Come inside if you wish.

UTTERSON [*walking in and taking off his coat and hat*]: Thank you. How are you?

MR. POOLE: As well as can be expected, sir; getting ready for this evening's party. How are you? It's been some time since you've called on the doctor.

UTTERSON: Actually I've been a bit troubled lately.

MR. POOLE: Is there anything I may assist you with, sir?

UTTERSON: Perhaps you can. Have you met Mr. Hyde?

MR. POOLE [*changes tone and turns away from UTTERSON*]: Yes. I have met him.

UTTERSON: I have seen him entering the laboratory through the back cellar entrance, so I thought you might have spoken to him.

MR. POOLE: We aren't actually allowed into the laboratory. Not even for cleaning. The doctor gave Hyde his own key. For the most part, we don't see him.

UTTERSON: Why do you think Jekyll would leave everything to him?

MR. POOLE: I'm not sure. The doctor was quite clear that we are to serve Mr. Hyde as we would serve the doctor.

UTTERSON: I am quite suspicious of this Hyde fellow. I think he may be blackmailing Dr. Jekyll, but I can't quite figure out for what exactly. Perhaps something when they were younger. I can't imagine why Jekyll would associate with Hyde otherwise.

MR. POOLE: I just do as instructed and keep the doctor happy. Are you attending the party this evening?

UTTERSON: I shall be here. I will show myself out.

MR. POOLE: Good day, Mr. Utterson.

UTTERSON [*grabs his things*]: Good day.

UTTERSON exits. MR. POOLE returns to dusting. End scene.

SCENE FIVE

Scene: *JEKYLL's townhouse. The party is wrapping up. JEKYLL, UTTERSON, LANYON, and CAREW are among the guests. LANYON is seen walking off stage and waving goodbye. JEKYLL walks to the edge of the stage with CAREW to see them off, but UTTERSON remains. He has a stoic look. CAREW stops at the edge of the stage and turns to JEKYLL.*

CAREW: Great party, doctor! We'll be seeing you again soon!

JEKYLL: Of course, Danvers!

CAREW [*sarcastically*]: That's Sir Carew, Dr. Jekyll.

    ALL laugh.

JEKYLL: Of course, *Sir Carew*. You won't be a stranger, will you?

CAREW: I may be a politician, but I always have time for old friends. Good night, doctor!

JEKYLL [*smiling*]: Goodnight, Danv—I mean, Sir Carew!

    CAREW exits; JEKYLL turns and notices, to his surprise, that UTTERSON is still seated.

JEKYLL: He's become quite the big shot, don't you say, Gabriel?

UTTERSON: Indeed he has. It is good to see he hasn't lost his good nature.

JEKYLL: We shall see. Parliament does tend to change people. [*sits at the table*] So what's on your mind, old chap?

UTTERSON: I've been waiting to speak with you, Jekyll.

JEKYLL: Come now, Gabriel. You may be my lawyer, but we are friends. Since when did you stop calling me Henry?

UTTERSON: All right, Henry. I'd like to speak to you about your will.

JEKYLL [*laughing*]: Quite a silly thing to want to talk about after I've just had a dinner party! Are you expecting my death any time soon?

UTTERSON: Not at all. If you remember, it also includes if you happen to *disappear*.

JEKYLL: I suppose I do recall that being included. Is there some problem you're having at the office?

    JEKYLL takes a drink.

UTTERSON: I've learned of this Edward Hyde to whom you have imparted all of your possessions.

    JEKYLL chokes.

JEKYLL: Is that so?

UTTERSON: I've come to counsel you on this matter.

JEKYLL [*forcefully*]: There are no words that can bring this matter to a close, Gabriel.

JEKYLL stands and straightens his posture. He becomes calm again.

JEKYLL: The moment I choose, I can be rid of Hyde. He is of great interest to me and I want him to be well taken care of for the time being.

UTTERSON: I think you're making a mistake. We can figure out how to get out of this. Is he somehow involved with your experiments?

JEKYLL [*seriously*]: As I said, Mr. Utterson, I can be rid of him the moment I choose. Hyde is proving to be quite important to my work at the time being. Promise me that you'll carry out my last will and testament should it become necessary.

UTTERSON [*frustrated*]: Of course I will, Henry.

JEKYLL [*more spirited*]: Wonderful! Now, I must be getting to sleep. You can find your way out, right, Gabriel?

UTTERSON stands and gets his things. He exits. JEKYLL remains. End scene.

SCENE SIX

Scene: *HYDE's apartment. It is completely withered and tattered. There are things all over. There is a bed that looks as if it has never been cleaned.*

UTTERSON [*off stage*]: This is the place!

UTTERSON enters with two POLICEMEN. Both of them begin turning and searching the apartment.

POLICEMAN 2: Edward Hyde! [*pause*] It looks like he's not here.

UTTERSON: I just can't believe it.

POLICEMAN 1: You saw Sir Carew lying there with your own eyes, Mr. Utterson.

UTTERSON: Who would ever want to kill Danvers? He was well-respected and a gentleman.

POLICEMAN 1: According to the woman who witnessed it, he didn't do anything to provoke Hyde. They exchanged a few words, and then Hyde attacked.

UTTERSON [*sits in a chair, looking pitiful*]: I just can't believe Danvers is gone.

POLICEMAN 1: Believe it. You saw him on the path. It's just lucky for us that Sir Carew had your card in his pocket or we might never have found Hyde's place.

UTTERSON: He was a client of mine. You know he's a member of Parliament.

POLICEMAN 2 [*turns to UTTERSON*]: *Was* a member of Parliament.

POLICEMAN 1: It isn't like anyone ever saw him anyway. These officials always disappear when you need them.

UTTERSON [*jumping to stand*]: Disappear!

POLICEMAN 1: Exactly.

UTTERSON: I've got to get to Jekyll!

UTTERSON runs off stage. POLICEMEN continue to search for clues. End scene.

SCENE SEVEN

Scene: *JEKYLL's house. JEKYLL is sitting at his dining table. He looks deathly ill. UTTERSON runs in from off stage.*

UTTERSON [*relieved*]: Henry! I'm glad to see you. Are you all right?

JEKYLL: I'm fine. Just a little under the weather. You seem quite stirred, though.

UTTERSON: Hyde has murdered Sir Danvers Carew! [*JEKYLL squirms in shock*] You have to help the police catch him, or they'll be coming for you when they discover how closely you've worked with him.

JEKYLL [*winded*]: I've ended any relationship I've had with him. The police shall never find him.

UTTERSON: How can you be so sure?

JEKYLL: Take a look at this letter.

JEKYLL picks up a letter from the table and holds it up to UTTERSON. He takes the letter.

HYDE [*off stage*]: Dear Henry: I have committed a terrible act. I have found a way to escape town safely. Do not worry about me. I'm not worthy of your generosity any longer. Signed, Edward Hyde.

UTTERSON looks up from the letter at JEKYLL.

JEKYLL: It was delivered today. I fear that if the police obtain this letter, my reputation will be marred.

UTTERSON: I've had a suspicious feeling about Hyde for quite some time. Did Hyde dictate your will and force you to sign over your assets to him?

JEKYLL nods in the affirmative.

UTTERSON: I think he meant to kill you.

JEKYLL: I say, he may nearly have taken over my life, but I need not worry about him anymore. It's the last anyone will see of him.

UTTERSON: I'll take the letter and keep it. I am your lawyer and confidant, after all.

JEKYLL: Thank you, my friend.

JEKYLL lays his head on the table. MR. POOLE enters from inside the house and walks to the door where UTTERSON is about to walk out.

UTTERSON [*addressing MR. POOLE*]: Can you describe who dropped off this letter today?

MR. POOLE [*confused*]: No one has delivered any such letters. In fact, there wasn't any mail today at all.

MR. POOLE passes by into another room, leaving UTTERSON alone.

UTTERSON [*perplexed*]: Why would Henry lie?

He exits. Fade to black. End scene.

END ACT I

ACT II

SCENE ONE

Scene: *JEKYLL'S townhouse. He is having a party. UTTERSON, LANYON, and ENFIELD are in attendance. JEKYLL is energetic and happy.*

UTTERSON: I'm glad to see you're back on your feet, Henry.

JEKYLL: It was quite an illness, but I'm much better now.

LANYON: I'm glad you've given up those silly experiments, if I may say so.

JEKYLL: It isn't that I've given up, Dr. Lanyon. I have chosen to stop.

LANYON: I suppose there is a difference.

JEKYLL: Certainly. The work was quite a wear on me.

UTTERSON: I can't agree more. That's all in the past now.

LANYON: I should hope so. It was all a waste of time.

JEKYLL [*angry*]: A waste of time?

UTTERSON: Surely he didn't mean that, Henry. Right, Lanyon?

JEKYLL: What would you know about it, doctor?

LANYON: I do know that you have nothing to show for it.

JEKYLL: Nothing to show? I'll show you something that will make your skin crawl!

UTTERSON [*stepping in between JEKYLL and LANYON*]: I think it's about time everyone gets going.

JEKYLL: That sounds like a wonderful idea to me. Mr. Poole? I'll be in my laboratory. Make sure everyone sees their way out.

JEKYLL exits into the house as MR. POOLE enters. All begin to head to the door as the lights turn to black. End scene.

SCENE TWO

Scene: *The prosperous London street with the neglected cellar entrance. Enter UTTERSON and ENFIELD.*

ENFIELD: I still say you should let sleeping dogs lie.

UTTERSON: I just want to take a look. No one has heard from Jekyll in some time.

ENFIELD: What happened to minding one's own business?

UTTERSON [*peeks inside the window of the cellar*]: Just a look. Henry! Are you in there?

ENFIELD: A waste of a nice stroll on this fine afternoon, I say.

UTTERSON [*calling out loudly*]: Dr. Jekyll!

JEKYLL [*from behind the cellar door, grumbling*]: Who's there? What do you want?

UTTERSON [*relieved*]: Henry! It's been a while, old chap. It's Gabriel Utterson. How are you?

JEKYLL: I'm fine. I'm at work in my laboratory. Please, leave me.

UTTERSON: Are you sure you're all right? You don't quite sound like yourself.

ENFIELD: The man said to leave him alone. We should go.

UTTERSON [*ignoring ENFIELD*]: You should get outside more. It'll do you some good, friend.

JEKYLL: I wish I were able, but I'm just too busy.

JEKYLL lets out a growl that startles UTTERSON away from the window.

ENFIELD: I told you we should leave, cousin!

UTTERSON: As we shall, but I will get to the bottom of this once and for all.

ENFIELD AND UTTERSON quickly exit. End scene.

SCENE THREE

Scene: *LANYON's house. It is well decorated and it is clear that LANYON is wealthy. LANYON is in his bed, under the covers. He is ill.*

UTTERSON enters.

UTTERSON: Dr. Lanyon?

LANYON [*sickly*]: Come in, Mr. Utterson.

UTTERSON: I've come to answer your call. I can see you are not well. I will come back another time.

LANYON: It is quite all right. I fear I shall not recover, and that is why I needed to see you.

UTTERSON: What is the matter? You were quite well not so long ago.

LANYON: I cannot say what has happened. I've experienced great trauma that is inexplicable. It has shaken me to the core. My entire structure and understanding of science is compromised.

UTTERSON [*confused*]: I don't understand. You've *experienced* something?

LANYON: I've written everything in this letter. [*hands to UTTERSON*] It is my wish that you do not read it until Dr. Jekyll has died or disappeared.

UTTERSON: Disappeared? Why would Jekyll disappear? Has he started working on his experiments with Hyde again?

LANYON [*curt*]: I will never speak of Dr. Jekyll again! Heed my word and do not read this letter until he has passed or disappeared.

UTTERSON: Of course, my friend. As your lawyer, I will maintain confidence.

LANYON: Promise me as my friend. You will not read the letter.

UTTERSON [*holding LANYON's hand*]: I promise.

LANYON: Very well, then. Leave me at peace.

UTTERSON: Farewell.

UTTERSON exits. End scene.

SCENE FOUR

Scene: *UTTERSON's house. UTTERSON sits at his desk. MR. POOLE knocks at the door. UTTERSON gets up to answer.*

UTTERSON: Welcome, Mr. Poole.

MR. POOLE: Thank you, Mr. Utterson. I've come to see you about the doctor.

UTTERSON: Has something happened to Henry?

MR. POOLE: He's been locked in his laboratory.

UTTERSON: Why would he lock himself in the laboratory?

MR. POOLE: I check on him, but he only grumbles and growls demands. He does not let me inside the laboratory, nor does he ever come out.

UTTERSON: That's ridiculous.

MR. POOLE: I think something is wrong. It doesn't sound like the doctor. I think there is some foul play afoot.

UTTERSON: Is it Mr. Hyde? Has he returned?

MR. POOLE: I'm not sure. The doctor has made some odd requests, but I haven't heard or seen anything that would indicate that it is Mr. Hyde. No one has come in or out of the house.

UTTERSON: Perhaps he is just having another bout with his illness.

MR. POOLE: I beg you, Mr. Utterson. Please come to the house for yourself and see.

UTTERSON: I don't need to be getting into Henry's personal business without his asking.

MR. POOLE [*more urgently*]: I fear that something has happened to the doctor and I need you to see for yourself. He doesn't sound like the same man. He is always asking for chemicals, to make his medicine.

UTTERSON: Medicine? Perhaps he is more ill than I thought. What medicine?

MR. POOLE: That I cannot say. He asks for chemicals. I can barely recite their names. I think he is making his own elixirs. But he doesn't seem to be getting any better. In fact, it seems he is only getting worse.

UTTERSON: You've convinced me that I should check on him. Surely there is an explanation, and as his friend, I am able to ask him. Let us go.

UTTERSON and MR. POOLE exit together. End scene.

SCENE FIVE

Scene: *JEKYLL's townhouse. MR. POOLE bursts through the door, while UTTERSON comes in more slowly and less energetically.*

UTTERSON: I don't see why you are so excited.

MR. POOLE: I have to admit that I've withheld my motives.

UTTERSON: I don't understand.

MR. POOLE: As the doctor's butler, I cannot enter the laboratory. I need you to break down the door.

UTTERSON: You are insane! Call for Henry. Let him know I am here and he will come out.

MR. POOLE [*turns away from UTTERSON*]: Dr. Jekyll? Mr. Utterson is here to see you.

JEKYLL [*gargling, off stage*]: Go away! I am not taking visitors!

UTTERSON is disgusted by the sound of JEKYLL's voice.

MR. POOLE [*to UTTERSON*]: Can you hear?

UTTERSON: There has to be an explanation.

MR. POOLE: Something is wrong. We need to get in there. I fear that it is not the doctor. He won't let us see him. I believe someone is imitating him.

UTTERSON: Perhaps the doctor has developed a disease that has caused him to have a physical disfiguration.

MR. POOLE: There is only one way to find out. You need to break down the door.

UTTERSON: Have some respect for your master! He requires privacy. Obviously he is sick, which is why he needs the chemicals. He does not want to be bothered during his recovery.

MR. POOLE [*shouting*]: You are wrong! Something far worse is going on and the doctor may need our help!

UTTERSON: Mr. Poole! I thought you knew your place.

MR. POOLE: I could say the same of you, Mr. Utterson. Your friend is in need and you refuse to help him.

UTTERSON [*excited*]: All right! I'll break down the door.

> *UTTERSON and MR. POOLE head off stage. Loud banging is heard until the door breaks down. JEKYLL lets out a loud yell and both UTTERSON and MR. POOLE run back on stage in fright. JEKYLL slowly enters and stands behind the dining table. He is dressed in his lab coat, tired and hunched over. He looks extremely ill.*

JEKYLL: I said to leave me alone!

UTTERSON: What has happened to you, Henry? Is this the result of your experiments?

JEKYLL: Yes, and I fear I've not long to explain.

> *MR. POOLE backs away toward the front door. UTTERSON moves a bit closer to JEKYLL.*

JEKYLL: All my life, I have had evil thoughts. Thoughts of meanness, cruelty…

UTTERSON: Naturally, Jekyll, we all have unsavory thoughts at times.

JEKYLL: Nonetheless, I wanted to remove this evil. I began experimentation. After many trials, I had found a way to isolate the parts of my personality that were evil.

UTTERSON: That is ridiculous. You must have created a potion that made you delirious. That would explain your sickness.

JEKYLL: It does not explain anything! I thought that I might create an elixir that would eliminate the evil inside me, but something else happened instead. I brought it to the forefront in the form of another person.

UTTERSON [*showing disbelief*]: You mean to tell me you created another person?

JEKYLL: No! He was inside me all along. My elixir didn't eliminate him. I transformed into him. He calls himself Edward Hyde.

> *UTTERSON and MR. POOLE gasp.*

UTTERSON: Surely, you are mistaken. I've met Mr. Hyde. He is smaller, and a nasty, greedy man. You aren't any of those things, my friend.

JEKYLL: But I am. I am all of those things, but they have been hidden inside me. Mr. Hyde is a physical manifestation of the evil inside me.

UTTERSON: This is quite preposterous. You are so delusional from your failed elixirs that you actually believe that you are a murderer who looks and sounds nothing like you.

MR. POOLE: Sir, if I may, please let me call for you a doctor.

JEKYLL [*angrily*]: There isn't a doctor in the world who can help me.

UTTERSON: Jekyll, if you are so certain of this, how is it possible that he has just disappeared after all this time?

JEKYLL: I couldn't control the time I spent as Hyde. I feared I would disappear completely and Hyde would take over permanently.

UTTERSON: Is that why you changed your will?

JEKYLL: Precisely, but after Carew's death, I knew I had to control him. I took enough antidotes that I thought it would eliminate any of the effects of the first elixir. It was working for a while.

UTTERSON: And then?

JEKYLL: I began to transform involuntarily. I was no longer intentionally turning into Hyde. I began changing randomly, against my own will.

UTTERSON: This is all still quite ridiculous. I don't see any reason to believe this isn't all in your head and that you are just a sick man.

JEKYLL: Dr. Lanyon has seen the transformation.

UTTERSON: Now you're just making things up. Dr. Lanyon is a sick man who cannot even leave his own bed. How could he have seen you transform if you haven't even left your laboratory?

JEKYLL: After my first involuntary transformation, I didn't have enough of the antidote to transform back. I had Mr. Poole get into contact with Dr. Lanyon for me so that he might collect the materials.

MR. POOLE [*scared to speak*]: That's right. You were asking for Dr. Lanyon to collect some medicines for you that I would not be able to buy.

JEKYLL: Exactly. He was collecting the chemicals needed for the antidote. Hyde took the elixir right in front of him and transformed back into me right before his eyes. He made Lanyon watch it happen, to punish him for doubting our experiments. That is why Lanyon is bed-ridden.

UTTERSON: Your story is stretching. Dr. Lanyon *did* say he never wanted to speak to you again, but perhaps it is only because you involved him with Hyde!

JEKYLL [*shouting*]: I *am* Hyde, and Hyde is me!

JEKYLL doubles over behind the dining room table, groaning out of sight. UTTERSON quickly backs away toward MR. POOLE in fright. The groaning turns into the growling of MR. HYDE. MR. HYDE pops up from behind the table in the same lab coat and clothes JEKYLL was wearing. MR. POOLE shrieks and runs out the door.

MR. POOLE [*off stage*]: Police! Police!

UTTERSON: You fiend!

MR. HYDE [*snickering*]: I'm just a part of your good pal, Dr. Jekyll! And now he'll be gone for good! I'll never take that antidote again!

UTTERSON: You'll never get away with this, Hyde!

MR. HYDE: Who will ever believe you? They'll call you the same crackpot names you were just calling your dear friend, Dr. Jekyll!

UTTERSON: The police are coming to get you now. You've been caught! They know who you are, you murderer!

MR. HYDE runs through the house toward the laboratory off stage. MR. POOLE and POLICEMEN enter quickly.

POLICEMAN 1: Where is he?

UTTERSON [*pointing*]: That way, to the laboratory!

POLICEMAN 1 runs off stage to the laboratory. POLICEMAN 2 remains with MR. POOLE and UTTERSON. UTTERSON, shocked, sits in a dining room chair.

POLICEMAN 2: You say it was Edward Hyde?

MR. POOLE: Yes, it was him. I'm certain.

POLICEMAN 1 [*off stage*]: He's run out the cellar door! I'm going after him!

MR. POOLE: Do you think he'll catch him?

POLICEMAN 2: He's a fast fellow, so he's got a good chance.

MR. POOLE: What's going to happen to Hyde?

POLICEMAN 2: I'll leave that to the judicial system. Where's the doctor? [*silence*] Is the doctor here?

UTTERSON [*interrupting, bluntly*]: The doctor is gone.

POLICEMAN 2: Where is he?

UTTERSON: He's... disappeared.

Fade to black. End play.

Mega Mountaintown: Come for a Visit!

written by Vincent J. Scotto
illustrated by David Rushbrook

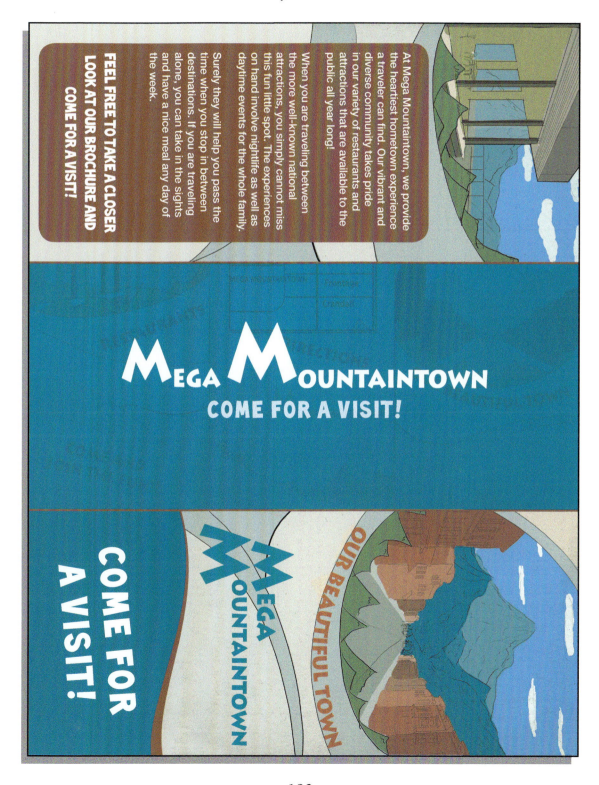

RESTAURANTS

GINO'S PIZZA AND DELI

Rating: 4 out of 5 stars
Category: Italian food
Price Range: $$
Dress: Casual

Have you ever tasted perfection? You haven't until you've eaten at Gino's. At Gino's Pizza and Deli, you will find artful masterpieces in the forms of pizzas, sandwiches, and a Mega Mountaintown favorite, Gino's Rolli Cannoli. Whether you're just stopping by to pick up a pizza or staying in for a full Italian feast, you will immediately become enthralled with the atmosphere the moment you step inside. Take a seat and watch your masterpiece unfold before your eyes. This is one you won't want to miss. The aroma coming from the rooftop vents alone is worth the trip!

MAIN STREET MARBLE ROOM

Rating: 5 out of 5 stars
Category: Steak house
Price Range: $$$$
Dress: Business casual (no hats)

If you like a juicy steak with fresh greens and a side of homegrown taters, look no farther! The Main Street Marble Room is a pillar of perfection that cannot be beat. Every table and counter is made with the finest marble, finished right here in Mega Mountaintown. If you plan on taking a break from traveling, the Marble Room offers sleeping quarters above the restaurant. At the Marble Room, our locals from Mega Mountaintown will treat you like a star. Don't just take our word for it; take it in with your own eyes by coming for a visit!

ATTRACTIONS

FRIDAY FEST IN DOWNTOWN MEGA MOUNTAINTOWN

Rating: 4 out of 5 stars
Category: Entertainment
Price Range: $
Dress: Casual

Entry is free to Mega Mountaintown's Friday Fest in downtown Mega Mountaintown! From food trucks of all kinds to various crafts, you can find anything you're looking for and more. With only a few dollars, you can spend the day alone or with the whole family. There are games for adults to win prizes while children can play in the bounce houses for hours. In the evening, we finish the night off on Mega Mountaintown Lake with a firework show. If you're passing through Mega Mountaintown for the night or spending the whole weekend, you won't want to miss this unique event!

MEGA MOUNTAIN

Rating: 5 out of 5 stars
Category: Natural preserves
Price Range: $$
Dress: Outdoor

When you see Mega Mountain from the highway, you'll know you need to take a moment to enjoy its splendor. For a simple entry fee that helps us protect and preserve the natural land, you will be granted access to the natural trails made from animal tracks and runoff. Between the wind rustling through the trees, the chirps from the birds, and the once-in-a-lifetime breathtaking views from the mountainside, a visit to Mega Mountain cannot be missed. But don't just take our word for it—come for a visit!

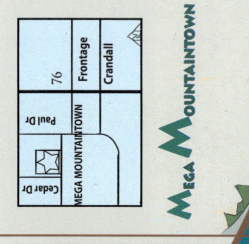

DIRECTIONS

RIGHT OFF THE EXPRESSWAY!

Coming Northbound

Take exit 76 toward Mega Mountaintown and turn left at the signal. Follow the road about a half-mile and we'll see you soon.

Coming Southbound

Take exit 76 toward Mega Mountaintown and turn right at the signal. Follow the road about a half-mile and we'll see you soon.

Meeting at a Bus Stop

written by Katie Catanzarite

"Oh, pardon me, but do you know what time the bus comes 'round?"

I turned as a cool, British voice blew into my ear. I faced a girl with wavy blonde hair. She had big blue eyes and front teeth that were separated by a substantial gap.

"The next stop is in twenty minutes—at two o'clock on the dot."

Relief flooded her face, and she smiled, flashing that endearing gap.

"Thank you so much." She stuck her hand out to me. "I'm called Lily. Pleasure to meet you." She sounded like she had introduced herself as *cold-Lily*, and I started having *Harry Potter* flashbacks because of how she said *pleasure* like *pleashah*.

I finally jolted out of my thoughts and shook her outstretched hand.

"You, too. My name's Jake."

"Hullo, Jake," she said again, and we both sat down on the bench in front of the bus stop.

"So, uh, are you from, um…"

"Liverpool, England. I'm studying abroad for the summer, but I major in English Literature at Uni."

"*You-nee*?" I asked, still thinking about how she said *lit-ra-chure*.

"Oh, I mean university. What do you call it?"

"Just college, mostly." I chuckled awkwardly, but she didn't seem to mind.

"I suppose 'college' works as well as anything."

"I do like 'Uni' though. Maybe I'll start calling BU 'Uni.'"

This time, Lily laughed, but then her eyes popped wide, and she asked, "Do you attend Boston University?"

"Yeah, I'm a junior. Chemical engineering."

"Oh, brilliant, that's where I'm taking classes for the summer."

"No kidding. I'll be up there for football practice soon."

"Maybe you could give me a proper tour around campus."

"Sure; I pretty much know the place like the back of my hand. Do you live in the dorms?"

"I do. My flat's on the fourth floor, and there's no lift, so I'll get my workout in every day."

I felt like I could listen to Lily talk for hours. I had never actually spoken to someone with a British accent in person before. I could probably listen to her read the phone book and never get bored.

"Which one? I've lived in Greenlee and Buckner."

"Yes, they've put me in Buckner. Despite the lack of lift, it's actually quite nice."

"Yeah, Buckner's pretty sweet—especially the air conditioning. Trust me, you don't want any part of Greenlee's rooms in the summer. They're like a sauna."

"I would take it. It doesn't rain here nearly as much as it does back home."

"So, what do you want to do with your English degree?"

"Oh, I would love to work in publishing. I've always loved books and reading; one of my classes is on Chaucer and I can't wait—I'm sorry, this must be boring for you."

"No, no, I'm into math, so I don't know much about the other side."

"Is that why you decided to study chemical engineering?"

"Kind of; I mean, I've always liked math, but my dad's an engineer, so it just kind of ran in the family."

"That's really excellent. My parents are both lawyers. They wanted me to study political science, but I found it too dull, I'm afraid. They're still getting over their disappointment."

Just then, the bus rumbled up the street, and the driver pushed open the door. Lily and I climbed onto the bus and settled down into the first row. It was practically empty inside, so Lily and I were able to continue the conversation, but the only thing I could come up with was, "Publishing sounds much more interesting." I was cringing on the inside, but Lily just smiled and scooted closer to me as more people got onto the bus.

"Well, I think chemical engineering sounds interesting, too. It's wonderful that you want to follow in your father's footsteps."

"Thanks. Maybe—um—maybe I could tell you more about it sometime. And you could tell me more about Chaucer…and Liverpool."

"I'd like that very much. When are you free? We could get a coffee together next week?"

"I can do Friday afternoons. Does that work for you?"

"That's right when my Chaucer class is dismissed; it's perfect!"

"Cool; so can I give you my number? I can text you the details. We could meet in the library."

"The library sounds great!"

I loved how she pronounced it *libe-ry*.

Wicked Storm

written by Bryon Gill

From the moment that Noah's plane touched down on the tarmac at Logan until they reached their townhouse in Cambridge, Richard couldn't contain his excitement. He hadn't seen his cousin since they were five years old. Richard's family had gone down to visit Noah's family in Florida for Christmas, but with the palm trees, humid heat, and beautiful sandy beaches, Noah had had a little trouble getting into the spirit. Now, the cousins were nine, and Richard was determined to show Noah what a real white Christmas was like.

"Have you ever been on the silver line?" Richard asked breathlessly. "We're gonna take that to South Station before we get on the red line."

"Is that like a highway or something?" Noah asked.

"No, it's the T," Richard explained. "You know, like a subway, except it goes above ground, too. Oh, and the silver line has a bus. You'll see; it's wicked cool."

The boys and Richard's parents made their way to the baggage claim area, where they found Noah's oversized Samsonite, first out of the chute. "You gonna put on your parka now?" Richard asked Noah.

"My *pah-ka*?" Noah asked. "What's a *pah-ka*?"

"You know," Richard replied, "your coat. It's cold out there."

"Oh! I'm wearing it," Noah said, indicating his Jaguars hoodie.

Richard looked to his father, who furrowed his brow with concern but said nothing. "That's all you got? Oh, man," Richard said. "You can borrow my Patriots flannel when we get home. You seriously didn't bring a parka?"

Noah shook his head. They reached the exit, and a frigid blast of air greeted them immediately. Richard's parents didn't seem to notice that the children had to fight to remain standing in the wind tunnel near the entrance. Noah's teeth set to chattering almost immediately.

"Cold enough for ya?" Richard asked, elbowing his cousin in the ribs. Noah wrapped his arms around himself protectively.

"I hope we don't have to wait long," Noah said. "The bus into Jacksonville always takes forever."

"Don't worry," Richard said. "The bus usually comes every couple hours or so. It won't be long." Noah's eyes went wide. "I'm just joshin', coz; it's every five minutes. Welcome to the big city."

When the snow began to fall, Richard's father noticed Noah shivering and took his coat off, draping it around the skinny boy; it made Noah look like a priest with long, flowing black robes that covered his feet and trailed behind him. If Richard's father noticed the cold, he didn't let it show. Noah continued to shiver until the bus arrived a few moments later.

The bus took them into a long tunnel. "This is the Big Dig," Richard said. "It took thirty years to dig a tunnel under the city. Dad says they could have done it in five, but, you know, *politics*." Richard gave Noah the same knowing wink that he'd seen his father give when he said that.

"Why would they build a tunnel under the city?" Noah asked. "Can't they just build a new road?"

"Oh, there's roads up there, too," Richard said. "They're too crowded, so we had to build roads under the roads."

"Oh," Noah said.

The four of them arrived at the T station and debussed. Once they had all swiped their tickets and entered the turnstiles, Richard noticed that their train was waiting; he began to run, heedless of whether Noah or his parents were following.

Noah bobbed and weaved through the crowd and caught up to Richard. The boys had beaten the train to the platform and now felt a bit foolish, flushed, and out of breath while the train crawled toward them. "So, what are we going to do tonight?" Noah asked.

"I think we're going to play a couple strings of candlepin," Richard said, "if we ever get out of this station." The train stopped, but the doors opened on the departing side first.

"What's candlepin?" Noah asked.

"You know, bowling, but without those giant balls," Richard said. "Just little ones that fit in your hands."

"Oh, like Skee-Ball?"

"No, there's no pins in Skee-Ball," Richard said. "This is just bowling with little balls and little pins."

"Oh, is it just for kids?" Noah asked. Richard shook his head, and as the doors opened, they entered and elected to remain standing, each holding on to a metal pole. "So, why is everything little, then?"

Richard shrugged. "I don't know; it just is. It's fun, you'll see."

A voice came over the speaker, announcing that this was a "Bwaintwee twain, Bwaintwee twain," which sent Noah and then Richard into a fit of hysterical laughter.

"Boston is weird," Noah said. "That guy sounds like Elmer Fudd."

"Yeah, it's just the way people talk around here," Richard agreed, "like, 'ya can't pahk your cah in Hahvahd Yahd.' It's not as thick as your accent, though."

Noah was taken aback. "My accent?"

"Yeah; when you say 'my,' it sounds like 'mah' or something."

Noah practiced saying it the way Richard said it. "'Mai.' 'Mahy.' 'May.'"

Richard shook his head. The announcer called out "Quincy," which was their stop, and they got off the train together.

"Did your dad park at the station, then?" Noah asked Richard.

"No, we don't have a car, remember?"

"I thought you were joking," Noah said. "You had one when you came to visit us—I remember."

"That was a rental," Richard replied. "We use Zipcars sometimes when we need to go somewhere, but mostly, if we can't take the T, we just don't need to go that bad."

"Is it a long walk to your house?"

"Our apartment is about a half-mile away, so maybe ten minutes?" Richard estimated. "We just walk up the hill there, bang a left and then a right, and we're home."

Noah looked apprehensively at the snow swirling in the wind. "I think I'd rather have gators than snow."

"Do you really have alligators where you live?"

Noah nearly burst with pride. "Yep—there was a big one in our back yard last spring. Mom had to call Animal Control, and I wasn't allowed outside for a month."

"Dang," Richard said. "Did it try to eat you?"

Noah nodded. "I looked it in the eye, and it looked at me like it was gonna make me its lunch," he said. "It started coming after me, but I'm wicked fast, so I got away."

Richard laughed, and they walked together into the winter air.

How to Build a House of Plastic Interlocking Bricks

written by Vincent J. Scotto

1. **Find a base.** Start with a plastic interlocking brick table or small platform. The size of the table or platform will depend on the size of the house to be built. Two-story houses can be built using multiple platforms.

2. **Plan the house.** Place the foundation bricks first and then lay initial bricks for interior walls. Make sure all rooms are included (kitchen, living room, bathroom, etc.). If a two-story house is being built, make sure there is room for stairs.

3. **Build the outside walls.** Lay the plastic interlocking bricks one row at a time, staggering the bricks in a diagonal pattern. Overlapping the bricks this way will make the house sturdy. Make sure to leave space for windows and doors.

4. **Build the interior walls.** Lay the brick in the same fashion as the outer walls.

5. **Make furniture.** Furniture can be made with basic plastic interlocking brick parts, but specialty parts can be used if available. Some typical furniture pieces include toilets, beds, couches, and tables with chairs.

6. **Add decorations (if desired).** Floor tiles can be made using flat pieces. Trees or fences can be added outside the house. The possibilities are only limited by the builder's imagination.

7. **Add the roof.** This should be the last step, as it will close the house. Designs can be made by overlapping pieces to form a triangular pyramid. The roof can be locked in or simply placed on top of the house for easier access.

Technical Writing Examples

written by Summer York
illustrated by Kimberly Stannard

Assembling the Modern Home Bookcase

You will need a flat head screwdriver and a hammer.

1 Remove all of the provided pieces from the packaging. There should be eight pieces labeled A through H.

2 Open the provided plastic bag of eight screws, eight nails, and twelve pegs.

3 Place the base labeled A face up on the floor and tilt it on its back side so the bottom is toward you and the top is facing away from you.

4 Align the holes on the left side of the base with the holes on the bottom of the side piece labeled B.

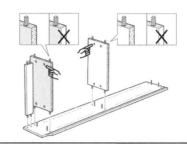

5 Attach the pieces with a screw in each hole, using the screwdriver to tighten the screws.

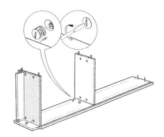

6 Attach the other side piece labeled C to the right side of the base and attach it in the same manner.

7 Place the top piece labeled D between the side pieces at the top and align the holes.

8 Attach the pieces with a screw in each hole, using the screwdriver to tighten the screws.

9 Turn the unit over so the back side is up.

page 1

10 Place the back cover piece labeled E over the unit with the right side facing down.

11 Align the back piece with the sides of the unit.

12 Attach the back piece to the unit using the hammer to lightly tap in the nails. Evenly distribute the eight nails around the back piece.

13 Stand the unit right side up.

14 Insert four pegs into the holes in the side pieces at the desired height of each shelf. Be sure that all four pegs are even at each height.

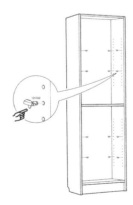

15 Pound in the pegs lightly with the hammer to secure them.

16 Insert each shelf piece (labeled F, G, and H) just above the pegs and let it rest on the pegs.

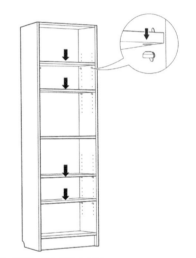

17 Dust the unit with a cloth or duster to remove any dust created during assembly.

page 2

LAB PROCEDURE

Testing Sugar Content in Foods

The following is a lab procedure by a team of scientists at a health food manufacturing company. The scientists needed to measure how much sugar the company's products contain in order to earn the endorsement of the American Diabetes Association.

First, the sugar content of the company's ten foods was measured. Each of ten test tubes was filled with 40 drops of distilled water. A small sample from each food was ground with a mortar and pestle. One gram of each sample was added to a test tube labeled with the name of the food. Ten drops of the chemical reagent Benedict's solution was added to each test tube. The test tubes were then heated in a hot water bath of 50°C for five minutes. Any color changes in the test liquids were recorded. This test was repeated three times to ensure accurate results.

Second, the sugar content of each of the company's five diet sodas was measured. Each drink was left uncovered to degas at room temperature for 48 hours before the test. A 300 mL sample of each drink was poured into a graduated cylinder. A Brix hydrometer was floated in each sample liquid for two minutes. After the allotted time, a reading was taken and recorded from each Brix hydrometer. The following equation was then used to determine the sugar content of an entire 22-oz. (651 mL) bottle of each drink: (Brix reading in grams)/100 mL = X g/651 mL. Solving for X gave the sugar content of each bottle. The test was repeated three times to ensure accurate results.

Works Cited

"Chemistry Experiments." *Science Company*, 2014, www.sciencecompany.com/Food-Chemistry-Experiments-W151.aspx. Accessed 11 Feb. 2014.

Patient Diagnosis:
Strep Throat

Your doctor has diagnosed you with strep throat. Strep throat is a bacterial infection in the throat and tonsils. It begins as a sore throat and becomes worse over a few days. Strep throat can cause any of the following symptoms:

- severe sore throat
- swollen tonsils
- fever
- white spots on the back of the throat
- difficulty or pain when swallowing
- headache
- rash
- nausea

To diagnose strep throat, your doctor may have performed a rapid strep test. In a rapid strep test, the throat is swabbed to collect bacteria. The bacteria are tested for strep in-office, and results are ready in about ten minutes. However, a rapid strep test is not always accurate. Your doctor may have performed further tests, including a throat culture. This type of test takes longer to obtain results.

Unlike a common sore throat, which is caused by a virus, strep throat is caused by streptococcal bacteria. Therefore, strep throat needs to be treated with antibiotics. Antibiotics are medicines that destroy bacteria and prevent them from spreading to other areas of the body. Your doctor may have prescribed penicillin, amoxicillin, or a similar antibiotic. Once you begin taking an antibiotic, you should begin to feel better in twenty-four hours. Additionally, drink ample fluids and get plenty of rest. Contact your doctor or pharmacist with any questions regarding your medication.

Strep throat is contagious. Avoid unnecessary contact with others while the bacteria are contagious. Strep throat is usually not contagious after the first twenty-four hours of treatment with an antibiotic. Wash your hands often to stop the spread of bacteria. Contact your doctor if your condition does not improve or symptoms get worse.

The Great Aluminum Knight

written by Steve Karscig
illustrated by Dave Rushbrook

Cast

DOUGRAY THE BRAVE	A boy looking for adventure through fantasy playtime
MARTIN THE TORMENTOR	A child with a mean streak
JOSIE THE KEEN	A smart girl
SYLVESTER THE SINISTER	Martin's friend; a follower
PHOEBE THE FEEBLE	A shy girl
HAWK	An ordinary predatory bird from the raptor family

Setting

A neighborhood playground with a swing set, merry-go-round, surrounding trees, and other playful structures.

Scene One

Scene: *A lively public playground filled with children, parents, and well-kept playground equipment. A four-person swing set stands at center stage, with a large tree in the background.*

Four children are swinging on the swing set: MARTIN, SYLVESTER, JOSIE, and PHOEBE. Enter DOUGRAY. He walks to the side of the swing set and slides off his backpack. He kneels down and opens the backpack. He pulls out a box of aluminum foil and a piece of old broken fence lattice.

MARTIN [*swinging on swing*]: Dou-gray…Douggie…Dooger…Hey, Dummy! [*laughing forcibly*] What are you doing in my playground?

DOUGRAY [*looking over from one knee*]: I am preparing to play something epic, if you must know.

SYLVESTER [*taunting*]: Oh, did you hear that? Somethin' epic.

DOUGRAY [*still kneeling*]: Do you even know what "epic" means?

MARTIN: 'Course we do. Whaddaya think we are, some kinda molasses-brained morons?

JOSIE [*swinging on swing*]: Ugh…. "Epic" means something that is part poetry-like and part adventure-like. Princesses and castles, heroic deeds and lost loves, swords and sorcery—a chosen warrior against the world they live in. It's something fantastical.

DOUGRAY: Yeah, roughly like that.

JOSIE: Dougie, I don't understand why you would do something like that in front of these two fools. You know they are just going to make fun of you.

DOUGRAY: Even a hero of experience must tolerate fools.

DOUGRAY begins wrapping the piece of old lattice with some aluminum foil.

MARTIN: What experience do you have? We're all in the same class. There is nothing special about you. You're a daydreamer. That's why Miss Thompson makes fun of you.

PHOEBE [*chewing on her hair, speaking meekly*]: Miss Thompson makes fun of everybody. She's not very nice.

SYLVESTER [*to DOUGRAY*]: What are you makin', anyway?

DOUGRAY: I am creating my own sword like Arthur's Excalibur, Roland's Durandal, and Beowulf's Naegling.

MARTIN: W-what?

JOSIE: They're famous sword names from legends. Don't you know that?

DOUGRAY holds up his wooden sword made from the broken lattice, which is now covered in aluminum foil. The light shines on it, allowing the foil to sparkle. The children on the swings giggle.

DOUGRAY: Behold! I give you the sword, the greatest of all warrior weaponry!

MARTIN: Man, I've thrown away better toys than that!

Enter the HAWK, a wild animal not particularly concerned with the children. The HAWK circles and then perches on a low-hanging tree branch in the playground.

SYLVESTER [*jumping off the swing*]: Whoa, would ya look at that! It's an eagle.

JOSIE: It's a hawk. Eagles are bigger. Sheesh.

MARTIN [*leaping from his swing*]: I'll bet I can knock it down with a rock.

SYLVESTER: Do it!

JOSIE: No! Leave it alone. It's a keystone species. It is important to the environment.

MARTIN: Shut it! I got this.

MARTIN picks up three small rocks from the ground. In the same moment, though, the HAWK flies off.

SYLVESTER: Aw, man!

MARTIN watches off-stage closely.

MARTIN: No, it's all right. He just went to that other tree by the merry-go-round. Let's go, nice and quiet.

PHOEBE: Please don't hurt the bird.

Scene Two

Scene: *MARTIN and SYLVESTER have moved around the tree to the area of the park where the merry-go-round is posted. All of the other children, except for DOUGRAY, have followed him. JOSIE and PHOEBE sit on the still merry-go-round. The HAWK curiously watches the children's movements.*

MARTIN: I need to get a clear shot. I don't want to miss this.

DOUGRAY enters. He is now dressed in epic aluminum armor, with sword in hand, looking like a knight. He steps up behind MARTIN and reaches his free hand out.

DOUGRAY: Stop!

MARTIN: What?

MARTIN turns to face DOUGRAY and laughs hysterically.

SYLVESTER [*pushing DOUGRAY*]: Shut up, Doogie.

DOUGRAY: Insolent peasant!

DOUGRAY swings at SYLVESTER with his makeshift sword and whacks him in the arm.

SYLVESTER: Ouch!

> *MARTIN turns from the HAWK and throws one of his three rocks at DOUGRAY. It dents his aluminum foil breastplate and makes him stumble backward.*

MARTIN: Not so tough now, are you?

> *DOUGRAY swings his sword at MARTIN but misses.*

DOUGRAY: Umph!

> *MARTIN throws his remaining two rocks at DOUGRAY, hitting him again in the chest.*

MARTIN: Take that!

> *DOUGRAY holds his chest painfully. He looks up at the HAWK.*

DOUGRAY: Fly! Fly, bird. Fly away!

> *DOUGRAY tosses his sword up toward the tree, hitting the branch upon which the HAWK is perched. The HAWK takes flight and soars well out of harm's reach, away from the children. DOUGRAY'S shining sword is stuck in the tree branches.*

> *MARTIN pushes DOUGRAY, ripping the aluminum armor from his chest.*

MARTIN: Was that epic enough for you, loser? You lost your fake sword and your pretend armor, and now you have nothing to play with. Not even friends.

> *MARTIN and SYLVESTER exit. JOSIE stands up on the merry-go-round.*

JOSIE: Hooray, Dougray the Brave, Defender of the Hawk! That was truly epic.

DOUGRAY: It felt epic. [*coughing and rubbing his chest*] Not particularly what I had in mind, though. I lost my sword.

PHOEBE [*chewing on her hair*]: Trees have been known to take all types of toys from kids.

JOSIE: You didn't lose it! You made a sacrifice play for the good of the hawk. You saved an animal from a cruel fate. Like the sword in the stone, your sword is now a majestic symbol. [*pointing to the sword hanging by the branches*] Talon should be its name!

DOUGRAY: Yeah, sure.

> *DOUGRAY pulls off the last bits of his aluminum armor and walks away, discouraged. PHOEBE pulls her hair out of her mouth.*

PHOEBE: Our hero!

END OF PLAY

The Hat

written by Bryon Gill
illustrated by C.J. Kuehn

Cast

PERRY .... 20s; wearing a silly hat

JESSIE .... 20s; overachieving sales clerk

Setting

The hats section of a major department store.

Scene: *It is a slow day at the department store. JESSIE moves from hat display to hat display, adjusting and perfecting each one. She is very eager to make some sales today. PERRY enters, wearing a tall, multi-colored hat.*

PERRY: Good day to you!

JESSIE: And a good day to you, too! How can I help you?

PERRY: My name is Perry, and I have a problem—a very particular and vexing problem. It has to do with hats.

JESSIE [*gesturing at hat displays*]: Well, you've come to the right place! We have caps and crowns, helmets and hardhats, and feathered fedoras and berry berets.

PERRY: Ah, yes. Well, you see, the problem is with this hat.

JESSIE: It's a lovely hat, if I may say so.

PERRY: You may.

JESSIE: It's a lovely hat.

PERRY: Yes, it is the loveliest hat I have ever worn, yet it causes me great sorrow.

JESSIE: How could such a perfect hat ever disappoint? You are obviously a person with taste and intellect. Your hat tells me everything I need to know about your sense of style.

PERRY: And it cradles my brain oh so gently. Alas! Just yesterday, I removed my hat while I was sitting on a park bench, and I laid it down gently beside me, just so.

> PERRY mimics taking the hat off and placing it on the counter, but he does not actually remove it.

PERRY: What a dilemma! Do I put the hat on the bench with the brim down, as if the bench were wearing the hat?

JESSIE: Surely not.

PERRY: Never in life! A bench cannot wear a hat—certainly not one so fine as this. Instead, I laid the hat down on the bench with the brim up.

JESSIE: Of course. You are a person who has a natural understanding of hats.

PERRY: Indeed! You are a keen judge of character! And yet, when one removes one's hat, one always takes a chance.

JESSIE: A gamble.

PERRY: A risk. It was a dangerous game, and I played it! I laid my hat down on the bench, and before you could say "Haberdasher," a creature dashed in and made vulgar use of my headgear.

JESSIE: No! A creature?

PERRY: A denizen of nature, a pleasant rodent. It was a gray squirrel. He wore the smartest real fur coattails I've ever seen, but sadly, he was as hatless as a newborn baby.

JESSIE: Until then.

PERRY: This squirrel—I can scarcely tell you what use he made of my hat. He crept up to the hat and dipped his head in as if he were going to try it on, but then, he immediately scurried off. I thought that was the end of it, until I looked inside.

JESSIE: What did you find there?

PERRY: A nut! An acorn. Then the squirrel returned with another, and another, and another! My fabulous cap has been demoted, as you will see…to storage shed.

PERRY takes off the hat, and acorns spill out of it onto the floor.

JESSIE: Oh, my!

PERRY: Oh! Help me pick these up, would you, please? Forgive me, but I have made a solemn promise—a vow—to this squirrel. I have sworn an oath, as it were.

JESSIE: How can I help?

PERRY: I informed my furry new friend that I would return in an hour. I promised that either I would bring him an even better hat than my own, or he would get to keep my hat for himself. This is what brings me to you today. I must have a hat so perfect that even a creature with a brain the size of a peanut can see its quality.

JESSIE: You have come to the right place! Would you follow me, please?

PERRY finishes gathering the acorns into the hat and stuffs the hat back onto his head.

JESSIE [*showing PERRY a hat*]: This one is from our new spring line. It's got secret pockets under the brim.

PERRY: Too obvious, I think. Squirrels are very smart, you know.

JESSIE: Of course, of course. [*bringing out a gigantic cowboy hat*] But perhaps this one? At ten gallons, this is our largest hat, very popular with rodeo clowns.

PERRY: Hm, the storage capacity impresses, but the style is perhaps a bit too much. This is a gray squirrel. Perhaps if he were a brown or a blue squirrel, this would suffice…but a gray squirrel is far too urban for a hat like this.

JESSIE: Indeed, but I think you'll agree that we're getting warmer.

PERRY: We are!

JESSIE [*taking a football helmet off the wall*]: Perhaps this fine football helmet would be suitable. It boasts an armored, shiny exterior to keep birds at bay, and a padded interior perfect for sorting and storing a variety of winter foods.

PERRY: Yes! If I were a squirrel, I would want to live in that hat! I am not a squirrel, though.

JESSIE: Certainly not!

PERRY spots a black baseball cap with a gold letter "P" on it.

PERRY: Hello…what about this one here?

JESSIE: Ah, yes, the Pittsburgh Pirates baseball cap. It has proven popular with fans of the game and people whose names begin with the letter "P."

PERRY: "P" is the finest of letters, and this is the finest of hats! It's exquisite! The yellow and black lines, the simple letter on the front, the fashionable brim…I have to tell you, I am in love! I'll take it!

JESSIE: Very good! Shall I help you place the acorns in it?

PERRY: Goodness, no, I will wear it right away! [*removing his current hat*] This old thing is perfectly awful—only fit for wild beasts. I don't know what I ever saw in it, to be honest with you.

JESSIE: It's dreadful.

PERRY: Awful.

JESSIE: Best to be rid of it.

PERRY: You've got a good head on your shoulders!

> *PERRY pays JESSIE and wears the new cap.*

JESSIE: If I may say so, you've got a fine hat on yours.

PERRY: Indeed!

END OF PLAY

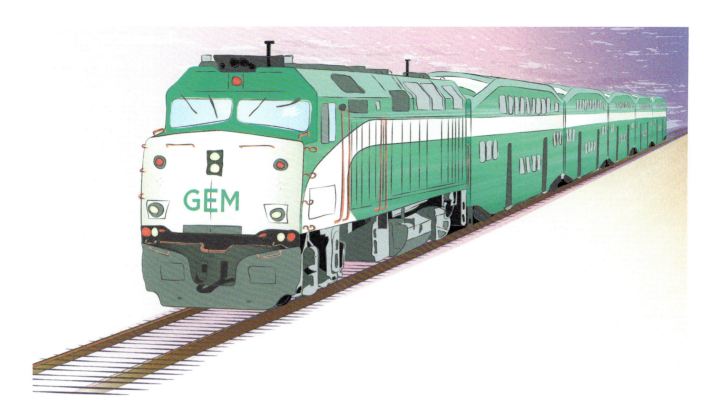

The Pacific Coast Gem: A Memorable Tour by Train

A Coastal Railways Travel Guide, written by Sarah Marino
illustrated by Mallory Senich

The California coast is perhaps one of the most wondrous sights to behold. From rugged mountains to pristine beaches, this stretch of the United States is a feast for the senses. Let Coastal Railways introduce you to this magical place and give you one of your best vacations yet. Make the Pacific Coast Gem train ride your next adventure!

To start, you will tour through the North Coast Redwoods. These are some of the biggest trees in the world! Glorious canopies of green surround you as you view the forest from every angle. Stopping in the small town of Eureka, you can smell fragrant air, some of the purest in the country. Whiffs of pine and salty ocean water will surely leave you refreshed and ready for the next part of the journey.

San Francisco is a city unlike any other. It is beautiful and rugged all at once. As it is the next stop on the Pacific Coast Gem tour, you will have time to explore. The Golden Gate Bridge is a marvel of engineering, and the mountains it is nestled between are likewise awe-inspiring. Whether under a clear, sunny sky or in the midst of the city's famed fog, this vista is one you will never forget. The deep red color of the bridge both contrasts and blends into the surrounding landscape. Be sure to walk across it to explore the bridge and see the view from this special place.

As you enter the city near Fisherman's Wharf, you may hear a strange barking sound. Don't be alarmed! That is simply the lovely sound of the sea lions who reside near Pier 39 at the wharf. These cute creatures add charm to an already picturesque tourist attraction.

Continue your tour by heading farther into the city. Hopefully you brought walking shoes because the hills of San Francisco are intense! They can be quite the workout. Beautiful homes of many different pastels and styles line the streets and please the eye. As you walk, don't forget to check out Lombard Street, whose first block consists of eight tight zig-zag turns. Remember, too, that San Francisco is on the Pacific Coast! Wander around Ocean Beach and dip your toes in the chilly water. Then head back through Golden Gate Park; inhale the scent of the cypress trees and the gorgeous roses at the Conservatory of Flowers.

Heading south and a bit inland, the Pacific Coast Gem train ride steams into Santa Clara Valley. There lies Silicon Valley, the technology headquarters of the United States. Nestled between the Santa Cruz Mountains and the Diablo Range is the city that is considered the heart of Silicon Valley, San Jose. The inland climate is much different from that of San Francisco. Temperatures can reach into the triple-digits in the summer months. The surrounding mountain hills are covered with dry grasses and desert vegetation. Mount Hamilton, the highest peak in San Jose, is home to Lick Observatory, an astronomy laboratory run by the University of California. The city of San Jose itself is quite flat, with none of the steep city hills for which San Francisco is famous. After briefly touring some of the major businesses in the area, you will get a chance to see Moffett Airfield, a NASA research center, as well as Stanford University.

Heading back out to the coast and along Highway 1, the Gem makes its way into some of the most pristine, gorgeous coastline of the United States, named Big Sur. Sharp, rocky cliffs jut out of the ocean, which sparkles a lovely aquamarine. Lush green vegetation and evergreens sit atop the rugged cliffs. These vistas will surely take your breath away!

The next stop is home to some of the most famous sea life in the world. Welcome to Monterey and the well-known Monterey Bay Aquarium. This city on the Pacific boasts beautiful seascapes and small-town charm. If you brought your wetsuit, be sure to check out the surfing scene!

The nearby town of Carmel is also a sightseeing favorite, with white-sand beaches and quaint tiny streets like those in European villages. The town is also home to one of the oldest Roman Catholic Mission churches in the United States, founded in the late 1700s. The cypress trees are extraordinary—especially to those who hail from the East Coast!

The coast past Carmel marks the southern edge of Big Sur. Its rolling green hills and rocky cliffs and beaches, with mountains off to the east, make for a delightful ride into Southern California. Soon you will enter the City of Angels! Los Angeles, in the San Fernando Valley, is a city of sprawl. However, it is beautiful nonetheless. Tour the beaches of Venice, Malibu, and Santa Monica, and make sure to check out the Hollywood spectacle. Continue south to San Diego to see world-famous beaches and more rugged, mountainous canyons. This last stop on the Gem train ride provides a fairytale ending to a fantastic exploration of the Pacific Coast. Book your seats today!

My Not-So-Fun Trip to the Zoo

written by Summer York
illustrated by Sean Kennedy

"Are we there yet?" asked my five-year-old sister from the backseat.

"Almost, sweetie," Mom replied patiently, smiling at her in the rearview mirror. I rolled my eyes. My sister was so excited to go to the zoo. I, on the other hand, was not. I didn't much care for the zoo. It made me sad to see those poor animals locked in cages. Plus, last time I visited the zoo, I had to hold my nose the entire time. No one bothered to tell me that the zoo smells.

We passed a sign for zoo parking and turned into the crowded lot. For a cold day in March, the place was packed. It might seem odd to visit the zoo in March, but we had come to see one of the last penguin parades of the winter. *Maybe the cold will take away the awful smell*, I thought as I put on my mittens and jumped out of the van.

People were already lining the parade path, so we hurried over to get a good spot. Soon a group of penguins came walking down the path toward us. They waved their wings at the crowd and hopped on their little webbed feet. My sister clapped with glee. Even I had to admit that it was fun to watch. But all of a sudden, one of the bigger penguins came right at me. I shrieked in fear and ran in circles as the penguin chased me. One of the zookeepers ran over and guided the animal back into line.

"Don't worry, he won't hurt you," laughed the zookeeper. I wasn't very reassured, though, since my pride was hurt quite a bit. I hung back as the parade went back to the aquarium building.

After my run-in with the penguin, we headed to the outdoor café for lunch. It was in the African section of the zoo, so it made you feel like you were eating in the jungle. However, several birds were hanging around the café that I don't think were part of the jungle atmosphere. There were many small birds pecking at crumbs on the ground. Some pigeons wandered here and there, their small heads bobbing as they walked. There were even two large peacocks, bright blue with colorful tail feathers dragging behind them. People commented on their beauty and fed them scraps.

We found a table at the edge of the café. I had just sat down with my basket of fries when one of the peacocks came boldly up to the table.

"Go away," I told it. I tried to cover my fries from the bird-thief with my arms. Mom got up to shoo it away from our table. But it must have gotten mad because its sharp beak came toward my food. I jumped back in surprise, accidentally sending my fries flying into the air. The mean peacock grabbed a fry from the ground and ran away with its prize. Mom went to buy me another basket of fries. Then we took our food to a bench outside the café to avoid any more bird encounters.

Once we finished eating, we walked to the petting zoo area. My sister wanted to pet the baby deer. As we approached, the stench I remembered came toward me. I pinched my nose in disgust. We petted the soft baby deer, which didn't smell that bad. Then my sister ran over to a pen with some baby goats. The little goats were leaping in the air and playfully head-butting each other. They were really cute.

In the next pen were soft sheep and funny-looking llamas. The zookeepers were handing out cups of food to feed the animals. I didn't want to get too close; I could see that the llamas had some big teeth. I stood to the side while Mom helped my sister feed one of the sheep. While I waited, a tall llama came near to where I was standing. I backed away, but it followed me along the fence of the pen. I glared at it and inched farther away. All of a sudden, the llama spit on me.

"Gross!" I yelled, looking down at the front of my jacket. One of the zoo workers brought a paper towel, and Mom wiped my jacket clean.

"Sorry," the zoo worker said. "Sometimes the llamas spit, but they usually don't spit on people."

"I didn't know," I replied unhappily, "or I would have stayed farther back."

We left the petting zoo area and went to see the other exhibits. We went to the aquarium and saw stingrays, dolphins, and many kinds of fish. Back outside, there were big brown bears. Then we saw snow leopards up in trees, tigers lying in the sun, and a big lion with lots of fur around its head.

In the African savannah section, we saw tall giraffes and slow rhinos. There were also a big grey elephant and a smaller baby elephant splashing in a pond near the path. We stopped to watch them drink with their long trunks. They flapped their ears at us and my sister waved back. My mom and sister were walking toward the flamingo area, but I wanted to stay and watch the elephants. At that moment, the bigger elephant launched a spray of water from her trunk. The wind carried some of the mist toward me, soaking the top of my head.

"I think it's time to go home," Mom told us. "I don't want you to get a cold."

"Good idea," I replied. We walked to the parking lot and got into the van, my hat dripping icy water down my neck. After this trip, I won't be ready to visit the zoo again anytime soon.

It's Party Time!

written by Debbie Parrish
illustrated by Brian Cibelli

I have an important decision to make. My nephew, Jeremy, is turning ten next month. Jeremy and his parents moved out of town last summer. They would like to surprise him with a birthday celebration here in town with his old friends. They have asked me to find a place to have the birthday party. I have gone to check out several places, asked some of my neighbors' children, and have even done some online searches to find just the right spot. I visited four or five last week and now I have it narrowed down to two really fun places. One is called Inflation Nation because it has inflatable slides and trampolines. The other place is called Party Times. The names of these two make them sound like they would be great fun! I need to consider the entertainment, the food, the facilities, and the cost of each before I make my final decision.

It was valuable to talk over the phone and look at different websites for information. Both helped me to narrow my choices down, but I still wanted to visit and see each place for myself. After all, I am taking this assignment very seriously. My sister, Jan, trusts me to make Jeremy's birthday a really special occasion. I do not want to let either one of them down. I set aside my whole Saturday afternoon to visit each place before phoning Jan with my decision.

Both places have all of their games and entertainment indoors. That's really good since it is cold and may even be raining the day of the party. They are both nearby, so Jeremy's old friends from school won't have to travel far. Even though one is called Inflation Nation, they actually both have inflatable slides, trampolines, and bouncy balls. Each has an arcade with skeeball, pinball machines, and video games. Party Times and Inflation Nation both have a bowling alley and a miniature golf course.

The managers at both places told me that they could provide all of the food. I liked that we would not have to shop for food and carry it in ourselves. They also said that our party guests could have all of the drink refills they wanted.

I was impressed that each party site checks a guest's invitation before he or she can enter. That seems very safe to me. Also, the games and entertainment stations of each place have adult supervision for safety purposes. Each place also has separate rooms available for eating and opening presents. I am so glad my sister asked me to help with Jeremy's party. He is a great kid, and I want this to be the best birthday ever.

Now, to make a final decision, I needed to consider the cost. I thought both places would be expensive, but they were actually quite reasonable. Each has a set price based on the number of people who are invited. This made it even harder to narrow the decision down. They both appeared to have everything we were looking for.

When I got home, I took out my notes and compared the two places. They looked almost identical until I started jotting down the pros and cons of each. Inflation Nation was much larger than Party Times. The games and inflatables at Party Times seemed to be bunched up on one another. Also, Inflation Nation had huge padded murals on the walls which muted much of the squeals and other party noise. At Party Times, I could hardly hear the manager when he was showing me around. I did, however, like that Party Times would allow us to decorate the separate room to personalize it for Jeremy. We cannot do this at Inflation Nation.

The entertainment at both places seemed to be about equal. Still, Inflation Nation has no limit on the number of times guests can play. Party Times gives tokens; when a guest runs out of tokens, his game time is finished. I also noticed that the trampolines at Party Times did not have safety nets. This worried me. Inflation Nation had safety nets and required each guest to wear a safety harness. Inflation Nation also had a climbing wall that I knew Jeremy and his friends would love.

As I mentioned, the food and beverage choices at both places were about the same, but the price at Inflation Nation did not include cake or ice cream. We could buy them separately or bring our own. The rest of the food in both places looked good and smelled delicious.

The cost to rent each place was nearly the same; both places charged by the number of guests. However, the whole amount for Party Times has to be paid two weeks in advance, and they do not give refunds for guests who end up not being able to attend. Inflation Nation only asks for a deposit and then charges for the actual number of people who come.

Inflation Nation it is! Considering the entertainment, the safety of the facility, the food, and the actual cost of each helped me to make an informed decision. I was so glad that I decided to visit each place before I made my final choice. Even if we do have to bring our own cake and ice cream, Inflation Nation is still the better place. I can hardly wait to tell Jan when she calls tomorrow. I think she will be just as excited as I am. The best part, however, will be seeing Jeremy's face when he walks into Inflation Nation and finds his old friends waiting to surprise him. Nothing will compare with that!